RTI Success

Proven Tools and Strategies for Schools and Classrooms

Elizabeth Whitten, Ph.D.
Kelli J. Esteves, Ed.D.
Alice Woodrow, Ed.D.

free spirit
PUBLISHING®

Library of Congress Cataloging-in-Publication Data
Whitten, Elizabeth.
  RTI success : proven tools and strategies for schools and classrooms / Elizabeth Whitten, Kelli J. Esteves, Alice Woodrow.
      p. cm.
  Includes bibliographical references and index.
  ISBN 978-1-57542-320-3
  1. Remedial teaching. 2. Slow learning children—Education. 3. Learning disabilities—Diagnosis. I. Esteves, Kelli J. II. Woodrow, Alice. III. Title.
  LB1029.R4W48 2009
  371.9'043—dc22
                                                                   2009005774

Edited by Douglas J. Fehlen
Cover and interior design by Michelle Lee; cover photo by Michelle Lee
Illustrations on page 62 by Nicholas Henchen
Illustrations on page 64: ©istockphoto.com/julichka and ©istockphoto.com/hypergon; page 193: ©istockphoto.com/kirstypargeter; page 210: ©istockphoto.com/CDH_Design

10 9 8 7 6 5 4 3
Printed in the United States of America

Free Spirit Publishing Inc.
217 Fifth Avenue North, Suite 200
Minneapolis, MN 55401-1299
(612) 338-2068
help4kids@freespirit.com
www.freespirit.com

Dedication

I am particularly indebted to my husband, Mike, who has continued to support me through the long process of writing and rewriting this book. I would like to dedicate this book to my three children, Mackenzie, Malley, and Matt, who make me smile and laugh. I have been blessed by their presence in my life. I also dedicate this book to my mother and sister, who have provided me with endless support and encouragement throughout my lifetime. —*Elizabeth Whitten*

I consider myself tremendously fortunate to have such wonderfully supportive parents and friends. Thanks for the guidance and encouragement over the years. I would also like to thank Dean, my husband, for his endless support, and my children, Ava and Alex, who bring me true joy each and every day. I love you very much and dedicate this book to you. —*Kelli J. Esteves*

I would like to thank my parents who have provided me with a loving and secure environment to personally and professionally grow. I dedicate this book to my children, Parker and Addison, who have given meaning to my life beyond my imagination. —*Alice Woodrow*

Acknowledgments

RTI Success would not have been possible without the input from many teachers and students who have influenced us on the development of the book. These individuals have shared with us countless classroom-tested strategies and creative approaches to working with students. Additionally, our sincere thanks go to our editor, Douglas Fehlen, for his careful attention and guidance through the editorial process. We also want to thank the staff at Free Spirit for their assistance. Finally, we would like to acknowledge the influence and support of many of our family and friends who over the years have provided us with the benefit of their wisdom.

Contents

List of Reproducible Pages

List of Figures

Introduction

Response to Intervention (RTI) is an innovative approach for meeting the challenges of today's diverse classroom. The model began to gain prominence after the 2004 reauthorization of the Individuals with Disabilities Education Act (IDEA) recognized it as an alternative means for identifying students with specific learning disabilities.

RTI is much more than a diagnostic process. It is designed to improve the achievement of *all* students. The RTI framework emphasizes the importance of quality teaching, early intervention, and progress monitoring through effective instruction. The intention is to address students' unique learning needs before severe academic problems requiring special education services can develop.

We have worked with many educators implementing RTI in schools, and we know that the model can lead to questions. Many teachers have heard or read about RTI as the "next big thing" in education but are unsure how it will affect their work in the classroom. Administrators intrigued by the potential benefits of the model are looking for assistance to help make it a reality in their schools. Even those educators who are very familiar with RTI may feel less clear on how to move from theory into practice.

RTI Success can help fill this need. The book provides comprehensive information on RTI, and then goes further, supplying hands-on, how-to tools teachers can use to help students succeed in the classroom. At the same time, it provides administrators with step-by-step implementation guidelines and practical solutions to challenges that can arise in building a strong RTI program and coordinating services throughout an entire school or district.

Whatever your role—teacher, special educator, or administrator—*RTI Success* is a one-stop resource for moving forward with the model in your environment.

The RTI Model

Response to Intervention is a multi-tiered instruction model designed to promote school success for all learners. RTI first calls for the use of high-quality, research-based instructional techniques proven to foster learning and limit learning difficulties. These teaching methods are geared toward a student's specific learning strengths and interests. A systematic screening process is set up to identify students at risk for academic failure. Those students who struggle in the classroom receive academic interventions based on learning deficits as well as thinking and learning styles.

Within the RTI framework, teachers use frequent progress monitoring to gauge student achievement. If initial instructional efforts do not produce adequate academic growth, more intensive interventions are introduced. Only after more vigorous intervention methods are shown to be unsuccessful (through comprehensive assessment) are students considered for special education services. The model can improve students' academic opportunities and help reduce costs associated with addressing learning disabilities.

RTI encourages a great deal of collaboration and teamwork among teachers, administrators, special educators, and other staff. As members of RTI teams (discussed in Chapter 2), staff members make decisions together about student instruction. Educators work together (along with parents) to assess students, monitor their progress, and implement interventions, which include differentiated grouping and instruction. Organizing and sharing information with one another is crucial as students receive instruction at each of the tiers.

In an era when many in education are being asked to do more with less, some educators have expressed reservations about RTI, fearing it will add responsibilities in what is already a full school day. It's important to recognize that RTI is not an add-on. In fact, it incorporates much of what educators already do. While RTI does present some new ways of doing things, these practices represent a step toward meeting an important objective—the success of all students.

RTI's Instructional Tiers

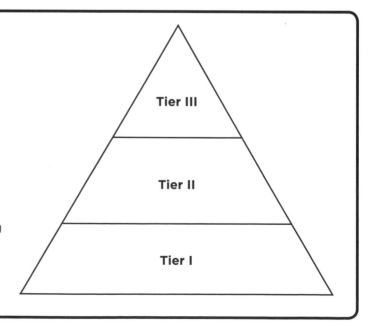

Tier III: Intensive interventions specifically designed to meet individual needs, instruction delivered in small groups or individually, frequent progress monitoring

Tier II: Focused supplemental instruction in small groups, research-based interventions targeted at specific strengths and needs, progress monitoring

Tier I: High-quality classroom instruction using research-based programs and instructional methods, universal screening a minimum of three times per year

Why Implement RTI?

The focus of RTI is on the use of high-quality instruction, screening and progress monitoring for early intervention, school-wide collaboration, and differentiated instruction within a multi-tiered service delivery model. This powerful formula has the potential to dramatically improve how we meet the needs of all students and transform how schools operate.

Increased focus on early intervention. RTI's emphasis on screening students at least three times each year can help identify those with learning challenges right away. Teachers can then implement interventions to remediate skill deficits before they lead to severe or chronic academic difficulties. Schools may use up to 15 percent of IDEA funds on these early intervention efforts for the whole school population.

> RTI can improve students' academic opportunities and help reduce costs associated with addressing learning disabilities.

Personalized instruction based on student needs. Teachers design instruction based on what they have learned about the strengths and skill deficits of each student. This attention on unique learner attributes keeps the classroom focus on delivering instruction that works for individual students (rather than a one-size-fits-all approach). Differentiated instruction, a staple of RTI, allows teachers to simultaneously address individual, small group, and large group needs.

Instruction driven by assessment. Within the RTI framework, student progress is frequently monitored to ensure learning is happening. If it is not, a different teaching strategy is put into place. This can help prevent time being lost in addressing academic difficulties. Rather than try something over a long period of time without knowing whether it's working, teachers can verify a strategy's effectiveness with a particular learner.

Improved quality of instruction. RTI emphasizes the need for quality teaching through use of research-based instructional methods. When teaching methods are grounded in research, students have the best chance of success. Additionally, the model involves ongoing professional development. This training in use of assessment tools and proven curriculum, teaching strategies, and academic interventions allows schools to raise the bar when it comes to instruction.

Focus on positive relationships in the classroom. Within the RTI framework, teachers identify students' unique characteristics. This information can be helpful in creating a classroom where learners feel supported and confident in who they are. They are also more likely to be motivated when instruction accounts for their learning strengths and interest areas. Students will learn to respect peers for their knowledge and individual strengths.

Increased school-wide collaboration. Administrators, classroom teachers, special educators, and other staff members work closely together within the RTI framework. School professionals participate on RTI teams, discussing student difficulties with one another and determining appropriate academic interventions. Diverse areas of expertise among these educators can help groups identify effective strategies. At the same time, shared knowledge of a student's challenges can ensure consistency in instruction. Collaborating together can also help staff members feel closer and more invested in one another's work. Many schools and teachers already follow principles on which RTI is based—it's the purposeful commitment to a consistent and comprehensive school-wide approach that gives it its strength.

What the Research Says*

More than a decade of research has established RTI as an effective model for addressing learning difficulties in schools. Many of the studies supporting the efficacy of RTI have been conducted by U.S. government agencies looking to establish best practices for identifying and addressing learning disabilities.

In 2001, the President's Commission on Excellence in Special Education issued a report suggesting that the discrepancy model (see page 12) be replaced as a basis for determining eligibility in the area of learning disabilities. The Commission recommended a system of early intervention and assessment directly tied to instruction. At the National Summit on Learning Disabilities that same year, RTI was called the "most promising" method for identifying learning disabilities. These developments were reflected in the 2004 reauthorization of IDEA recognizing RTI as an option for the identification process. Ongoing studies by the National Institute for Child Health and Development confirm that the discrepancy model delays appropriate education services to students. The organization endorses the early intervention services integral to RTI.

> Many of the studies supporting the efficacy of RTI have been conducted by U.S. government agencies looking to establish best practices for identifying and addressing learning disabilities.

In addition to studies supporting the overall effectiveness of RTI principles, many others have been conducted within academic subject areas. To date, studies supporting RTI's effectiveness in reading instruction at the elementary level have dominated this research. Studies within various content areas are ongoing. The RTI Action Network (see page 11) is one place where you can monitor research related to RTI.

---

*Batsche et al. (2005), Fuchs and Fuchs (2006), Bender and Shores (2007), and Hughes and Dexter (2009).

About This Book and CD-ROM

RTI Success has been written with the needs of the entire school staff in mind. Some sections may be more useful to one reader or another.

Part I: Implementation. Here are tools for developing a successful RTI program.

- **Chapter 1: Response to Intervention** provides comprehensive information helpful for all staff toward understanding RTI as a school-wide model. The section explains the core beliefs behind RTI and provides a full analysis of the multi-tiered service delivery model.

- **Chapter 2: Setting Up RTI Teams and the Problem-Solving Process** details how staff can work together to support the RTI initiative and includes information for administrators who are putting together RTI teams in a school- or district-wide effort. Descriptions of RTI meeting structures and the problem-solving process illuminate staff roles in making decisions about instruction.

Part II: Assessment. A crucial aspect of RTI is ongoing learner assessment. This part of the book provides tools for developing a comprehensive evaluation program.

- **Chapter 3: Personalized Learner Assessment** provides tools for understanding students as individuals and learners. Gathering this information helps base instructional decisions on how students best learn. Tools in this section also help promote strong classroom relationships.

- **Chapter 4: Academic Assessment** provides information on achievement indicators important within the RTI framework. Tools for screening and progress monitoring are covered in depth, as are guidelines for making determinations about movement between tiers. RTI team members can use the Educational Profile at the end of the chapter to make and record decisions about instruction.

Part III: Instruction. The final section of the book offers practical strategies for the classroom.

- **Chapter 5: Purposeful Grouping** provides differentiation strategies teachers can use to meet student needs. The chapter includes information for creating groups that challenge and meet the learning needs of all students within diverse classrooms.

- **Chapter 6: Research-Based Teaching** features hundreds of proven instructional methods to use with learners of diverse backgrounds. "What to Try When" charts allow teachers to identify promising instructional methods based on student attributes and learning deficits.

Within each of these chapters, you'll find a wide range of helpful elements. The figures located throughout provide at-a-glance information about RTI. "Spotlight" features detail key information about the framework and demonstrate how to carry out important RTI processes. The "RTI in Action" elements offer instructive examples of how the model is being carried out in other schools. The "Tech Tools" provide Web links where you can learn more about important aspects of RTI.

Throughout the book you will also find reproducible forms that can be used in planning, implementing, and carrying out RTI. The forms can be filled out electronically by accessing them on the accompanying CD-ROM.

Does RTI Come with Challenges?

Because RTI is evolving at the same time schools are implementing it, certain challenges are inevitable. This book has been written with the challenges in mind and is designed to help address them.

One challenge, noted earlier, is that much of the existing research on best practices for RTI has been conducted in reading achievement at elementary levels. Guidelines for other content areas and secondary grades are less established. Additionally, confusion remains about the framework's role in the determination of Specific Learning Disabilities (SLD). While some states do provide guidance on best practices, it is often up to individual districts to develop procedures on their own.

How *RTI Success* can help . . .

This book features examples from across grade levels and subject areas to give you an idea of how the model can take shape in diverse environments. Additionally, you'll find a discussion of the model's role in special education referrals (pages 113–114) in Chapter 4. The Web links included throughout the book can also connect you with updates on best practices as RTI procedures evolve.

Another potential difficulty that can arise in schools implementing RTI is confusion about the model within the school community. Administrators, classroom teachers, special educators, and support staff must work together in new ways to support a school's RTI initiative. Significant changes in staff relationships and roles may be necessary and create the potential for misunderstanding (or even resentment).

How *RTI Success* can help . . .

Carefully crafted professional development can help increase confidence in your RTI initiative and ensure consistency in the delivery of services. This book and CD-ROM provide comprehensive information on RTI and a PowerPoint presentation that can be used for staff development. Ready-to-use reproducible forms can also help stream-line RTI processes.

Misperceptions about the scope of RTI within the school community can also present challenges. Classroom teachers may think of RTI as a "special education thing." Even those who understand RTI as a model designed to meet the needs of all students might perceive its potential benefits to be limited to students with learning disabilities. Some parents and advocates of gifted students, for example, may worry that RTI will move resources away from teaching students who already thrive in the classroom. While the model strives to meet the needs of all students at their current level, that message may sometimes be difficult to get across.

> **RTI can be implemented in stages. Schools may start, for example, by either piloting the program in limited locations or at specific grade levels across the district. Training and resource decisions can thus be made on a limited scale.**

How *RTI Success* can help . . .

Students benefit when teachers learn more about them as unique learners. With this information, teachers can plan lessons that engage and challenge all learners. It's important to highlight this information with parents or advocates who may have reservations about RTI. (You might share the PowerPoint presentation on the included CD-ROM in a parent-teacher organization meeting.) You'll also find tools for the practical work of identifying students' unique attributes, capitalizing on their areas of strength, and differentiating instruction.

Rapid, full-scale implementation of Response to Intervention has the potential to be costly. Depending upon a school or district's readiness for RTI, there may be a need for in-depth staff development and extensive curriculum resources. Considerable funding and time requirements may appear to be a barrier to implementation for schools looking to adopt the model.

How *RTI Success* can help . . .

The practical tools in this book are offered toward reducing potential costs related to training, progress monitoring, and resource requirements. Also, the resources that appear throughout provide Web links where additional tools (often cost-free) can be found. One other thing to keep in mind: RTI can save districts money (and in effect "pay for itself") by reducing the number of special education referrals.

This last potential concern highlights a very important point: RTI can be implemented in stages. Schools may start, for example, by either piloting the program in limited locations or at specific grade levels across the district. Training and resource decisions can thus be made on a limited scale.

Before You Begin

While this book presents a structure to follow and a wealth of tools to support your RTI initiative, it is not a rigid blueprint. All of the recommendations are offered with the caveat that specific situations at your school or in your classroom may call for doing things in a different way. The goal of RTI is not to complete some "official" version of the model. Rather, the very nature of the framework calls for meeting the unique needs of each student. Just as there is no single way to teach, there is no uniform way in which to administer RTI. This will be left to each school or district.

When implemented well, RTI can reduce the over-identification of students with learning disabilities and better unify general education and special education services. This convergence of resources can have positive effects as the importance of labeling some students is diminished and greater focus is placed on the skill development of all students.

We wish you all the best in your RTI journey. We are interested to learn about your progress and any strategies that have proven especially helpful in your setting. Please share your thoughts with us throughout your journey. You may contact us in care of our publisher:

Elizabeth Whitten, Ph.D., Kelli J. Esteves, Ed.D., and Alice Woodrow, Ed.D.
Free Spirit Publishing Inc.
217 Fifth Avenue North, Suite 200
Minneapolis, MN 55401-1299
help4kids@freespirit.com

Part I

Implementation

Response to Intervention (RTI) is a school-wide initiative designed to raise student achievement. As a result, implementing the model involves coordinating multiple processes among staff members. Some of the procedures supporting RTI are most likely already in place in your school or district. In these cases, only slight adaptations to existing processes may be needed. Other procedures may be new to your environment and require larger-scale change to school schedules and staff responsibilities.

The two chapters in Part I are intended to help in your school's transition to RTI. Chapter 1 offers a comprehensive overview of the model that can be useful in familiarizing staff members with RTI. The section offers explanation of the core beliefs behind RTI and analysis of its three instructional tiers. Chapter 2 gives step-by-step recommendations administrators and other school leaders can use in school- or district-wide implementation. The section also details the problem-solving process that RTI teams will use to make decisions about instruction.

While Part I is written with the expectation that RTI is a new instructional framework for you and your school, the information can also be helpful in environments where programs are already up and running. In these settings, the book may be of help as you seek to improve existing group processes and provide additional staff development.

Chapter 1

Response to Intervention

Response to Intervention (RTI) has emerged as a promising framework for meeting the challenges of today's classroom. But even as many educators embrace RTI as a proactive approach for addressing unique learner needs, others have questions. What are the three instructional tiers? Who is ultimately responsible for delivering intervention services? What does RTI look like in practice at the school-wide level?

This chapter offers a comprehensive review of the RTI model. Whether you are a teacher wondering about the implications RTI will have on your classroom role or an administrator involved in implementation, the section can provide you with information helpful in carrying out the model in your setting.

What Is RTI?

RTI is an assessment and intervention process designed to help schools meet students' diverse learning needs. The model emphasizes the importance of high-quality, research-based instruction in the classroom. The intent is to foster student achievement and limit learning difficulties through use of proven teaching methods. This instruction also takes into account a student's specific learning strengths and interests.

An important component of RTI is comprehensive learner assessment. Screening measures are used to gauge academic achievement, diagnostic evaluations are conducted to identify specific strengths and needs, and early interventions are put in place to help students who are not achieving benchmarks. Progress is monitored closely, and more intensive academic interventions are introduced for learners who continue to struggle. Only after more vigorous intervention methods are shown to be unsuccessful (through comprehensive assessment) may students be referred for special education services.

RTI has many advantages over previous models used to address learning difficulties. First, it eliminates ineffective instruction or curriculum as possible explanations for student struggles. Additionally, early intervention efforts can help resolve learning problems before they severely distance a student from peers. Another benefit: progress monitoring and diagnostic assessment can allow educators to target the most effective ways in which students learn. In short, RTI is an instructional model that is truly *responsive* to student needs.

While RTI has emerged from special education legislation, the model's focus on early, classroom-based interventions makes it primarily a general education initiative. RTI is designed to ensure vigorous, research-based education and meaningful, intentional progress monitoring for *all* students—not just those at risk of learning difficulties. Additionally, many interventions for those learners struggling academically (especially early on) are administered in the general education classroom. In this way, RTI represents a marriage of general and special education services. It provides a problem-solving process for making decisions about instruction (detailed in Chapter 2) that can be valuable in working with any student.

> **While RTI has emerged from special education legislation, the model's focus on early, classroom-based interventions makes it primarily a general education initiative.**

Tech Tools

RTI Action Network
www.rtinetwork.org

Visit the RTI Action Network site for guidance on critical issues related to Response to Intervention. The site is a collaboration of some of the nation's most important education advocacy organizations. You'll find comprehensive information on RTI, planning and implementation tools, and professional development and networking opportunities. A one-stop place for vital best practices information, the site also features instructive profiles of RTI in practice.

U.S. Department of Education—IDEA
idea.ed.gov

Visit this site for information on how RTI can be used for SLD determination and procedures required by law. You'll also find up-to-date information on specific regulations for implementing RTI in your state and details on how up to 15 percent of IDEA funding can be used for Early Intervention Services (EIS).

Spotlight

The Evolution of Special Education

Since passage of the Education of All Handicapped Children Act in 1975 (later renamed the Individuals with Disabilities Education Act), schools have been required by law to address the unique needs of students with disabilities. While this legal imperative has been a constant for more than 30 years, how schools have fulfilled these responsibilities has changed over time. Initially, students with disabilities were largely separated from peers in pull-out settings. A strong inclusion movement in the mid-1980s led many educators to condemn this practice, and schools began to (as much as possible) accommodate students with disabilities in the general education classroom.

In addition to debate over best practices for educating students with special needs, questions remain about how to identify learning disabilities. Students were identified for services under the learning disabilities category when a severe discrepancy was shown between ability and academic achievement. The most commonly used method for identifying a discrepancy was to compare IQ testing results and scores on achievement tests.

In recent years, many educators have criticized the discrepancy model as a "wait to fail" approach for addressing learning disabilities.

In the model, students cannot be identified as learning disabled (and thus eligible for special education services) until they demonstrate a significant discrepancy between their ability and achievement. Years of struggle might pass before learners receive the intensive instruction or remediation in problem areas that they might need. Other flaws have been cited: for example, the identification process does not account for cultural, linguistic, or other individual attributes that might influence testing results. It also does not consider the quality of instruction students received.

Policy makers sought to design a more responsive way to address students' needs—a proactive model that could prevent chronic failure in the classroom. The reauthorization of IDEA in 2004 presented language setting up RTI as an alternative to the discrepancy model for identifying students with learning disabilities. The legislation was influenced by other education reforms that had preceded it, including the No Child Left Behind Act of 2001. The emphasis on research-based instructional strategies included within that law also became a signature component of RTI. Data collection and progress monitoring, represented in Reading First programs, were also included within RTI provisions.

Within the RTI model, general and special educators work together closely to address learner needs in the classroom. This collaborative approach to instruction is not new but based on another movement: the Regular Education Initiative (REI). Introduced in the 1980s, it also featured educators of diverse teaching backgrounds collaborating in the general education classroom. Although the initiative had the support of special education teachers, it was unsuccessful because it lacked the support of general educators, a fact that underscores the importance of school-wide engagement. (Chapter 2 features ideas for building support for the model.) Implemented well, RTI represents a distinct change in the way teachers teach and schools think.

The Three Tiers of Instruction

RTI incorporates a multi-tiered approach to instruction. While the specific designation of these levels can vary, most school districts implementing RTI to this point have favored a three-tiered model. Tier I is the universal level of instruction available to all students within the classroom; assessments are routinely administered to screen for learning difficulties. Tier II interventions represent more targeted teaching methods directed toward students at risk of academic failure. For those students not responding to Tier II instruction, Tier III interventions may be required. These are the most intensive interventions designed to support students with the most severe academic needs. Frequent progress monitoring and diagnostic evaluation determine any changes in instruction over time.

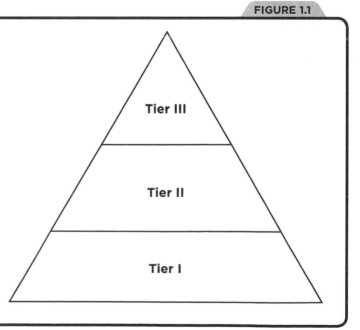

RTI's Instructional Tiers   **FIGURE 1.1**

Tier III: Intensive interventions specifically designed to meet individual needs, instruction delivered in small groups or individually, frequent progress monitoring

Tier II: Focused supplemental instruction in small groups, research-based interventions targeted at specific strengths and needs, progress monitoring

Tier I: High-quality classroom instruction using research-based programs and instructional methods, universal screening a minimum of three times per year

Tier III

Tier II

Tier I

Tier I

Tier I (universal level) instruction emphasizes use of high-quality, research-based core curricula and teaching methods that have been shown to promote learning and limit learning difficulties. Tier I instruction includes:

Research-based curricula. Access to quality education programs is a vital first step toward ensuring student success. RTI emphasizes the need for schools to use learning materials that have been proven effective; it's important that these programs also be used in the way they have been designed.

Research-based instructional methods. Teachers use a wide range of instructional methods that have been shown to work in the classroom. These teaching strategies are often geared to a specific population of students (to meet unique needs). Chapter 6 features strategies teachers can use with diverse learners.

RTI in Action

Mr. Aiden at Tier I

Mr. Aiden is a second-grade teacher at Malley Elementary School. He and his colleagues at the school share a literacy curriculum and support strategies that have been compiled and sanctioned by the school as examples of research-based methods. As part of this reading instruction, Mr. Aiden regularly gauges student progress using curriculum-based measurements. These assessments measure factors such as word recognition and reading fluency. In the fall, Mr. Aiden screens his class to establish a baseline and determine if any of his students may be at risk for reading failure. This screening process is carried out in all Malley Elementary classrooms.

Assessment of student learning strengths, interests, and academic performance. RTI acknowledges the individuality of every student. Teachers collect comprehensive data on learners so that a full portfolio of strengths, deficits, and interests can be compiled. Chapter 3 includes ready-to-use assessments that are helpful in this process.

Teaching strategies targeted toward individual academic needs, interests, and learning strengths. Techniques for raising achievement are not "one size fits all." Instead, instructional methods are selected based upon students' individual learning needs, strengths, and interests. Chapter 6 features interventions that can be used to target specific student needs.

Differentiated instruction within the classroom. Teachers instruct diverse learners within the general education classroom by providing teaching based on individual student need.

Flexible grouping. The need to provide differentiated instruction makes flexible grouping an essential classroom practice. Groups are based on academic skills, learning characteristics, and interests (rather than only ability levels). Chapter 5 features suggestions for grouping learners.

Screening of student achievement. As part of Tier I instruction, students are to be screened in content areas a minimum of three times each year to gauge progress. Many schools elect to gauge student performance in fall, winter, and spring. Chapter 4 provides comprehensive information on screening learners.

Ongoing professional development. Research-based education programs and methods on their own cannot ensure achievement. It's important that schools fully train classroom teachers and support staff in delivering Tier I curricula and instructional strategies. Staff members should have continuing opportunities to expand their knowledge in innovative, research-based teaching and assessment methods. Chapter 2 features extensive information on staff development.

Components of Tier I Instruction

FIGURE 1.2

Target Audience	For all students
Instructional Focus	Research-based programs, strategies, and instructional methods
Grouping	Differentiated and flexible grouping formats within the general education classroom
Instructional Time	90 minutes per day or more for literacy, 60 minutes per day for math
Assessment	Universal screening at beginning, middle, and end of academic year, assessment of students' learning strengths and interests, outcome assessment after units of instruction
Service Provider	General education classroom teacher
Setting	General education classroom

Tier II

Tier II (targeted level) instruction is designed to address learning challenges that emerge during screening and diagnostic evaluation. Students who are identified as at risk receive additional instruction (often for 30-minute intervals in small group settings). Students receive this instruction in addition to the general education curriculum. Tier II interventions include:

Diagnostic evaluation of students' academic strengths and needs. Learning strengths, deficits, and interests of students are identified. Fully understanding learners is important toward tailoring interventions to unique learner attributes.

Collaborative problem solving by RTI teams. RTI teams meet to review and discuss the learning attributes of students who are struggling. These team members work together to identify instructional approaches that are likely to work with learners. RTI teams and the problem-solving process these teams use to make decisions about instruction are detailed in Chapter 2.

RTI in Action

Mr. Aiden at Tier II

Screening tests conducted by Mr. Aiden in the fall reveal that several of his second-grade students struggle to identify basic words peers recognize. Further analysis reveals that these students are on track to score below grade-level standards established by the state. In accordance with RTI guidelines at Malley Elementary, Mr. Aiden refers these students to his grade-level team. Upon reviewing scores and learning profiles, the team decides these students can benefit from additional instruction in a small group setting. An intervention is designed in which the school's literacy specialist works with these students an additional 30 minutes (three times a week) for six weeks, or until grade-level proficiency is reached. Progress is monitored biweekly through curriculum-based measurements.

Parent involvement in the problem-solving process. Parents (or legal guardians) are notified when children are identified as struggling. Parental input about student difficulties can be helpful in determining appropriate intervention strategies.

Supplemental research-based interventions that target the identified areas of need. When a learner's specific needs have been determined, an intervention can be chosen. These strategies for raising achievement should account not only for student difficulties, but also learning interests and strengths.

Small group instruction. At Tier II, interventions are often administered to small groups of struggling learners within the classroom. Special educators, classroom aides, and other support staff trained in implementing interventions generally assist classroom teachers.

Monitoring of interventions. Staff members collaborate to ensure interventions are implemented in the way they have been designed. Peer observation is the most common method for monitoring strategies. It's important that at least one educator is fully trained in using the selected Tier II strategy.

Components of Tier II Instruction

FIGURE 1.3

Target Audience	For students identified with marked difficulties and those who have not successfully responded to Tier I efforts
Instructional Focus	Research-based interventions that consist of programs and/or strategies designed and employed to supplement, enhance, and support Tier I
Grouping	Small group instruction based on skill deficits
Instructional Time	Minimum of 30 minutes per day, three to four times per week in small group, in addition to Tier I instruction
Assessment	Progress monitoring weekly or biweekly on target skills to ensure adequate progress and learning
Service Provider	Personnel determined by the school (literacy specialist, intervention specialist, Title 1 teacher, speech and language pathologist, etc.)
Setting	General education classroom or pull-out

Progress monitoring. Progress monitoring is a vital element of RTI and should be conducted at least twice a month in Tier II interventions. This performance data is the basis for future decisions on student instruction. Chapter 4 provides comprehensive information on monitoring learner progress.

Tier III

Tier III (intensive level) interventions are administered when learners do not make sufficient progress after Tier II interventions have been put in place. Students generally receive an additional 30 minutes of instruction on an individual level or in a small group. Tier III instruction should involve:

More intensive interventions. Tier III interventions are more vigorous attempts to raise student achievement. They build on what's been learned from instructional strategies employed during Tier II.

Increased one-on-one or small group instruction. When Tier II interventions fail to raise student achievement, it becomes important to provide more individualized attention through increased group or individual work. A combination of both may also be provided or necessary.

Research-based strategies targeted to learner attributes. As in Tier II, interventions are based on a student's academic needs, interests, and learning strengths. Learner inventories and progress monitoring data can provide additional insight to guide instruction.

Monitoring of interventions. Staff members again collaborate to ensure interventions are implemented correctly. It's important that at least one educator is fully trained in using the selected Tier III strategy.

Progress monitoring. More frequent progress monitoring is called for as the intensity of interventions increases. At Tier III, student progress should be monitored at least once a week.

RTI in Action

Mr. Aiden at Tier III

After six weeks of additional instruction time, only one student from Mr. Aiden's original group has not progressed to grade-level proficiency. Two reached proficiency after only a couple of weeks; they are now matching or surpassing their peers' performance on curriculum-based measurements. Two other students had preliminary struggles, but achieved proficiency with the benefit of the full six-week intervention. The remaining student has not met intervention targets and has, in fact, regressed. The grade-level RTI team reviews the data from the preceding weeks and decides that this student would benefit from more intensive intervention. They establish a plan for the student to be taught literacy skills under the close oversight of a literacy specialist for 30 minutes three times each week. The intervention plan calls for a special education referral in the event this weekly progress monitoring does not reveal grade-level achievement in another six weeks.

Components of Tier III Instruction		FIGURE 1.4
Target Audience	For students identified with marked difficulties who have not fully responded to Tier II efforts	
Instructional Focus	Research-based interventions that consist of programs and/or strategies designed and employed to supplement, enhance, and support Tier I and Tier II	
Grouping	Small group instruction or individual instruction	
Instructional Time	Minimum of 30 minutes per day, three to four times per week individually or in small groups, in addition to Tier I instruction	
Assessment	Weekly progress monitoring on target skills to ensure adequate progress and learning	
Service Provider	Personnel determined by the school (special education teacher, literacy specialist, intervention specialist, Title 1 teacher, speech and language pathologist, etc.)	
Setting	Appropriate setting designated by the school	

Five Principles of RTI*

1. **All children can learn.** RTI is a model designed on the principle that every student can learn and achieve his or her full potential. It recognizes that helping students succeed is about *how* they are taught and *what* they are taught. In an RTI model all students are assured quality teaching, thus eliminating weak instruction as potential cause for failure. Students' individual learning strengths and deficits are accounted for in the classroom by teachers able to differentiate instruction for diverse needs. Learners in need of extra support receive it at varying levels of intensity in a multi-tiered service delivery model. This framework of research-based, differentiated instruction and early intervention has the potential to minimize the severity of learning problems and prevent negative impacts on a student's self-esteem that can result from sustained school failure.

2. **Quality assessment informs instructional practices.** It's important that decisions about student instruction are driven by data. While progress monitoring is essential to the RTI process, it is not the only type of assessment needed. Personalized learner assessments allow for understanding of students' learning strengths and interests. Diagnostic evaluation targets specific academic strengths and needs. Outcome assessment reveals whether or not the instruction was effective. And universal screening identifies students who might be at risk. A multifaceted approach to assessing learners is most effective in determining appropriate instruction.

---

*These principles encompass important aspects of RTI identified by the National Association of State Directors of Special Education (NASDSE) in *Response to Intervention: Policy Considerations and Implementation* (2006).

3. **Quality teaching makes a difference.** A critical element of RTI is the proper use of research-based teaching methods. The focus is on proactively creating an instructional environment that sets up students for high levels of achievement. Core curriculum, interventions, and instructional methods should all be grounded in research and have a high probability for success. Research-based teaching goes beyond validated programs and strategies to include proven instructional methods such as differentiated instruction. This is an important principle of RTI because all learners must have the opportunity to learn (and demonstrate their learning) in ways that allow them to be successful. Instruction should be designed to account for students' learning strengths, interests, and academic readiness.

   The No Child Left Behind Act of 2001 defines scientific, research-based interventions as those that have been accepted or reviewed by peers who are experts in the appropriate field of study. The strategy, program, or intervention, must be subjected to rigorous, systematic, and objective procedures to obtain and provide reliable and valid data using experimental or quasi-experimental designs across multiple settings. This book features many such methods in diverse content areas as well as resource connections to many others.

> When students feel safe and accepted by teachers, they demonstrate greater academic growth. Respecting students' learning strengths and interests promotes learning and fosters an environment where students can thrive.

4. **Positive relationships within the classroom maximize learning.** Studies show the importance of positive and supportive student-teacher relationships. When students feel safe and accepted by teachers, they demonstrate greater academic growth. Respecting students' learning strengths and interests promotes learning and fosters an environment where students can thrive. Flexible grouping and peer-assisted learning, both essential components of RTI, allow teachers to simultaneously build students' social and academic skills; as relationships are strengthened, so too are students' academic skills.

5. **Educators must work as a team.** RTI is a general education initiative. Responsibility for carrying out the model, however, should not fall solely on the shoulders of classroom teachers. Rather, educators of all backgrounds and experiences participate in various forms of teamwork to meet the needs of students. For example, it is through a group problem-solving process that academic interventions are determined. Educators also engage in teaming to differentiate instruction for diverse learner needs. Successful teaching within the RTI framework is not an isolated act. Instead, educators support one another in efforts to ensure academic success for all students. Parents are also involved in the teaming process as they provide insight into children's learning strengths, interests, and academic needs.

Core Beliefs and Key Elements of RTI

FIGURE 1.5

Core Belief	Behavior	Key Element of RTI
All children can learn.	Promote early intervention to prevent big problems by addressing them when they are minor.	Early intervention
	Help students achieve their personal best by differentiating instruction through a multi-tiered service delivery model.	Differentiated instruction in a multi-tiered service delivery model
	Monitor academic growth through progress monitoring and intervene when sufficient progress is not made.	Progress monitoring
Quality assessment informs instructional practices.	Collect meaningful data and use that data to drive instruction.	Academic assessment Personalized learner assessment
Quality teaching makes a difference.	Use research-based teaching strategies and programs with fidelity of implementation.	Research-based teaching
	Design instruction so that all students have access to the material presented.	Differentiated instruction
	Assess students' learning strengths, interests, and academic readiness.	Personalized learner assessment
Positive relationships within the classroom maximize learning.	Get to know students on a personal level.	Personalized learner assessment
	Facilitate positive relationships among peers.	Flexible grouping and peer-assisted learning
Educators must work as a team.	Use a team approach to problem solving.	
	Participate in collaborative team teaching.	Transdisciplinary teaming
	Partner with parents.	

RTI in Action

RTI: One School's Story

Leonard Elementary began its Response to Intervention journey when the first-year principal realized the child study team was unable to keep up with the number of academic referrals for special education testing. Additionally, the number of students identified as eligible for special education services was increasing at a rate in which the existing staff could not provide adequate service.

In order to determine students' needs on a group basis (rather than by individual students), the principal moved the child study team process to grade-level teams. Each group of grade-level teachers began meeting on a monthly basis with the purpose of analyzing student data and creating instructional groups. These groupings were based on student performance on formative assessments in reading and math. As the teachers observed the performance of students in their classrooms, they began to identify learners whose data showed that they needed more intense instruction than that provided by the curriculum.

The principal supported teachers by purchasing intervention materials for reading and math. As

teachers identified students in need of additional instruction, more intensive interventions were provided using strategies from these sources. These interventions occurred in addition to regular time allotted for reading and math instruction. Running records were kept on the students and weekly progress monitoring was conducted with curriculum-based measurements.

At monthly grade-level meetings, teachers looked at the progress monitoring data to determine whether students showed sufficient progress, or if changes to interventions were needed. Only when data indicated inadequate progress and numerous interventions did these groups refer students for a comprehensive evaluation for special education.

Success of the RTI process at Leonard Elementary hinged on the ability of school leaders and teachers to work together. Collaboratively staff members were able to analyze student data, group students for appropriate interventions, and document progress monitoring data toward making future instructional decisions.

Tech Tools

National Center on Response to Intervention
www.rti4success.org

A common criticism of RTI has been a lack of information on best practices and standardized guidelines for movement between the tiers. The National Center on Response to Intervention serves as a clearinghouse for practices that are being shown effective in schools throughout the country. For example, it provides best practices for middle school implementation, a subject previously under-explored in research on RTI. Visit the Web site for comprehensive information, practical tools, and opportunities to collaborate and network with others interested in these issues.

National Research Center on Learning Disabilities
www.nrcld.org

The National Research Center on Learning Disabilities is an initiative of the U.S. Department of Education. Its Web site offers diverse resources for implementing and carrying out RTI at the classroom, school, and district levels. It also provides insight on the interplay between RTI methods and the Specific Learning Disability (SLD) distinction outlined in IDEA. The relationship between RTI and SLD is explored in great depth with tools provided for use in the classroom.

Chapter 2

Setting Up RTI Teams and the Problem-Solving Process

Response to Intervention calls for a great degree of collaboration and teamwork among staff members. Teaching students with academic difficulties does not fall to a particular individual or group of professionals within a school. Instead, classroom teachers, special educators, literacy specialists, counselors, school psychologists, and administrators all have a role in meeting the needs of learners. From the delivery of effective instruction in the general education classroom to diagnostic testing for learning disabilities, RTI as an initiative calls for full staff collaboration at every stage toward raising achievement.

Some of the teaming processes within the RTI model may be new to you and your school. Shifts in staff roles and responsibilities might also be required as the general education classroom becomes a focal point for addressing learning difficulties. But once implemented, RTI as a model allows schools to take full advantage of personnel strengths and building resources. More importantly, it provides a realistic blueprint for meeting the learning needs of a diverse, inclusive population at a school-wide level.

The first part of this chapter details step-by-step guidelines for getting programming up and running in your school. Directed to administrators and other school leaders involved in implementation, this information can also provide other staff members with important insight. The chapter concludes with a closer look at RTI teams and the problem-solving process they use to make decisions about instruction. Teachers, special educators, literacy specialists, and other members of RTI groups can start here (beginning on page 34) to learn how the model plays out at the classroom level.

Response to Intervention Teaming Designs

Response to Intervention relies on multiple teams to identify and address the needs of students. These teams incorporate different staff members and fulfill specific functions within the model.

RTI Navigation Team (pages 24–34). The RTI Navigation Team is responsible for implementing and maintaining RTI programs within a school or district. This group oversees staff development, screening, and other important RTI processes. The Navigation Team has a major ongoing role in ensuring the effectiveness of the framework at the organizational level.

RTI Grade Level Team (pages 34–35). RTI Grade Level Teams are typically comprised of classroom teachers. These teams are responsible for guiding instruction within their respective grade levels. In addition to implementing the grade-level curriculum, Grade Level Teams work with other RTI teams to address students' academic difficulties within the general education classroom.

RTI Support Team (pages 35–36). RTI Support Teams often consist of literacy specialists, speech and language therapists, school psychologists, and other staff members familiar with strategies effective for teaching students who are academically struggling. Members from Support Teams often implement Tier II-level interventions in general education classrooms or pull-out settings and help guide instruction for students experiencing persistent difficulties. Support Team members can also help general education teachers strengthen Tier I instruction.

Spotlight

Transdisciplinary Teaming*

Implementing RTI benefits from the use of *transdisciplinary teaming.* In this teaming process, staff members meet on a regular basis to systematically address students' academic challenges. Team members bring their own professional expertise (such as grade level or content area knowledge) to the group as well as a shared knowledge of assessment tools, progress monitoring techniques, research-based programs, instructional strategies, and data collection methods. It is this shared knowledge of RTI process among members that distinguishes transdisciplinary teams from multidisciplinary or interdisciplinary groups. Open communication, collaboration, and consensus building are all vital in this teaming process so members may work together in determining strategies that will most benefit students.

*Information on transdisciplinary teaming incorporates ideas from Vonde, et al (2005), Lyon and Lyon (1980), and Siders, (1987).

RTI Evaluation Team (page 37). The RTI Evaluation Team becomes involved in cases where students are experiencing severe, prolonged academic difficulties. This team may put in place intensive, Tier III-level interventions for students who have continued to struggle. The Evaluation Team is also the group that considers the potential need and benefit of special education services.

Staffing for RTI teams will vary from school to school as program goals, personnel, and resources will be unique in each environment. In all cases, these groups should feature personnel with diverse backgrounds and skills; the teaming process, then, presents an excellent opportunity to match staff abilities and expertise with group needs. When working within their interest and strength areas, teachers can better oversee RTI processes and stay engaged in their roles.

> **For the purpose of providing a ground-level analysis of RTI teams, this section of the book presumes schools are initiating Response to Intervention for the first time. This does not mean, however, that information on Navigation Teams cannot be useful for schools with groups already in place. Instead, reviewing your processes alongside this material can get you thinking about efficiencies your school might consider to improve existing team structures.**

Keep in mind that RTI teams can incorporate existing structures already functioning within your school. For example, a single team (often called the child study team) may currently be responsible for developing interventions for students who are struggling academically or providing support for the general education teacher. This team may be comprised of a principal, special education teacher, general education teacher, literacy specialist, speech and language therapist, school psychologist, or others. While RTI represents a contrast in this traditional teaming approach (since it requires multiple teams and multiple tiers to address student needs), you needn't completely dismantle child study teams; rather, you can think of how you might meld existing teams into RTI groupings in your school.

The RTI Navigation Team and Its Implementation Responsibilities

The RTI Navigation Team is responsible for initiating and overseeing implementation of RTI at a school- or district-wide level. This group is responsible for "big picture" issues related to the RTI model, both in the model's infancy and over the course of time. The Navigation Team has many important responsibilities, including conducting baseline assessment, staff development, and ongoing evaluation of the teams' effectiveness. The decisions made by this group will often have far-reaching consequences for the success or failure of RTI as an initiative at the organizational level. In effect, the Navigation Team is simultaneously the public face and sustaining engine of RTI within the school community.

The Navigation Team has these important functions:

1. Establish Timeline and Scope of Initiative

2. Involve Staff and Parents in RTI Development

3. Establish School Baseline

4. Inventory and Supplement School Resources

5. Provide Targeted Professional Development

6. Draft RTI Procedures and Programming

You can use the "RTI Navigation Team Initial Meeting Form" on pages 45–46 to strategize how and when you will complete tasks related to implementation. The form includes places where you can record planning dates, plan for RTI development, and identify personnel who will head up respective implementation efforts.

1. Establish Timeline and Scope of Initiative

Many planning decisions surrounding RTI will be the responsibility of the Navigation Team. For example, when will the model officially be put into practice? On what scale will your initial efforts occur? What's needed to ensure implementation stays on track? Establishing answers to these and

 Spotlight

Selection of the Navigation Team

Who makes up the Navigation Team? Like all groups within the RTI framework, it's important that this team reflect wide representation of the school community. Among those who may be included: building principal, special education teacher, general education teachers, literacy specialist, selected parents, and others deemed appropriate by your school. Some schools model the Navigation Team after leadership groups already in place (such as the Curriculum Steering Committee or School Planning Committee).

It's important that those on the Navigation Team be fully knowledgeable about RTI and prepared to be strong advocates for the model. Members of the group also should have a thorough understanding of a school's procedures and resources as well as be realistic about what may be possible over time. Finally, it is important that group members be respectful individuals who can appreciate others' perspectives about RTI and its effect on the school. An open attitude can allow team members to provide leadership and enthusiasm for the model from the beginning.

other important questions will be vital toward smooth adoption of the model. Following are some issues your Navigation Team should address early on in your RTI initiative. Preliminary RTI meetings might take place a full year in advance of when you plan to have programming in place.

Scope of Initiative. RTI can be a large undertaking, what will the scope of the effort be at your school? Establishing programming and procedures for your entire school or district currently may not be realistic. Perhaps staff or resource limitations make it possible for you to pilot the model only in first-grade classrooms at your school. Or maybe one of the smaller schools in your area is well positioned to utilize the framework but the district at large is in need of more training before the model can be implemented on a wider scale. Whatever your situation, articulating the scope of RTI programming is an important step toward ensuring that everyone has a similar vision of how the model will look in your school. A good rule of thumb: Starting small and doing a few things well is often preferred to a large sprawling initiative that may be well intentioned, but ultimately ineffective. This strategy can allow momentum to build for RTI and minimize the risk of failures that may sabotage the framework in a school or district.

Timeline. When will the model go into effect at your school? When will professional development be scheduled? Identifying times for these and other events can help you keep your RTI initiative on track. As a group, establish when you will introduce the RTI model to staff and parents, acquire baseline data, and provide staff training. It can help at this meeting to have a full calendar of upcoming school events and in-service dates. The schedule you prepare should include all of the different tasks that must precede programming and include target dates for completion.

2. Involve Staff and Parents in RTI Development

One of the key responsibilities of the Navigation Team is to build support for RTI among the entire school community—including administrators, classroom teachers, specialists, and parents. It's important that all stakeholders are familiar with RTI and realize its potential to improve student achievement. Without favorable attitudes about the model, implementing it can prove difficult. RTI as a practice is very much dependent on the full collaboration and teamwork of school personnel, parents, and learners. Failing to establish full support for the instructional framework can hamper a school's RTI efforts since resistance or resentment among even a few individuals can potentially undermine the efficacy of the entire initiative.

Introducing RTI to Staff

How can you ensure that RTI is well received by administrators, teachers, and other school staff? Part of this task lies in fully explaining the benefits of the model to your school. Administrators, for example, are likely to appreciate that RTI, while potentially requiring start-up resources, can ultimately reduce costly special education expenditures. Teachers may be happy to realize that RTI's collaborative approach can mean greater sharing of labor-intensive responsibilities associated with teaching students with learning difficulties. Additionally, the model has the potential to increase overall engagement and collaboration among school staff.

It's a good idea to be systematic in how you present information about RTI. Random or incomplete communication about the model can lead to misinformation or misunderstanding that can set back efforts to implement the model in your school. A way to avoid this difficulty is by presenting comprehensive information about RTI at staff meetings or in-services. You may, for example, use the PowerPoint presentation on the CD-ROM included with this book. At the same time you provide this background information, your Navigation Team can outline what is planned for your school. Previewing what is to occur can prepare those in your school community for the implementation rollout that is to occur. In these informational meetings, be sure there is adequate time for people to raise questions or voice concerns they may have.

> **It's important that all stakeholders are familiar with RTI and realize its potential to improve student achievement.**

Parent Introduction

Staff members may not be the only individuals with limited knowledge of RTI practices. Many parents in your district might also be unfamiliar with the model or how it can best help meet the learning needs of their children. Without ensuring parent support for the framework, your RTI initiative has the potential to fall flat before it even gets started.

Why should parents be pleased with the introduction of RTI at your school? It gives their children the best opportunity for academic success and diminishes the likelihood of learners falling behind. RTI is designed to address and resolve academic challenges right away—before they become persistent problems that can have broader effects not only on academic achievement but also create social and emotional challenges (such as low self-esteem).

Parents can provide tremendous insight to best meeting students' needs. RTI emphasizes the importance of instruction that targets learners' strengths and interests. Who better than caregivers to provide this kind of individualized information about children? Chapter 3 features forms that can be used to get to know learners, including inventories that glean insights from family members. Making parents aware of the importance of their role early on will help develop a stronger partnership and provide on-going support for RTI.

As with educators, misconceptions about RTI have the potential to hinder your efforts among parents. For this reason, it's important to be thoughtful and thorough in presenting information to them. It can be helpful to discuss RTI well in advance of its implementation, perhaps at your school's curriculum night, PTO meetings, or other special events.

Spotlight

RTI Resources for Parents

Parents can be important partners in the education of their children. Making sure they are also strong supporters of RTI can help your initiative thrive. As mentioned, sharing information on RTI at school meetings is important. It's also a good idea to provide a method by which parents can ask questions about the model. They might be encouraged, for example, to contact a particular member of the Navigation Team. Another way to share information about RTI: Include updates on your initiative at a school Web site. You might include links to the following online resources for those parents interested in more information.

A Parent's Guide to Response-to-Intervention by Candace Cortiella. This parent briefing from the National Center for Learning Disabilities (NCLD) features accessible information about RTI and student profiles from the classroom demonstrating the model in practice. There is also a list of frequently asked questions and resources where parents can learn more. The briefing can be found under the "Parent Center" menu at the NCLD Web site (www.ncld.com).

"Response to Intervention (RTI): A Primer for Parents" by Mary Beth Klotz. This online article is available from the National Association of School Psychologists (NASP). The document covers key elements and terms of RTI, the model's benefits, and its role in special education eligibility. The article can be found by entering "RTI" in the search box of the NASP's Web site (www.nasponline.org).

"A Parent's Guide to Response to Intervention (RTI)" by Susan Bruce. Appearing at Wrightslaw, a Web site specializing in special education advocacy, this article explains how RTI works and what it means for student instruction. There is also a description of IDEA 2004 and how RTI has emerged from the legislation. Find the article by selecting "RTI" from the "Topics" menu at the Wrightslaw Web site (www.wrightslaw.com).

3. Establish School Baseline

Informing the school community about RTI is an important step, but it is only the beginning of the Navigation Team's work. Another important function of the group is to conduct an evaluation of a school's readiness for RTI by administering a baseline assessment that gauges a school's ability to carry out important RTI processes.

Why is the assessment essential to readiness in your school? The information you collect on this survey will guide many of the Navigation Team's decisions. For example, these groups will have targeted dates for RTI training during preliminary meetings, but exactly what professional development efforts are needed in advance of implementation? Are classroom teachers familiar with intervention strategies they can use with struggling learners? Do staff members know how to screen and monitor progress? How familiar are educators with the teaming structures used in RTI? What is staff experience with the problem-solving process (detailed beginning on page 38) that guides instructional decision making? Establishing a baseline assessment in your school can answer these and other questions essential to training efforts and prioritizing resources.

It's important to schedule a time at which the baseline assessment should occur. Many schools elect to stage implementation so that the survey is administered shortly after RTI has been introduced as a model to staff. For example, the Navigation Team might conclude an in-service about RTI by handing out the baseline questionnaire and asking that teachers return it by a specific date. You'll find the "RTI School Baseline Survey" on pages 47–48.

The amount of training staff members may need can vary significantly among schools. The Navigation Team may learn that teachers from grades targeted for RTI are already quite familiar with framework processes; full teaming and problem-solving capabilities may be very close to being in place. In other situations, a great deal of professional development may be needed before a school is ready to take on the initiative. It's possible that, upon compilation of data, it's necessary to revisit the proposed scope for your initiative, keeping in mind that implementing it in stages may be the best approach.

4. Inventory and Supplement School Resources

Staff development is one potential area of need that must be addressed before RTI can be successfully implemented. Another potential challenge for schools or districts is the need to purchase or reorganize curricular tools. RTI as a model emphasizes the use of materials that have been proven effective toward raising student achievement and that are research-based. In some situations, schools may need to purchase new or updated materials to meet research-based criteria called for by the framework. Additionally, RTI's emphasis on continuous progress monitoring may seem to require the need for costly assessment tools. You might worry about your school's ability to come up with funds for resource requirements.

While some have the impression that RTI features prohibitive implementation costs, the reality is that most schools already have teaching modes and measures in place that support RTI principles. Also, many low-cost and no-cost progress monitoring techniques (including some of those offered in this book) can be used by staff members in lieu of expensive assessments.

> You can use the "RTI Navigation Team Ongoing Planning Form" (pages 51–52) to plan for the events that will follow administration of the "RTI School Baseline Survey."

A good first step is to compile a list of all the programs, subject curricula, instructional techniques, assessment methods, and other tools currently being used within your school. Ask the curriculum coordinator to provide a full listing of materials being used. Have teachers provide information on any additional tools or research-based instructional strategies they may be employing in the classroom. (You can take advantage of professional development settings

text continues on page 32

Spotlight

Administering RTI School Baseline Survey

47

RTI School Baseline Survey

Section 1: Professional Skill and Development.

Please indicate the extent to which you use or are familiar with the below practices.	Use	Familiar	Unfamiliar
Transdisciplinary teaming			
Differentiated instruction			
Student thinking and learning styles			
Multiple intelligences			
Grouping strategies			
Progress monitoring			
Universal screening assessments			
Diagnostic evaluation			
Research-based instructional strategies			
Research-based programs			
Curriculum-based measurements			

Section 2: Collaborative School Climate

Please indicate how you feel about collaborating with other teachers at your school. Circle "6" to show that you strongly agree with a statement and "1" to indicate that you strongly disagree.	Disagree					Agree
Given the busy schedule of a teacher, collaboration with other colleagues is not a practical idea.	1	2	3	4	5	6
It is easier for me to figure out solutions to student learning problems rather than rely on input and opinions of others.	1	2	3	4	5	6
I don't understand the collaborative teaming process or how it can benefit me in the classroom.	1	2	3	4	5	6
In collaborating with others, I will probably be required to agree with them or use their ideas when I may actually disagree.	1	2	3	4	5	6
The ability to be a successful collaborator is a special gift some educators may not be able to develop.	1	2	3	4	5	6
Collaboration is too time consuming to be an efficient means for resolving student difficulties.	1	2	3	4	5	6

CONTINUED ➤

48

RTI School Baseline Survey (continued)

Section 3: Teaming Process

Please rate the following statements on team building by identifying how important you feel each area is. Circling a "6" indicates you believe a statement is very important. Circling "1" indicates you don't believe it is important.	Not Important					Important
Teams should develop appropriate academic interventions for student needs, starting with the identification of a learning goal.	1	2	3	4	5	6
Team members should encourage fellow educators to consult RTI teams when they have student-specific or class-wide concerns.	1	2	3	4	5	6
When appropriate, parents should play a role in the work of RTI teams.	1	2	3	4	5	6
Teams should clearly define the role each member has in working on a specific student concern or group task.	1	2	3	4	5	6
As much as possible, teams should effectively support teachers in meeting the needs of students in the general education setting.	1	2	3	4	5	6
Team members should be respectful and work together.	1	2	3	4	5	6

Section 4: Intervention Readiness

Please indicate the extent to which you use or are familiar with the below practices for academic interventions.	Use	Familiar	Unfamiliar
Skill areas for determining interventions:			
Develop step-by-step intervention plan			
Identify others who can assist in intervention			
Define academic difficulties in observable, measurable terms			
Collect pre-intervention (or baseline) data			
Implement ongoing progress monitoring			
Skill areas for determining effectiveness of intervention:			
Assess whether intervention was implemented as planned			
Chart and graph the results			
Compare baseline data with post-intervention data			
Use systematic classroom observation			
Refer to group standardized test scores			
Use progress monitoring			
Administer outcome tests			

"RTI School Baseline Survey" on pages 47–48.

The "RTI School Baseline Survey" helps you determine areas that must be shored up for successful support of transdisciplinary teams working at the three tier levels. This assessment is divided into four sections.

Section 1. Professional Skill and Development.
This section gauges staff members' familiarity with instruction, assessment, and grouping methods that are important in RTI.

Section 2. Collaborative School Climate. Teachers and administrative staff offer their feelings about collaborating in various school environments.

Section 3. Teaming Process. This portion of the survey determines attitudes about RTI teaming processes.

Section 4. Intervention Readiness. The last section of the baseline survey allows staff members to report their familiarity with intervention and progress monitoring strategies.

Summary Report
Once a school has conducted a baseline, the information can be compiled into a summary report. (You can use the "Summary Form of RTI School Baseline Survey" on pages 49–50.) Members of the Navigation Team can perform this analysis, and a meeting of the group should follow the report's preparation. The team at this stage will have enough information on which to base decisions for allocating professional development resources toward preparing staff for RTI implementation. You can use the "RTI Navigation Team Ongoing Planning Form" (pages 51–52) to plan for the events that will follow administration of the "RTI School Baseline Survey."

The Navigation Team at Ava Elementary conducted the School Baseline Survey to determine how prepared staff members were for RTI processes. After compiling a summary report, members of the Navigation Team analyzed baseline data. It was clear that there was a

Summary Form of RTI School Baseline Survey

Ava Elementary School

(School Name)

Section 1. Professional Skill and Development. This section gauges staff members' familiarity with instruction, assessment, and grouping methods that are important in RTI.

Staff members are most skilled in the following areas:

Differentiated instruction

Student thinking and learning styles

Multiple intelligences

Curriculum-based measurements

Progress monitoring

Staff members are least skilled in the following areas:

Transdisciplinary teaming

Universal screening assessments

Grouping strategies

Diagnostic evaluation

Research-based instructional strategies

Section 2. Collaborative School Climate. Teachers and administrative staff offer their feelings about collaborating in various school environments.

The baseline score for our collaborative school climate is based on a 6-point scale with 6 being high agreement and 1 being low agreement. Our averaged collaborative school climate score is __3.2__. Following are averages of staff responses for each question.

Staff attitudes about collaborating with other teachers. A "6" shows strong agreement with a statement and "1" indicates strong disagreement.	
Given the busy schedule of a teacher, collaboration with other colleagues is not a practical idea	3.3
It is easier for me to figure out solutions to student learning problems rather than rely on input and opinions of others.	3.2
I don't understand the collaborative teaming process or how it can benefit me in the classroom.	4.1
In collaborating with others, I will probably be required to agree with them or use their ideas when I may actually disagree.	2.7
The ability to be a successful collaborator is a special gift some educators may not be able to develop.	2.1
Collaboration is too time consuming to be an efficient means for resolving student difficulties.	3.5

CONTINUED

Summary Form of RTI School Baseline Survey (continued)

Section 3. Teaming Process. This portion of the survey concerns attitudes about RTI teaming processes.

The baseline score for our teaming process is based on a 6-point scale with 6 being high importance and 1 being low importance. Our averaged teaming process score is __4.6__. Following are averages of staff responses for each question.

Staff attitudes about priorities within the teaming process. A "6" indicates respondent feels idea is very important; "1" indicates respondent feels sentiment is not important.	
Teams should develop appropriate academic interventions for student needs, starting with the identification of a learning goal.	4.9
Team members should encourage fellow educators to consult RTI teams when they have student-specific or class-wide concerns.	3.8
When appropriate, parents should play a role in the work of RTI teams.	3.3
Teams should clearly define the role each member has in working on a specific student concern or group task.	4.5
As much as possible, teams should effectively support teachers in meeting the needs of students in the general education setting.	5.3
Team members should be respectful and work together.	5.5

Section 4. Intervention Readiness. The last section of the baseline survey allows staff members to report their familiarity with intervention and progress monitoring strategies.

Staff members are most familiar with and/or are using these methods for determining interventions and evaluating their effectiveness:

Identify others who can assist in intervention

Develop step-by-step intervention plan

Define academic difficulties in observable, measurable terms

Assess whether intervention was implemented as planned

Use systematic classroom observation

Refer to group standardized test scores

Administer outcome tests

Staff members are most unfamiliar with these methods for determining interventions and evaluating their effectiveness:

Chart and graph the results

Implement ongoing progress monitoring

Collect pre-intervention (or baseline) data

Use progress monitoring

Compare baseline data with post-intervention data

Sample "Summary Form of RTI School Baseline Survey."

need for training in transdisciplinary teaming. Areas of relative strength were differentiated instruction, thinking and learning styles, multiple intelligences, and curriculum-based assessments. Staff attitudes about collaboration confirmed that teachers would benefit from learning more about how it could benefit them in the classroom. The Navigation Team decided to emphasize initial professional development in this area, particularly in relation to the process of transdisciplinary teaming structures in RTI meetings. Future staff trainings would address screening, grouping students, conducting diagnostic evaluations, and using research-based instructional strategies. These settings would capitalize on the knowledge

of staff members. Those with vast experience in collecting baseline data and conducting ongoing progress monitoring (including charting and graphing results) would lead groups of colleagues in teaming exercises, thus reinforcing skills from the initial staff development setting. Having established these areas of strength and weakness ten months in advance of the implementation year, Ava Elementary was able to spend nearly a full year addressing these areas of need through professional development and teaming exercises. By the time August of the following year came, educators were well trained in RTI principles because key components of the model had been targeted at several in-service dates over the course of the preceding year.

text continued from page 29

to gather this information.) Get full feedback on what people are using and establish what's working—and what isn't.

When a full list of resources has been compiled, the Navigation Team can conduct a needs assessment to target any gaps that might exist in the delivery of services via the RTI framework. It's a good idea to rate these areas of need in a manner that aligns with the priorities you established for your RTI initiative.

5. Provide Targeted Professional Development

After the Navigation Team has informed staff about RTI and established a school baseline, it can begin to target professional development needs. As the problem-solving model relies on the participation of all staff, failure to provide adequate training in RTI processes can lead to ineffective execution of the framework (ultimately failing learners) and also to frustration and difficulties that cause staff to lose faith in its effectiveness. Providing this training, on the other hand, can help staff members feel empowered and valued as team members.

An important part of the Navigation Team's planning is determining how and when training will be provided. You might, for example, target administrative and staff meetings for this professional development, or in-services could be held over the course of days (through intensive workshops) or months (in regular school meetings). Training efforts may involve the entire school staff or selected educators who are involved in a staged implementation of the framework. Your team could elect to use outside RTI experts or you could share information on RTI techniques and tools from this book.

This stage can also be helpful with another important process in RTI: the selection of team members. As professional development is underway, candidates for RTI teams may emerge. During this professional development period, your goal will be to provide staff with the skills and experience they'll need to meet the objectives of your RTI initiative.

6. Draft RTI Procedures and Programming

After staffing capabilities and resources have been accounted for, it's possible for the Navigation Team to make preliminary plans for how education services will be delivered at your school within the RTI framework. For example, what literacy program will constitute Tier I instruction at respective grade levels? What procedures will your school follow for student referrals? How will eligibility for special services be established? Following are some of the issues that will need to be addressed before you implement RTI in your school.

Screening Procedures. RTI calls for screening at least three times over the course of the school year. When and under what circumstances will this screening take place? Additionally, what forms of assessment will be designated for respective grade levels and subject areas? Will teachers need to be trained? Will Support Team members take the lead on screening and diagnostic assessment? Answering these questions is important toward ensuring everyone has the same expectations for screening. Given the large amount of work this process can entail, it's also important to assign responsibilities toward its completion. (For example, will special educators or other support staff help aid general education teachers on screening days? Who will compile and review results?)

Referral Practices and Documentation. It's important that your school have in place official procedures for documenting when particular students are at risk for academic failure. Additionally, what process will respective RTI teams follow when students are referred for interventions? What forms must be filled out? The "RTI Student Referral Form" (page 53) and "RTI Collaboration Log" (pages 54–55) can be helpful. The "Educational Profile" (pages 118–133) detailed in Chapter 4 can also be useful in RTI documentation.

> **Instructional decision-making will be driven by the learners' respective challenges, strengths, and progress over the course of time; this responsive approach to a student's unique attributes is the foundation of RTI principles.**

Schedule RTI Meetings. RTI meetings, to some extent, will occur as needed. Some meetings, though, will need to be determined in advance of your implementation date. For example, when you've established your school's initial screening dates, you can also anticipate subsequent meetings that will be needed for adjustments to instruction. And, it will be important that grade-level teachers be able to meet together on a frequent basis to discuss learners' achievement levels. Many administrators will need to ensure that these educators' schedules allow for meetings on at least a weekly basis.

Determine Tier Movement and Instruction. Instructional decision-making will be driven by the learners' respective challenges, strengths, and progress over the course of time; this responsive approach to a student's unique attributes is the foundation of RTI principles. Some general guidelines for instruction, though, will also have to be made at the macro level by the Navigation Team. For example, how many interventions may be tried at Tiers II and III? At what point will testing for special education occur? In addition to answering these questions, you might also provide staff members with a full compilation of curriculum resources and strategies that have been approved for use for respective tier levels, grades, and content areas.

Implementation Schedule. For those implementing RTI in stages (such as beginning with a single grade level), it's important to think about how you will expand the process. While taking manageable steps can help in implementation, the ultimate objective of your Navigation Team should be school- and district-wide participation. Use Navigation Team meetings to strategize how RTI might best be rolled out over time.

In addition to answering large administrative questions, the Navigation Team will be the leadership group others look to for guidance on important matters. At least some advocacy efforts will be required at every stage of preparation for RTI as well as throughout its implementation. Let's now examine the other teams instrumental in the RTI process.

RTI Grade Level Teams

The RTI Grade Level Team is responsible for providing research-based teaching that is differentiated to meet unique learners' needs within the classroom. Representing the full student population of an entire grade level, this team of general educators meets on a weekly basis to discuss learners who might be struggling and intervention strategies that could be helpful in raising achievement. In addition to student progress, Grade Level Teams also discuss the overall effectiveness of the curriculum and cite potential instructional improvements that might benefit their classrooms.

> **Grade Level Teams continually monitor the effectiveness of their instruction methods in the classroom and conduct ongoing student-centered assessment. Teachers in these groups chart student results and together in weekly meetings identify students who may be in need of academic interventions.**

The work of Grade Level Teams does not begin when students encounter difficulties with the curriculum. Rather, RTI requires a proactive approach toward identifying the circumstances in which students learn best. This work starts at the beginning of the school year, when learning profiles should be compiled for each student. These summaries of student achievement, strengths, needs, interests, and learning preference are used for a variety of purposes. First, these profiles help familiarize educators with students whose learning they will oversee for the year. Second, this information helps group students for differentiating instruction in the general education classroom. Third, the profile serves as a formalized collection point for documentation of ongoing instructional strategies tried with students, progress monitoring data, and other achievement modes. (In-depth information on the "Educational Profile" and reproducible forms are included in "Chapter 4: Academic Assessment" on pages 115–134.)

Grade Level Teams continually monitor the effectiveness of their instruction methods in the classroom and conduct ongoing student-centered assessment. Teachers in these groups chart student results and together in weekly meetings identify students who may be in need of academic interventions. In addition to making determinations about Tier I instruction, Grade Level Team members also aid in decision making and instruction at advanced tier levels. These teachers refer students for more intensive interventions and collaborate with the Support Team (usually literacy specialists, classroom aides, and special educators) to determine and implement instructional adjustments. They are also called upon to provide

Team	Members	Function
Grade Level Team	General education teachers by grade	1. Meet together on a weekly basis.
		2. Assist team members in compiling Educational Profile.
		3. Work together to ensure curriculum is aligned with state and school-wide standards.
		4. Problem-solve various ways to address individual academic and behavioral needs and differentiate instruction through purposeful grouping.
		5. Determine when to move students not meeting benchmarks to Tier II.

Tier I Teaming Structure FIGURE 2.1

information for and work with the Evaluation Team when even more intensive interventions or full special education referrals may be necessary. Discussions about learners take place within the context of the problem-solving process, detailed on pages 38–43. Grade Level Teams also meet at least three times a year with the Navigation Team to discuss screening data, students struggling academically, curriculum effectiveness, and other RTI considerations.

RTI Support Teams

The RTI Support Team becomes involved at Tier II of the RTI framework. This group of educators often includes special education teachers, a literacy specialist, a speech and language therapist, and any other professionals who can be helpful in meeting the needs of struggling students. As the name implies, this group offers support for teachers in the general education classroom. When learning assessments and progress monitoring techniques reveal that select students are struggling to meet benchmarks in core content areas, Support Teams and Grade Level Teams collaborate to determine and administer interventions designed to raise achievement.

The Support Team has multiple roles in Tier II-level interventions. First, educators from the group are responsible for helping Grade Level Teams analyze student performance and learning attributes in order to determine appropriate interventions. Their training in addressing special needs also makes them ideal staff members to administer interventions. For example, a literacy specialist may be called on to provide remedial instruction to a small group within a general education classroom. As the classroom teacher utilizes Tier I-level curriculum and teaching strategies, this literacy specialist employs a Tier II intervention providing more intensive instruction in a particular skill area (such as decoding or fluency) that select students have exhibited difficulty with while participating in the core curriculum.

Tier II interventions should begin as soon as possible upon a student being identified for more intensive instruction. The frequency and time period for these strategies can vary depending upon the subject area and instruction level as well as specific student difficulties. An example of a Tier II intervention, however, might be one that is implemented for 30 minutes a day, three to five times a week, for approximately nine weeks. The involvement of Support Team members at Tier II is intended to provide early intervention toward remediating students' learning deficits—before sustained failure over long periods leave learners well behind peers. If these prevention efforts are successful, students will be able to return to Tier I services as delivered by the general education teacher.

Instrumental in determining students' responsiveness to respective interventions is progress monitoring. Support Team members often provide assistance in administering assessments and collecting data. This may be with specific learners they are working with or a whole classroom of students. The objective of collecting this assessment data is to determine whether students are responding to Tier II interventions. If a learner continues to achieve at a significantly lower level than peers, it may be necessary to consider Tier III interventions.

Tier II Teaming Structure

FIGURE 2.2

Teams	Members	Function
Grade Level Team	General education teachers by grade or adjacent grades	1. Identify students not meeting benchmarks and discuss observations with the Support Team. 2. Collaboratively teach with identified member of the Support Team. 3. Collaborate with the Support Team to determine if students not demonstrating progress at Tier II should be referred to the Evaluation Team for more intensive interventions or a specific learning disability.
Support Team	Literacy specialists, special educators, speech and language teachers, other appropriate specialists	1. Meet with Grade Level Teams and discuss identified students and determine appropriate intervention. 2. Collaboratively teach with classroom teacher by providing intensive Tier II instruction to a small group of students (for 30 minutes three to five times a week for nine weeks). 3. Collaborate with Grade Level Teams to determine if students not demonstrating progress at Tier II should be referred to the Evaluation Team for more intensive interventions or a specific learning disability. 4. Report results of achievement testing and progress monitoring to Tier II team.

RTI Evaluation Teams

The RTI Evaluation Team becomes involved when students do not respond to instruction at Tiers I and II. This group works closely with the Support and Grade Level Teams and may include members from each. Members of the Evaluation Team often include a principal (or another school administrator), special educators, general education teachers, speech and language therapists, literacy specialists, school psychologist, and others involved in the delivery of special services.

The work of the Evaluation Team includes overseeing the implementation of intensive interventions and referrals for special education. Part of this group's work is to closely examine all learner information available, including a student's background, health history, formal and informal achievement tests, and any progress monitoring data that has been compiled at Tiers I and II. The group also looks closely at interventions that have been tried with learners and considers factors that may have caused them to fail.

The Evaluation Team, upon examining available student data, may recommend that another intervention be tried. An example might be intensive instruction in a specific area of need with an interventionist four times a week for 30-minute sessions. Tier III interventions are designed to remediate students' skill deficits through individual or small group (one to three students) instruction. Students in these settings are closely monitored by a special education teacher or another qualified staff member. Those showing adequate progress may return to Tier I or II services if the "boost" is effective.

The severity of some students' learning difficulties may simply be beyond those that can be addressed through instruction at Tiers II or III. In these situations, the Evaluation Team may refer students for additional testing to determine whether a specific learning disability is causing academic difficulties.

Spotlight

Outstanding RTI Questions

Clear consensus has not yet emerged on standardized guidelines for movement between Tiers II and III of the RTI framework. For example, some models feature multiple interventions with the aid of Evaluation Teams at Tier II so that Tier III is synonymous with special education referrals. In other frameworks, Evaluation Teams may not get involved until Tier III, at which point more intensive interventions are tried before special education testing is performed. Regardless of which tier structure interventions are employed, the objective is to ensure that proven strategies are used for learners' unique needs to raise achievement and limit special education referrals.

Another issue concerns best practices for individual intervention strategies. The frequency and time period for interventions, for example, have not been definitively determined. The guidelines offered throughout this book reflect current suggested practices, but it's also a good idea to monitor developments of the Department of Education and organizations devoted to advancing RTI (see the "References and Resources" section on pages 225–238). As additional research is performed, more clearly defined guidelines for the RTI framework are likely to emerge.

Tier III Teaming Structure

FIGURE 2.3

Teams	Members	Function
Grade Level Team	General education teachers by grade or adjacent grades	1. Engage in ongoing collaboration with appropriate members of Support Team and Evaluation Team to provide current information on Tier III students. 2. Coordinate instruction with Tiers II and III.
Support Team	Literacy specialists, special educators, speech and language therapists, other appropriate specialists	1. Collaboratively teach with members of Grade Level Teams to provide intensive Tier II instruction (to a small group of students for 30 minutes three to five times a week for twelve weeks) and provide Tier III intensive instruction (to individual students or a small group of 3 or less for at least two 30-minute sessions per week). 2. Collaborate with Grade Level Teams when students are not successful at Tier II and make referrals to the Evaluation Team for more intensive interventions or special education testing. 3. Each specialist serving on the Tier III team serves as a liaison between Tiers II and III. They have the responsibilities of co-teaching, reporting achievement testing results, assisting in developing interventions and ensuring fidelity of interventions.
Evaluation Team	Principal, special education teachers, general education teachers, speech and language therapists, literacy specialists, school psychologist, and other appropriate personnel	1. Meet with appropriate personnel from Grade Level Teams and Support Team to gather data on the student referred to Evaluation Team for more intensive interventions or special education testing. 2. Conduct formal evaluations of students utilizing data from previous intervention efforts. 3. Provide members of Grade Level Team and Support Team with evaluation results and recommendations for successful instruction of the student.

The RTI Problem-Solving Process

Grade Level, Support, and Evaluation Teams have different functions within the RTI framework. These groups may be involved at different points in the process and responsible for carrying out specific RTI objectives. One important element shared between teams, however, is the use of a standardized problem-solving process for instructional decision-making. This model for making decisions is used to guide, implement, and assess instruction across the three tiers of RTI.

Following a common problem-solving process allows RTI teams to operate efficiently. Team members have a shared understanding of the process that governs all instructional decisions. All of those involved, regardless of team assignment, know what to expect from the process, as well as expectations that may be asked of them.

The problem-solving process generally occurs in meetings of RTI teams profiled in this chapter. For example, Grade Level Teams use this decision-making process at weekly meetings to address preliminary difficulties that arise in the classroom. Members from Grade Level and Support Teams use it to guide instruction for students not responding to early intervention. Grade Level, Support, and Evaluation Teams use the problem-solving process to determine intensive interventions for students experiencing severe, prolonged difficulties.

Team Member Roles in the Problem-Solving Process

Within the problem-solving process, some roles must be filled by RTI team members during meetings. Because these groups include qualified staff members of diverse backgrounds, there should be no difficulty in matching individuals' respective areas of expertise with requisite group roles.

Referring Teacher. Classroom educators who refer students for interventions join the Support Team for Tier II meetings. It's up to these teachers to share information about referred students in order to determine appropriate academic interventions. If adequate progress is not demonstrated and Tier III-level meetings become necessary, referring teachers will participate in those discussions as well.

Facilitator. Facilitators oversee meetings and are responsible for ensuring the RTI framework is followed, keeping groups on task, and adhering to time limits for meetings.

Recorder. Recorders are responsible for documenting the discussions and decisions of RTI teams. The "RTI Collaboration Log" on pages 54–55 can serve as a template for keeping meeting minutes and documenting intervention strategies.

> Grade Level, Support, and Evaluation Teams have different functions within the RTI framework. These groups may be involved at different points in the process and responsible for carrying out specific RTI objectives.

Case Manager. The case manager is assigned toward the conclusion of meetings. One function of this role is ongoing communication between referring teachers and RTI teams. The case manager is also responsible for verifying that interventions are correctly implemented and students are closely monitored, while providing any support referring teachers may need.

These group roles are, for the most part, administrative. For example, the recorder is not necessarily limited to that role. All staff members should feel welcome to offer their input throughout the teaming process and at every juncture of RTI meetings. The collective brainstorming process, for example, is vitally important toward determining the best solutions for students' academic challenges. Some teams shift responsibilities among individuals throughout the school year so that all group members can be trained in each of these roles. Other groups prefer to capitalize on individuals' respective areas of expertise by assigning roles to specific staff members for the school year. In smaller schools or districts with severe staff limitations it may be necessary for educators to fill multiple roles in RTI meetings.

RTI Team Roles

FIGURE 2.4

All Members	Facilitator	Recorder	Referring Teacher	Case Manager
Are effective listeners monitoring nonverbal language	Guides the discussion, redirecting team to task as needed	Records information on RTI Collaboration Log	Identifies academic concerns and shares them with group	Conducts follow up after RTI meetings
Are empathetic and encouraging of all team members	Moderates team pace	Organizes information	Presents details about students' challenges	Communicates with referring teacher and RTI team
Generate ideas through brainstorming	Mediator	Reiterates statements	Identifies strategies used and background information	Verifies interventions have been put in place
Are accepting of others' ideas	Organizes the meeting	Clarifies from notes	Collects academic data	Ensures strategies implemented correctly
Ask questions, paraphrase, and clarify information	Is the timekeeper	Provides timekeeper support	Establishes baseline	Provides referring teacher with support
Attend follow-up meetings	Evaluates the intervention	Records dates for follow-up meetings	Participates in the problem-solving process	Sets up meeting to monitor student progress
Evaluate team effectiveness	Brings closure to the meeting	States ground rules for meeting	Implements the intervention	Contributes to the evaluation plan

Using the Problem-Solving Process in RTI Meetings

RTI is most effective when the problem-solving process is consistent and all team members have shared expectations for meetings. The "RTI Collaboration Log" (pages 54–55) can serve as a basis for meeting minutes and documentation of the student intervention. This form focuses on seven steps of the standardized problem-solving process.

1. Identify Academic Strengths and Challenges

The referring teacher provides background and baseline information about the student. Referring teachers should be organized with relevant information on performance; they should be able to offer precise information on students' struggles as well as how they best learn. This will usually include an overview of achievement levels and assessment data. Biographical information that may have a bearing on achievement can also be brought up at this time.

2. Analyze Challenges

After the referring teacher has talked about a student's challenges, team members discuss the concerns raised. They may ask additional questions or clarify points about student performance. After a full group analysis of student challenges, the recorder documents them in the "RTI Collaboration Log."

3. Establish Academic Baseline and Learning Preferences

RTI team members use the relevant background data and information gathered through steps 1 and 2 to establish a measurable baseline of student achievement. This baseline incorporates information that has been presented by referring educators as well as any other useful data collected by the school such as past district or state testing scores, student samples, or other work demonstrating skill deficits. The baseline determined by RTI groups will be compared against future data to establish whether students have or have not progressed. If there is inadequate information for establishing a baseline, more data will have to be gathered prior to the team moving to step 4. Chapter 4 offers a full examination of assessment criteria and tools you can use to establish an academic baseline.

In addition to collecting academic information, it's important also to account for personalized learner data that provides insight into how students best learn. Without this information, RTI teams are not able to select interventions that are specifically geared toward student interests and strengths—a vital component of RTI. The "Student Interest Inventory," "Thinking and Learning Styles Inventory," and "Multiple Intelligence" surveys found in Chapter 3 help you collect this information. Generally, grade-level teachers have collected this data early in the year as they get to know their students and differentiate instruction to meet unique needs.

> **Following a common problem-solving process allows RTI teams to operate efficiently. Team members have a shared understanding of the process that governs all instructional decisions. All of those involved, regardless of team assignment, know what to expect from the process, as well as expectations that may be asked of them.**

Team members at this stage should collect as much information as possible toward establishing an adequate baseline and student learning preferences. Descriptive statements about student achievement and interests can be helpful. Consider asking referring educators "how" or "what" questions (for example, "How does the student respond to . . ." or "What happens when . . .") to gather adequate information for a full learning profile.

4. Brainstorm Teaching Strategies and Interventions

Step 4 of RTI teams' work consists of brainstorming and listing as many strategies and interventions as possible. These options should be chosen based on the preceding discussion of student academic challenges and strengths. It can help to have on hand a full listing of your school's curricular resources and intervention strategies to stimulate the discussion. It's important to remember that all ideas are welcome and should be respectfully considered. While some of the instructional ideas may not work for the student in question, listing all possibilities can provoke thoughtful discussion and produce solutions that otherwise might not have been suggested.

5. Develop an Intervention Plan

Provided you have enough academic baseline and personalized learner data, you should be able to develop an intervention plan for students experiencing academic difficulties. In accordance with RTI principles, it's important to fully document the implementation of the intervention. Important aspects to note include:

- The name or type of intervention.

- The frequency with which it will be implemented.

- The period of time over which it will be tried.

- The person responsible for implementing the intervention.

- The person responsible for ensuring it is correctly carried out.

All team members should be clear on the details of these interventions and understand their roles in carrying them out.

6. Develop an Evaluation Plan

At this time, the team establishes clear benchmarks that represent adequate academic progress. For example, if an intervention addresses difficulties in reading comprehension, a series of curriculum-based measurements can be put into place to monitor a student's progress. The intervention is successful if the student consistently achieves a set benchmark score. If this standard is not met over a specified time period, another more appropriate alternative is put in place by the RTI team.

Without clear guidelines for what constitutes sufficient progress can compromise a team's ability to determine the effectiveness of an intervention. Clearly outlining what success will look like, on the other hand, allows team members to have a shared vision for student expectations. Making arrangements to ensure that interventions are used correctly is similarly important; if strategies aren't put in place as they have been designed, it's impossible to determine whether they can effectively address specific student needs.

7. Establish a Case Manager

The case manager is responsible for providing ongoing communication between the referring teacher and RTI teams. This person verifies that interventions are in place and are being implemented correctly. The case manager also provides any follow-up support the referring teacher may need. A follow-up meeting for a discussion of student progress should also be scheduled at this time.

RTI in Action

Tier II Fourth-Grade Team Meeting

Jamal is in Mrs. Mackenzie's fourth-grade classroom. He has demonstrated some difficulties in reading fluency and comprehension since the beginning of the year. Mrs. Mackenzie has already discussed Jamal's challenges with Mrs. Willis and Mr. Martinez in her Grade Level Team. At that time, the group decided to pair Jamal with a reading buddy and his reading assignments were modified when appropriate. After three months, Jamal continues to struggle in the areas of fluency and comprehension. Mrs.

Mackenzie is concerned that the Tier I instruction has not provided the support Jamal needs. She completes a referral form, and a Tier II meeting is arranged. In addition to Mrs. Mackenzie's fourth-grade colleagues, this meeting features members of the Support Team, including Ms. Perry (the principal), Mrs. Lowry (the special education teacher), and Mr. Spagnola (the literacy specialist). These team members use the problem-solving process to determine an appropriate intervention for Jamal.

Reproducible | 54

RTI Collaboration Log

Student Name: _Jamal Royal_

Date: _November 25th_   Grade: _4_   Tier: _II_

Team members:

Mrs. Mackenzie	_Ms. Perry_
Referring Teacher	Facilitator
Mr. Martinez / _Mr. Spagnola_	_Mrs. Willis_
Recorder / Case Manager	Support Staff
Mrs. Lowry	
Support Staff Support Staff	Support Staff

1. Identify Academic Strengths and Challenges. Referring teacher provides student academic information to the group to initiate problem-solving process (reference "RTI Student Referral Form").

Jamal has been the subject of Tier I intervention efforts to address reading fluency and comprehension difficulties for approximately three months. He has been paired with a reading buddy and reading assignments are modified when appropriate. Jamal is still having difficulty in the areas of reading fluency and comprehension. He is currently only reading 70 words per minute in a third-grade text. Jamal's comprehension improves if he slows his reading, but he tends to read fast to be like peers. Many days, Jamal is able to answer questions about the beginning of the reading text but not the middle or the end.

2. Analyze Challenges. Team members paraphrase academic challenges and ask questions to clarify their understanding of student performance.

—Mr. Martinez asked about Jamal's comprehension at a second-grade reading level. Mrs. Mackenzie stated he comprehends 85 to 90% of what he reads in a second-grade reading text. He understands the main idea and theme but has difficulty recalling details. When he reads second-grade-level text he reads about 100 words per minute.
—Mrs. Lowry inquired how the reading buddy was being used. Mrs. Mackenzie described the process, which everyone agreed was appropriate.
—Ms. Perry brought up the fact that Jamal struggles with attention and wondered if reading text in his interest areas would increase his oral reading fluency scores as well as comprehension.

3. Establish Academic Baseline and Learning Preferences. Use data to establish measurable baseline of student achievement and document learning strengths.

— Jamal is currently reading 70 words per minute with third-grade text.
—At a third-grade reading level he has difficulty recalling facts and details but he can get the main idea and/or theme.
—When reading second-grade text, Jamal can answer 85–90% of the questions.
— Jamal is interested in snowmobiling, hunting, football, and hockey.

CONTINUED ▶

Reproducible | 55

RTI Collaboration Log (continued)

4. Brainstorm Teaching Strategies and Interventions. List strategies and interventions that may be used to remediate skill deficits, accounting for personalized learner data.

—Keep the reading buddy and implement use of thinking maps.
—Give Jamal reading material in the second and third grade exclusively until he masters that level.
—Include Jamal in the Read Naturally intervention group for 30 minutes daily after the 90-minute language arts block.

5. Develop an Intervention Plan. Determine and document intervention plan, including who will be responsible for carrying it out and ensuring fidelity of implementation.

Jamal will join the Tier II level Read Naturally group following the 90-minute language arts block. Mr. Spagnola, the literacy specialist, will work with Jamal to increase fluency and focus on guided reading to improve comprehension. Jamal will also continue to work with a reading buddy. Reading choices will be based on interest areas. The reading buddy will read aloud while Jamal follows along in his text. Then Jamal will read out loud while the buddy follows along. Once they have completed a chapter or book together they will complete a thinking map. The thinking maps will be turned in to Mrs. Mackenzie so she can monitor comprehension.

6. Develop an Evaluation Plan. Document method by which effectiveness of intervention will be determined.

Progress monitoring from Tier II intervention program and documentation of reading buddy and high interest reading material will occur for four weeks. The team will review Jamal's progress at the Grade Level Team meeting in four weeks.

7. Establish a Case Manager. At the same time you determine a case manager, you can also set a date for a follow-up meeting.

Mr. Spagnola will be the case manager. He will support Mrs. Mackenzie in implementing the intervention and assist in efforts to monitor progress. Jamal's progress will be discussed at the fourth-grade team meeting in four weeks.

Sample "RTI Collaboration Log."

RTI Navigation Team Initial Meeting Form

Date: _____

Team members: _____ _____

_____ _____ _____

_____ _____ _____

Target RTI implementation date: _____

Participating grade levels/schools: _____

_____

_____

School or district priorities in implementing RTI: _____

_____

_____

_____

_____

Staff member(s) overseeing development:

_____ _____

Timeline and planning for staff introduction: _____

_____

_____

_____

_____

Staff member(s) overseeing development:

_____ _____

CONTINUED ➤

RTI Navigation Team Initial Meeting Form *(continued)*

Timeline and planning for establishing school baseline: _____

_____

_____

_____

_____

_____

Staff member(s) overseeing development:

_____   _____   _____

Timeline and planning for parent introduction: _____

_____

_____

_____

_____

_____

Staff member(s) overseeing development:

_____   _____   _____

Notes: _____

_____

_____

_____

_____

_____

RTI School Baseline Survey

Section 1: Professional Skill and Development.

Please indicate the extent to which you use or are familiar with the below practices.	Use	Familiar	Unfamiliar
Transdisciplinary teaming			
Differentiated instruction			
Student thinking and learning styles			
Multiple intelligences			
Grouping strategies			
Progress monitoring			
Universal screening assessments			
Diagnostic evaluation			
Research-based instructional strategies			
Research-based programs			
Curriculum-based measurements			

Section 2: Collaborative School Climate

Please indicate how you feel about collaborating with other teachers at your school. Circle "6" to show that you strongly agree with a statement and "1" to indicate that you strongly disagree.	Disagree					Agree
Given the busy schedule of a teacher, collaboration with other colleagues is not a practical idea.	1	2	3	4	5	6
It is easier for me to figure out solutions to student learning problems rather than rely on input and opinions of others.	1	2	3	4	5	6
I don't understand the collaborative teaming process or how it can benefit me in the classroom.	1	2	3	4	5	6
In collaborating with others, I will probably be required to agree with them or use their ideas when I may actually disagree.	1	2	3	4	5	6
The ability to be a successful collaborator is a special gift some educators may not be able to develop.	1	2	3	4	5	6
Collaboration is too time consuming to be an efficient means for resolving student difficulties.	1	2	3	4	5	6

CONTINUED

RTI School Baseline Survey (continued)

Section 3: Teaming Process

Please rate the following statements on team building by identifying how important you feel each area is. Circling a "6" indicates you believe a statement is very important. Circling "1" indicates you don't believe it is important.	Not Important					Important
Teams should develop appropriate academic interventions for student needs, starting with the identification of a learning goal.	1	2	3	4	5	6
Team members should encourage fellow educators to consult RTI teams when they have student-specific or class-wide concerns.	1	2	3	4	5	6
When appropriate, parents should play a role in the work of RTI teams.	1	2	3	4	5	6
Teams should clearly define the role each member has in working on a specific student concern or group task.	1	2	3	4	5	6
As much as possible, teams should effectively support teachers in meeting the needs of students in the general education setting.	1	2	3	4	5	6
Team members should be respectful and work together.	1	2	3	4	5	6

Section 4: Intervention Readiness

Please indicate the extent to which you use or are familiar with the below practices for academic interventions.	Use	Familiar	Unfamiliar
Skill areas for determining interventions:			
Develop step-by-step intervention plan			
Identify others who can assist in intervention			
Define academic difficulties in observable, measurable terms			
Collect pre-intervention (or baseline) data			
Implement ongoing progress monitoring			
Skill areas for determining effectiveness of intervention:			
Assess whether intervention was implemented as planned			
Chart and graph the results			
Compare baseline data with post-intervention data			
Use systematic classroom observation			
Refer to group standardized test scores			
Use progress monitoring			
Administer outcome tests			

Summary Form of RTI School Baseline Survey

_____

(School Name)

Section 1. Professional Skill and Development. This section gauges staff members' familiarity with instruction, assessment, and grouping methods that are important in RTI.

Staff members are most skilled in the following areas:

_____

_____

_____

_____

_____

Staff members are least skilled in the following areas:

_____

_____

_____

_____

_____

Section 2. Collaborative School Climate. Teachers and administrative staff offer their feelings about collaborating in various school environments.

The baseline score for our collaborative school climate is based on a 6-point scale with 6 being high agreement and 1 being low agreement. Our averaged collaborative school climate score is _____. Following are averages of staff responses for each question.

Staff attitudes about collaborating with other teachers. A "6" shows strong agreement with a statement and "1" indicates strong disagreement.	
Given the busy schedule of a teacher, collaboration with other colleagues is not a practical idea.	
It is easier for me to figure out solutions to student learning problems rather than rely on input and opinions of others.	
I don't understand the collaborative teaming process or how it can benefit me in the classroom.	
In collaborating with others, I will probably be required to agree with them or use their ideas when I may actually disagree.	
The ability to be a successful collaborator is a special gift some educators may not be able to develop.	
Collaboration is too time consuming to be an efficient means for resolving student difficulties.	

CONTINUED ➤

Summary Form of RTI School Baseline Survey (continued)

Section 3. Teaming Process. This portion of the survey concerns attitudes about RTI teaming processes.

The baseline score for our teaming process is based on a 6-point scale with 6 being high importance and 1 being low importance. Our averaged teaming process score is _____. Following are averages of staff responses for each question.

Staff attitudes about priorities within the teaming process. A "6" indicates respondent feels idea is very important; "1" indicates respondent feels sentiment is not important.	
Teams should develop appropriate academic interventions for student needs, starting with the identification of a learning goal.	
Team members should encourage fellow educators to consult RTI teams when they have student-specific or class-wide concerns.	
When appropriate, parents should play a role in the work of RTI teams.	
Teams should clearly define the role each member has in working on a specific student concern or group task.	
As much as possible, teams should effectively support teachers in meeting the needs of students in the general education setting.	
Team members should be respectful and work together.	

Section 4. Intervention Readiness. The last section of the baseline survey allows staff members to report their familiarity with intervention and progress monitoring strategies.

Staff members are most familiar with and/or are using these methods for determining interventions and evaluating their effectiveness:

Staff members are most unfamiliar with these methods for determining interventions and evaluting their effectiveness:

_____

_____

_____

_____

_____

RTI Navigation Team Ongoing Planning Form

Training needs revealed by RTI School Baseline Survey: _____

_____

_____

_____

_____

_____

_____

Timeline and planning for RTI professional development: _____

_____

_____

_____

_____

_____

_____

_____

Staff member(s) overseeing development:

_____   _____   _____

Material needs revealed by inventory of school resources: _____

_____

_____

_____

_____

_____

_____

CONTINUED ➤

RTI Navigation Team Ongoing Planning Form (continued)

Planning for addressing material needs: _____

_____

_____

_____

_____

_____

Staff member(s) overseeing development:

_____   _____   _____

Planning for screening measures: _____

_____

_____

_____

_____

_____

Staff member(s) overseeing development:

_____   _____   _____

Special education referral process: _____

_____

_____

_____

_____

_____

Staff member(s) overseeing development:

_____   _____   _____

RTI Student Referral Form

Student Name: _____ Date: _____

Referring Teacher: _____ Grade: _____

Academic challenges for which student is being referred. Please indicate the specific academic difficulty student is exhibiting.

_____

_____

_____

_____

Have interventions previously been implemented to address this difficulty? If yes, please describe

Yes _____ No _____

Tier _____

_____

_____

_____

_____

Tier _____

_____

_____

_____

_____

Notes: _____

_____

_____

_____

RTI Collaboration Log

Student Name: _____

Date: _____ Grade: _____ Tier: _____

Team members: _____ _____
                       Referring Teacher   Facilitator

_____ _____ _____
Recorder   Case Manager   Support Staff

_____ _____ _____
Support Staff   Support Staff   Support Staff

1. Identify Academic Strengths and Challenges. Referring teacher provides student academic information to the group to initiate problem-solving process (reference "RTI Student Referral Form").

_____

_____

_____

_____

2. Analyze Challenges. Team members paraphrase academic challenges and ask questions to clarify their understanding of student performance.

_____

_____

_____

_____

3. Establish Academic Baseline and Learning Preferences. Use data to establish measurable baseline of student achievement and document learning strengths.

_____

_____

_____

_____

RTI Collaboration Log *(continued)*

4. Brainstorm Teaching Strategies and Interventions. List strategies and interventions that may be used to remediate skill deficits, accounting for personalized learner data.

_____

_____

_____

_____

5. Develop an Intervention Plan. Determine and document intervention plan, including who will be responsible for carrying it out and ensuring fidelity of implementation.

_____

_____

_____

_____

6. Develop an Evaluation Plan. Document method by which effectiveness of intervention will be determined.

_____

_____

_____

_____

7. Establish a Case Manager. At the same time you determine a case manager, you can also set a date for a follow-up meeting.

_____

_____

_____

_____

Part II

Assessment

Assessment plays a vital role with Response to Intervention. The model emphasizes the importance of identifying learning difficulties early, before students fall significantly behind their peers. But the need for assessment extends beyond simply testing for academic achievement. It's also essential for getting to know student interests and discovering the ways they best learn. When we know our students well and account for their unique needs, we are able to provide the most effective instruction.

Part II helps you develop a comprehensive assessment program at your school. Chapter 3 features personalized learner assessments that identify learning styles, multiple intelligence preferences, interest areas, and other student qualities. In addition to providing insight for designing instruction, these tools can be helpful in affirming children and building student-teacher and peer relationships within the classroom. Chapter 4 provides information on assessment procedures—including screening and progress monitoring—important within the RTI model. The chapter also features tools you can use to compile assessment data, document interventions, and make decisions about student instruction.

It's likely that you and your school already rely on many of the assessments discussed in Part II. Chapters 3 and 4, though, can help you streamline your current assessment efforts so that they directly support RTI procedures. These tools can simplify your efforts to document interventions and allow you to effectively share information about students with different RTI teams.

Chapter 3

Personalized Learner Assessment

Getting to know students through personalized learner assessment is an important component of RTI. The model requires that instructional decision-making be based on students' specific strengths, weaknesses, and interest areas.

Identifying students' interest areas and learning styles might seem overwhelming because of the already enormous demands upon educators' time. But discovering sources of student motivation and strength is essential if teachers are to make meaningful learning connections. Incorporating interests and learning styles into instruction can help you engage students and best meet their unique learning needs.

This chapter presents a variety of fun and educational tools you can use to learn more about your students—including their hobbies, motivations, multiple intelligences preferences, and learning and thinking styles. Among these are welcoming activities, such as those presented in the opening weeks of school. You can also ask that children (individually or with the help of an adult) complete inventories of their preferences. These activities and instruments can be used in conjunction with other tools in this book.

Benefits of Personalized Learner Assessment

Understanding the unique attributes of learners can help you design effective instruction, but the advantages of getting to know students extend far beyond drawing up lesson plans for the classroom.

One key to fostering academic success is convincing students it is possible for them to succeed. When you show them you want to know more about their strengths and preferences, you send the message that the unique things about them are important. Incorporating these individual qualities and interests into your instruction can promote positive attitudes about learning, help students maintain focus and explore new areas of creativity, and push students to reach higher levels of potential. Building relationships with students can take time, but increased academic achievement and greater emotional well-being make it time well spent.

Another benefit of personalized assessment is the effect it can have on peer relationships. Research shows that students' academic growth increases when they feel part of a safe and supportive environment—both in regard to staff and peers.* Personalized learner assessments have the potential to reveal connections between students and thus build community in the classroom. Learners will be involved in activities that allow them to share personal stories and strengths. Showing that these unique attributes are valued can help you foster a classroom community that is built on acceptance. Structured activities like "Coat of Arms" (page 62) and "School Yellow Pages" (page 63) can help you accomplish this goal.

Beyond the social benefits of identifying personalized learner information are the academic implications. Understanding students' multiple intelligences and learning and thinking preferences can help you design academic interventions tailored to students' respective strengths and learning styles at all three tiers of RTI. These learner attributes can present you with a variety of options for the kind of instruction you use, how you deliver lessons, and what students can do to demonstrate what they know.

Another benefit of personalized learner assessments is creating flexible learning groups. This grouping component becomes very important in RTI because of every teacher's need to vary the curriculum. In cooperative groups, students can contribute to the greater effort while capitalizing on their given learning strengths. The result: meaningful and productive group work that supports all students.

Tools for Personalized Learner Assessment

This chapter includes several reproducible forms to help with personalized learner assessment. These activities and inventories can be administered in a variety of ways based on your needs. Additionally, time restrictions or other circumstances specific to your setting may guide how you prioritize administering the assessments.

*Goodenow (2003), Klern and Connell (2004), and Ryan and Patrick (2001).

Assessments on pages 61–64 can be useful in identifying student interests and building community in your classroom. Results from the assessments on pages 65–70 (concerning thinking and learning styles and multiple intelligences preferences) will be instrumental in determining appropriate academic interventions for students. Assessments include:

What Makes a Great Teacher? (page 61). Use this classroom activity to better understand the expectations that students and parents have of you as a teacher. This information can be helpful in communicating with learners and their families, planning instruction, and setting individual student goals.

The Perfect Classroom (page 61). Students map out their preferred learning environments. Analyze this information to identify and implement within the classroom any themes that emerge.

Coat of Arms (page 62). This activity gives students the opportunity to share things that are important to them—from interest areas to fundamental personal beliefs they hold. The exercise can help students develop a better sense of themselves and their classmates through sharing personal experiences and interests.

Yellow Pages (page 63). This activity highlights the many talents, strengths, and interests of your students. Sharing this information at the classroom level can help build feelings of community among learners.

Student Interest Inventory (page 64). This assessment helps you get to know students on a deeper level and establish strong teacher-learner relationships. This information helps set learning objectives, group students, and ensure student interest.

Thinking and Learning Styles Inventory (page 65). This classroom activity can help you understand how students best process information and communicate what they know. The information can assist in planning instruction that accounts for each student's thinking and learning styles.

Parent Checklist (page 68). Parents usually know their children better than anyone else. Involve parents by asking them to contribute information about their children's multiple intelligences to help you teach to the respective strengths of your students.

Multiple Intelligences Teacher Observation (page 70). Use this form of assessment to document observations of students' multiple intelligences within the classroom. Designing instruction that accounts for multiple intelligences can help you effectively meet individual learning needs.

Each of the assessments is set up similarly. Descriptions of the exercises are followed by guidelines for administering them and recommendations for integrating students' interests and strengths into instruction. You can use the "What to Try When" charts in Chapter 6 to match up learner attributes with research-based strategies.

In addition to the exercises provided here, you can find assessment tools in "Web-Based Learning Strengths Assessments" on page 71.

What Makes a Great Teacher?

Knowing what students value in a teacher is helpful in the classroom. The "What Makes a Great Teacher?" form (page 72) can give you insight into how to effectively communicate with students and shape instruction to best meet their needs. Another benefit: Gathering this information can improve the classroom climate, because learners feel validated and part of a community when their opinions are taken into account.

The "What Makes a Great Teacher?" questionnaire is useful at the beginning of the year. As you share your expectations with students, you can demonstrate your genuine interest in their feelings and wishes for the year. Secondary students should be able to complete the form in one sitting without assistance. You could ask students to write a brief essay on one of the questions (such as writing about their favorite teacher from the past and why). You might offer the option of completing the form electronically.

> Personalized learner assessments can help you identify student interests, build community in the classroom, and determine appropriate academic interventions.

For elementary grades, you might elect from a few different options for collecting the information. With very young students, you could hold a classroom discussion of the questions on the form, writing students' answers on the board. Another option is to send the form home with younger students, asking them to complete it with the help of parents. You might send two copies so parents can share their expectations of you. It's also a good idea to include a note enlisting their support as strong partners in the education of their child. Emphasize that you want children to feel welcome in your classroom and that you're interested in how they best learn.

The Perfect Classroom

Another useful activity for the beginning of the year is "The Perfect Classroom." How students construct an ideal learning environment can tell you a lot about what makes them feel comfortable. The activity can also reveal a lot about learning preferences. Students who put many desks or beanbags together might value collaborating with peers and have a high degree of interpersonal intelligence. This may affirm the need for a place in the classroom where small groups can assemble. Information from this activity can be especially helpful when viewed alongside other interest and learning style inventories.

When introducing "The Perfect Classroom" activity to students, explain that it should be a model of a real classroom (rather than a fantasy learning environment). The form on page 73 includes a list of some items that might be included in the room.

Elementary students may enjoy drawing their ideal learning environments. For secondary students, you may want them to complete the activity on a computer. You can provide the electronic form from this book's CD-ROM and students can insert clipart or other graphics. Another option: Ask students to design classrooms online using the "Classroom Architect" feature at the 4Teachers "Teach with Technology" Web site (classroom.4teachers.org). When all of your students have completed the activity, it is up to you to analyze their creations. You may wish to have a group discussion about how you can best set up your classroom. (Be sure to check with your principal for any policies on school furniture or classroom design.) While you probably will not be able to accommodate all suggestions offered by students, you can observe trends and make adjustments to account for individuals' needs.

Coat of Arms

"Coat of Arms" is a fun exercise that can build community in the classroom and reveal student interests. Learners create a coat of arms using images and words that represent things important to them. Then they share what they have done with their classmates. Coats of arms can be posted in the room or hallway as affirmation of students' unique qualities.

The type of information you elicit from students will vary depending upon the ages and abilities of your students. Here are some of different questions you might ask learners as they complete the activity.

- What is an important event that you can remember—something that has made you the person you are today?

- What is your favorite game, hobby, or activity?

- What is the best part of the school day?

- Who is your most favorite person in the world?

- What are you most proud of or happy about?

- What is a motto you have for everyday living?

The idea is to engage students in a way that builds confidence and community in the classroom. With younger students, you might ask them to complete the activity at home with parents.

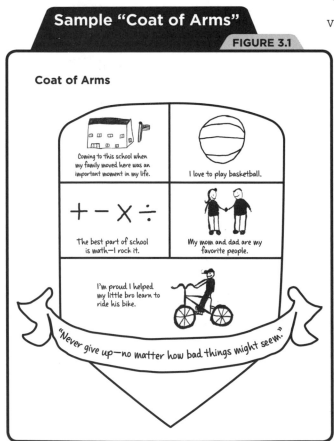

Sample "Coat of Arms"

FIGURE 3.1

Coat of Arms

Coming to this school when my family moved here was an important moment in my life.

I love to play basketball.

$+ - \times \div$

The best part of school is math—I rock it.

My mom and dad are my favorite people.

I'm proud I helped my little bro learn to ride his bike.

"Never give up—no matter how bad things might seem."

"Coat of Arms" on page 74.

A coat of arms template is provided on page 74, but any type of display that enables children to highlight themselves could be used. You might ask students to use photos, hand-drawn pictures, magazine cuttings, or other images to represent responses. If you work with secondary students, you may wish for them to create products in an electronic format. The options are limitless.

When students have finished displays, designate class time to allow learners to introduce their creations to the larger group. You might do this all at once or space the presentations over the course of a few days. The objective is to ensure students are able to talk about some of the things that are important to them and promote acceptance of others within the larger group. As you watch the presentations, facilitate discussion that highlights the unique qualities of students. These qualities can also help you group learners for future lessons.

Yellow Pages

Another great way to promote the unique individual abilities and interests of students is the "Yellow Pages" activity. Students identify themselves as knowledgeable or skilled in specific areas; learners then are listed in a "telephone book" of experts and may be consulted when a question in their area of expertise arises. The "Yellow Pages" activity gives you insight into learners' interests, and it can also help students—especially those who may be shy—to connect with peers. The activity can bring together students with common interests who previously may not have made a connection.

The "Yellow Pages" activity can be conducted in a variety of ways to suit your specific purposes. For example, it can be done on a school-wide level or within a single classroom. In the elementary grades, the "Yellow Pages Expert Form" (page 75) may be sent home so students can confer with their parents. For secondary students, you might allow them to work in small groups to brainstorm about their respective areas of expertise. Before the activity, you might distribute a list of expert areas you would like to see filled or allow student preferences to determine those represented.

After the expertise areas have been determined, the Yellow Pages are compiled, bound, and disseminated to each participating classroom. They can also be made available in electronic format. The form features space for three possible expert areas, so students could be listed in three different sections within the bound Yellow Pages. You can, however, use the template on the CD-ROM to adjust this as necessary. You can encourage students to refer to the Yellow Pages when they need help with a task. For example, a student searching for a picture for the coat of arms might search within the reference under "graphic arts."

Sample "Yellow Pages Expert Form" and Completed Yellow Pages Activity

FIGURE 3.2

Yellow Pages Expert Form

Name: Shelby Lanois

Grade: 6th   Age: 11

Teacher's Name: Mr. Raymond   Room Number: 603

Expert Area 1: Working on the computer

I spend __8__ hours a week at this activity.

I consider myself to be _____ at this activity. (circle one)
(excellent)   good   fair

Comments: I don't just play games when I'm on the computer. I like to figure out how programs work and do cool stuff online. I even have my own blog! But I guess I like playing games, too.

Expert Area 2: Basketball

I spend __7__ hours a week at this activity.

I consider myself to be _____ at this activity. (circle one)
excellent   (good)   fair

Comments: I love basketball. We have practice after school and I play with my mom on the weekends. Coach says I have a great jump shot.

Expert Area 3: Performing in front of others (like in the theater)

I spend __4__ hours a week at this activity.

I consider myself to be _____ at this activity. (circle one)
excellent   (good)   fair

Comments: I'm in the drama club. We're practicing to put on a performance of "A Christmas Carol" during the holiday season. I have the part of Scrooge!

"Yellow Pages Expert Form" on page 75.

Sixth Grade Yellow Pages

C

Computer

Expert	Homeroom Teacher
Callie Anderson	Mrs. Kay
Rashard Daniels	Mr. Raymond
Kristin Humphrey	Mr. Raymond
Marianne James	Ms. Robertson
Shelby Lanios	Mr. Raymond
Avery McDonald	Ms. Robertson
Rachel Nance	Mrs. Kay
Leilani Samuels	Mrs. Kay

8

Sixth Grade Yellow Pages

Zamzam Sharif	Ms. Robertson
Jing Tan	Mr. Raymond
Charlie Waters	Mrs. Kay
Sam Youngston	Ms. Robertson

D

Dance

Expert	Homeroom Teacher
Abby Boettcher	Mrs. Kay
Lize Brouhan	Ms. Robertson
Emily Haynes	Mr. Raymond
Alejandro Diaz	Ms. Robertson

9

Student Interest Inventory

Similar to the other activities in this chapter, the "Student Interest Inventory" compiles information that helps to determine classroom instruction—including how to engage learners, set academic goals, and group students. The more you know about your students, the better your relationships with them can be.

Two versions of the "Student Interest Inventory" are at the end of this section. Level I (pages 76–78) is more basic and geared for elementary grades. Level II (pages 79–81) is intended for secondary students. You can determine which inventory level is appropriate for your students. Additionally, how you administer the inventory might vary depending on the level at which you teach. Following are some variations you might consider:

- Administer the inventory over multiple days (for example, one page per day)

- Allow students to complete the form on a computer (using the Word form on the enclosed CD-ROM)

- Use a game format (for example, put the questions on popsicle sticks, ask a student to draw a popsicle stick, read the question, and write down an answer)

- Ask older students to help younger learners complete the questions (students eight years or older ask questions and document the responses of younger students)

- Design your own inventory (select questions appropriate for an individual or group of students, adding others you deem important)

Infusing student interests into lesson plans can help you ensure engagement, design instruction that accounts for individual student choices, and effectively differentiate content for unique needs.

Thinking and Learning Styles Inventory

How we try to reach students and ask them to demonstrate their knowledge will have a great impact on their academic achievement. The "Thinking and Learning Styles Inventory" helps determine the ways students best take in and process information. Level I of the inventory (page 82) is for elementary grades and Level II (pages 84–85) is for secondary education. You can determine which version is appropriate for your classroom.

Understanding students' thinking and learning styles can give you powerful insight into assigning school tasks. But what are the ways in which students process information?

Thinking Styles

Analytic thinkers. Those who think analytically tend to be logical in their approach to learning and problem-solving. They generally prefer order and are deliberate in carrying out tasks. These students are usually detail-oriented and timely in completing work. They typically prefer to work on projects in a step-by-step process without interruption.

Global thinkers. Students who think globally are typically less structured in how they learn and perform at school. These learners may seem disorganized and less cognizant of time limitations or deadlines. They generally prefer to work on multiple projects simultaneously. Students who are global thinkers usually bring a big-picture mentality to problem solving and concepts make more sense to them when they are able to understand the greater context. They are generally "idea" people who prefer open-ended tasks.

Spotlight

Using the Results of Thinking and Learning Style Inventories

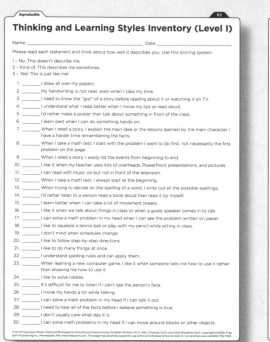

"Thinking and Learning Styles Inventory (Level I)" on page 82.

"Thinking and Learning Styles Inventory Scoring Guide (Level I)" on page 83.

"Thinking and Learning Styles Inventory (Level II)" on pages 84–85.

"Thinking and Learning Styles Inventory Scoring Guide (Level II)" on page 86.

After you have administered the appropriate "Thinking and Learning Style Inventory" to your students, transfer student responses to the "Thinking and Learning Styles Inventory Scoring Guide." Total each of the five columns to find out the types of learners in your classroom. The highest score of the first three columns indicates the learning style the student favors (visual, auditory, or kinesthetic). The highest score of the final two columns indicates the preferred thinking style (global or analytic).

If two of the three learning style scores are close to the same, students likely prefer a combination of styles. Typically a person thinks either globally or analytically. If a student's scores are close to the same, the test results may not be valid. In this case, you might go through the form with learners to ensure they have understood the questions.

In this example from a secondary classroom, the student is clearly a global thinker who processes information visually. Knowing this, you can adjust your instruction as necessary. For example, if the student struggles with a particular academic skill, you can identify promising teaching strategies for global thinkers who prefer visual learning in the "What to Try When" charts in Chapter 6 (reference the "Key Learning Styles and Multiple Intelligences" column).

Reproducible 86

Thinking and Learning Styles Inventory Scoring Guide (Level II)

Student Name: _Alyssa Knox_   Date: _October 5th_

Transfer student scores to the grid below. For example, if a student scored the first item with a 3 (This often describes me.) enter a 3 in the blank. When you have entered all the scores for each question, total each of the five columns.

Item Score	Item Score	Item Score	Item Score	Item Score
1. 3	2. 2	4. 2	5. 2	6. 1
3. 2	7. 1	10. 2	11. 3	13. 2
8. 3	9. 1	14. 2	12. 3	18. 2
15. 3	17. 1	20. 1	19. 2	22. 1
16. 2	21. 1	24. 2	23. 2	29. 1
26. 3	25. 2	27. 1	28. 3	31. 1
33. 3	32. 2	36. 2	30. 3	34. 1
35. 3	37. 1	40. 2	39. 3	38. 1
TOTAL 22	TOTAL 11	TOTAL 14	TOTAL 21	TOTAL 10
Visual	Auditory	Kinesthetic	Global	Analytic

Learning Style   **Thinking Style**

Within the first three columns, the highest total indicates a student's favored learning style (visual, auditory, or kinesthetic). The highest score within the last two columns suggests a student's preferred thinking style (global or analytic).

The lowest score possible for learning or thinking style is 8; this score suggests that students do not feel a particular style describes them. A score of 24, on the other hand, suggests that students strongly prefer a given mode of learning or thinking. A high score of 18 or more is a strong indicator of a student's preferred learning or thinking style. A score of 10 or less is a strong indicator that students are not inclined to a particular style of learning or thinking.

Sample "Thinking and Leaning Styles Inventory Scoring Guide (Level II)."

Learning Styles

Visual learners. Visual learners generally learn best through seeing. These students are skilled in remembering and processing information that comes in the form of images and presentations.

Auditory learners. Students who are auditory learners learn best by listening. For these learners, lectures and other spoken information can be easily remembered and synthesized.

Kinesthetic learners. Kinesthetic learners generally process information best when they are able to incorporate touch or movement into learning.

Parent Checklist

Multiple intelligences (MI), identified by Howard Gardner, have revolutionized what it means to be "smart." This grouping of eight intelligences allows for the fact that children (as well as adults) have unique aptitude strengths, areas that can be tapped to improve overall academic achievement.

Limitations in verbal/linguistic ability, for example, may result in a student struggling with writing papers in different subject areas. The same students who struggle with essays, however, might have strong visual/spatial intelligence, which allows them to create presentations that demonstrate what they know about a topic. Without accounting for these learning strengths, it might be assumed that students writing incoherent essays don't understand the subject material. When the same students are given an alternative product to create, however, they are able to demonstrate their knowledge.

The "Parent Checklist" is designed to help you establish students' strongest areas of aptitude. Multiple intelligences are an important part of a child's full learning profile. For this reason, it's important to try to obtain parent feedback on strength areas early in the school year. (If you receive your class list during the summer, you may even consider sending the checklist along with a letter of introduction.) You might also share what you learn about students' MI preferences in parent-teacher conferences. The information can be helpful to parents to understand children's unique strengths and get them on board as partners in education.

Multiple Intelligences Preferences

Student abilities within MI categories can vary. Multiple intelligences are:

Verbal/Linguistic. Students with strong verbal/linguistic intelligence tend to excel in language (spoken and written). These learners usually enjoy reading, writing, and speaking with others.

Spotlight

Using Multiple Intelligences Preferences to Guide Instruction

After you've received the completed checklist from parents, use the "Parent Checklist Scoring Guide" (page 89) to determine students' MI preferences. As with thinking and learning styles, this information can then be referenced as you design instruction and academic interventions for specific learning challenges (reference the "Multiple Intelligences Preferences and Key Learning Styles" column of the "What to Try When" charts in Chapter 6).

In this example, the parent's responses strongly suggest this student has a strong preference for bodily/kinesthetic modes of learning and a high level of aptitude in the naturalist multiple intelligences category.

89

Parent Checklist Scoring Guide

Student Name: _Alyssa Knox_   Date: _October 5th_

Transfer the checks the parents gave next to each item below. When you have entered all the checks, total the number of checks in each of the eight columns. Some items are listed twice because the statements on the checklist are related to two intelligences. The highest number of checks indicates the parents' perception of their child's strongest multiple intelligence.

Item	Item	Item	Item	Item	Item	Item	Item
6. ___	1. X	7. ___	2. X	3. X	4. ___	10. ___	5. ___
11. X	12. X	9. ___	10. ___	16. ___	8. X	17. X	7. ___
15. ___	19. ___	18. ___	14. ___	21. ___	22. X	20. ___	13. X
41. ___	23. X	25. ___	26. ___	24. ___	31. X	29. X	32. ___
43. ___	27. X	35. ___	34. X	33. ___	42. X	30. ___	38. ___
44. ___	28. X	37. ___	45. ___	36. ___	46. ___	39. ___	40. X
Verbal/ Linguistic	Bodily/ Kinesthetic	Intra-personal	Logical/ Mathematical	Musical/ Rhythmic	Naturalist	Visual/ Spatial	Inter-personal
TOTAL 1	TOTAL 5	TOTAL 0	TOTAL 2	TOTAL 1	TOTAL 4	TOTAL 2	TOTAL 2

Note: Numbers 7 and 10 appear twice because the statements apply to more than one intelligence.

"Parent Checklist" on pages 87–88.

Sample "Parent Checklist Scoring Guide."

Logical/Mathematical. Those with advanced logical/mathematical skills generally enjoy working with numbers and coming up with solutions through use of established problem-solving methods. Math and science are generally subjects favored by these students.

Visual/Spatial. Students who have high levels of visual/spatial intelligence are typically skilled in learning through images. These learners also generally perform well when they are asked to demonstrate their knowledge by visual means.

Bodily/Kinesthetic. Those with bodily/kinesthetic intelligence tend to have well-developed motor skills. These students often enjoy learning (and showing what they have learned) through movement.

Musical/Rhythmic. Learners with high levels of musical/rhythmic intelligence are usually skilled in understanding different elements of sound and rhythm. These students learn well through music and also often write or play it well.

Interpersonal. Strong interpersonal intelligence allows students to get along well with others. These learners are often good leaders and enjoy working in groups.

Intrapersonal. Students who have high levels of intrapersonal intelligence are typically introspective. While they may enjoy working with others at times, they usually excel in individual tasks that allow them to reflect on their own.

Naturalist. Students with talents as naturalist learners usually feel comfortable in diverse environments and often enjoy exploring their surroundings. These learners often enjoy the outdoors.

Multiple Intelligences Teacher Observation

The "Multiple Intelligences Teacher Observation Form" (pages 90–92) supplements the parent feedback on MI preferences with observations of your own. To begin, list students' names on the blank lines along the left margin. Then review the list of characteristics (listed on the second and third pages of the form). Reading across each row, check the qualities that apply to the student. The multiple intelligences with the most checks are considered strengths of that student.

When reviewed alongside the "Student Interest Inventory" and the "Thinking and Learning Styles Inventory," this data can provide great insight into students' unique learning needs. Reference the "Key Learning Styles and Multiple Intelligences" column of the "What to Try When" charts in Chapter 6 to find out how to use this information to best reach learners.

 **Spotlight**

Web-Based Learning Strengths Assessments

Web-based assessments can be used to supplement the tools found in this book. Many of the following sources offer student-friendly versions, which can be taken online or printed off and scored by hand. Due to the reading level and technological skills needed, most of these online thinking and learning styles and multiple intelligences assessments are designed for secondary students. Many assessments can be used with younger students if an adult or older student is available to read and explain the items.

Abiator's Online Learning Styles Inventory
www.berghuis.co.nz/abiator/lsi/lsiframe.html

Two Learning Styles tests, a Multiple Intelligences Assessment, and an Analytic/Global Test are available at this Web site. Tests range from 30–56 questions.

Learning Styles Online
www.learning-styles-online.com

This site offers a Web version of the Memletics learning styles inventory. Students can answer the 70 questions online or download the test in Microsoft Excel or Adobe PDF. Results are presented graphically and organized in the following categories: visual, aural, verbal, physical, logical, social, and solitary. The site also offers easy-to-read explanations of the categories.

Literacy Works
literacyworks.org/mi/home.html

The 56-question assessment found at this Web site is based on Howard Gardner's multiple intelligences. Results indicate a student's top three intelligences.

Personal Thinking Styles
www.thelearningweb.net/personalthink.html

Personal Thinking Styles offers a different take on learning styles by assessing how students think versus how they learn. Thinking styles include: concrete sequential, concrete random, abstract random, and abstract sequential.

What Makes a Great Teacher?

1. What are the five most important qualities in a great teacher? Number these qualities 1–5 (1 being most important). Place an X by any other qualities you feel are important but not in your top five.

____ Caring	____ Answers all questions
____ Fair	____ Good listener
____ Creative	____ Positive role model
____ Makes me want to do my best	____ Understanding
____ Respectful	____ Calm
____ Praises students	____ Disciplinarian
____ Believes in me	____ Tries new things
____ Enthusiastic	____ Gives me extra help
____ Smart	____ Grades papers right away
____ Teaches in a variety of ways	____ Other: _____
____ Enjoys teaching	____ Other: _____

2. Look back at what you marked as the most important quality. Why must a great teacher have this quality?

_____

_____

_____

_____

3. What strategies have teachers taught you that have helped you become a better student?

_____

_____

_____

_____

4. Who is the best teacher you have ever had? Why?

_____

_____

_____

_____

The Perfect Classroom

Draw a picture of the perfect classroom. Here are some things you might include:

Tables	Teacher's Desk	Student Desks	Computers	Bean Bags
Study Center	Shelves	Listening Center	Rug	TV/Projector
Art Center	Bulletin Boards	Class Library	Kitchen	Science Center

Coat of Arms

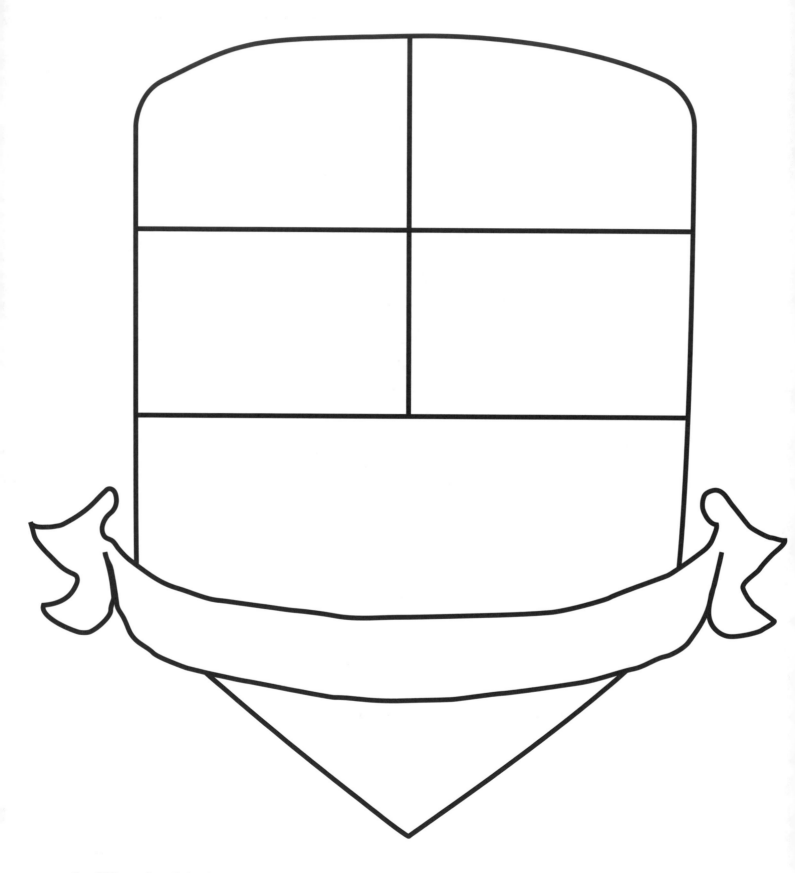

Yellow Pages Expert Form

Name: _____

Grade: _____ Age: _____

Teacher's Name: _____ Room Number: _____

Expert Area 1: _____

I spend _____ hours a week at this activity.

I consider myself to be _____ at this activity. (circle one)

　　　excellent　　　good　　　fair

Comments: _____

_____

Expert Area 2: _____

I spend _____ hours a week at this activity.

I consider myself to be _____ at this activity. (circle one)

　　　excellent　　　good　　　fair

Comments: _____

_____

Expert Area 3: _____

I spend _____ hours a week at this activity.

I consider myself to be _____ at this activity. (circle one)

　　　excellent　　　good　　　fair

Comments: _____

_____

Student Interest Inventory (Level I)

Name: _____ Date: _____

Answer each of the questions as best as you can. Remember, there are no wrong answers—this activity is for learning more about you.

1. Circle the feelings you experience most in school.

Happy	Frustrated	Sad	Angry
Excited	Bored	Interested	Confused
Other: _____	Other: _____	Other: _____	Other: _____

2. What is something you liked about school last year? Why? _____

_____

3. What is something you didn't like about last year? Why? _____

_____

4. What is your favorite thing to do after school? _____

_____

5. Who do you think is the smartest person in the world? Why? _____

_____

6. What is one thing every child should have? Why? _____

_____

7. If you could give an award to someone in your family, what would it be? _____

_____

8. Who is one of your best friends? Why? _____

_____

CONTINUED ➜

Student Interest Inventory (Level I) *(continued)*

9. What do you get excited about? _____

_____

10. What kind of books do you like to read? _____

_____

11. Circle your favorite way to work in class.

a) by myself   b) with a partner   c) in a small group   d) as a whole class

12. Circle the way you learn best.

a) by listening   b) by doing   c) by watching   d) by reading

13. What is a special compliment you have received? _____

_____

14. What can I do as a teacher to make learning more interesting for you? ____

_____

15. What is something you want to learn more about this year? _____

_____

16. Where would you like to sit in the classroom? _____

_____

17. What do you worry about? _____

_____

Student Interest Inventory (Level I) (continued)

18. What do you need help with in school? _____

_____

19. When do you laugh? _____

_____

20. What is one thing you want me to know about you? _____

_____

Rate how much you like the subjects listed below:

Subject	Love it	It's okay	Not very much	Not at all
Reading				
Math				
Spelling				
Writing				
Social Studies				
Science				
Music				
Art				
P.E.				
_____				
_____				

Student Interest Inventory (Level II)

Name: _____ Date: _____

Answer each of the questions as best as you can. Remember, there are no wrong answers—this activity is for learning more about you.

1. What is something you liked about school last year? Why? _____

_____

2. What is something you didn't like about last year? Why? _____

_____

3. What hobbies or special interests do you have outside of school? _____

_____

4. Do you think you will be different in 20 years? How? _____

_____

5. Who is one of your best friends? Why are you so close? _____

_____

6. Who is one of the luckiest people you know? Why is he or she so lucky? _____

_____

7. What is the best compliment someone could ever give you? _____

_____

8. Do you ever feel shy? If yes, when? _____

_____

9. Do you want to go to college? Why or why not? _____

_____

CONTINUED ➤

Student Interest Inventory (Level II) (continued)

10. What would you like to do for a job when you finish school? _____

_____

11. Circle your favorite way to work in class.

a) by myself   b) with a partner   c) in a small group   d) as a whole class

12. Circle the way you learn best.

a) by listening   b) by doing   c) by watching   d) by reading

13. What TV shows do you like to watch? _____

_____

14. Who do you think is the smartest person in the world? Why? _____

_____

15. Does being in school motivate or drain you? Why do you think that is? _____

_____

16. What subject would you like to teach if you were a teacher? _____

_____

17. Whose advice do you listen to? Why can you trust this person? _____

_____

18. What can I do as a teacher to make learning more interesting for you? _____

_____

19. What is something you want to learn more about this year? _____

_____

Student Interest Inventory (Level II) (continued)

20. What do you most fear about becoming an adult? _____

_____

Complete the following statements:

21. I can't understand why _____

_____

22. I need extra help with _____

_____

23. Activities I like to do with friends include _____

_____

24. Activities I like to do by myself include _____

_____

25. The accomplishments I am most proud of are:

a)

b)

c)

Rate how much you like the subjects listed below:

Subject	Love it	It's okay	Not very much	Not at all
_____				
_____				
_____				
_____				
_____				
_____				

Thinking and Learning Styles Inventory (Level I)

Name: _____ Date: _____

Please read each statement and think about how well it describes you. Use this scoring system:

1 – No. This doesn't describe me.
2 – Kind of. This describes me sometimes.
3 – Yes! This is just like me!

1. _____ I draw all over my papers.

2. _____ My handwriting is not neat, even when I take my time.

3. _____ I need to know the "gist" of a story before reading about it or watching it on TV.

4. _____ I understand what I read better when I move my lips or read aloud.

5. _____ I'd rather make a poster than talk about something in front of the class.

6. _____ I learn best when I can do something hands on.

7. _____ When I retell a story, I explain the main idea or the lessons learned by the main character. I have a harder time remembering the facts.

8. _____ When I take a math test, I start with the problem I want to do first, not necessarily the first problem on the page.

9. _____ When I retell a story, I easily list the events from beginning to end.

10. _____ I like it when my teacher uses lots of overheads, PowerPoint presentations, and pictures.

11. _____ I can read with music on but not in front of the television.

12. _____ When I take a math test, I always start at the beginning.

13. _____ When trying to decide on the spelling of a word, I write out all the possible spellings.

14. _____ I'd rather listen to a person read a book aloud than read it by myself.

15. _____ I learn better when I can take a lot of movement breaks.

16. _____ I like it when we talk about things in class or when a guest speaker comes in to talk.

17. _____ I can solve a math problem in my head when I can see the problem written on paper.

18. _____ I like to squeeze a tennis ball or play with my pencil while sitting in class.

19. _____ I don't mind when schedules change.

20. _____ I like to follow step-by-step directions.

21. _____ I like to do many things at once.

22. _____ I understand spelling rules and can apply them.

23. _____ When learning a new computer game, I like it when someone tells me how to use it rather than showing me how to use it.

24. _____ I like to solve riddles.

25. _____ It's difficult for me to listen if I can't see the person's face.

26. _____ I move my hands a lot while talking.

27. _____ I can solve a math problem in my head if I can talk it out.

28. _____ I need to hear all of the facts before I believe something is true.

29. _____ I don't usually care what day it is.

30. _____ I can solve math problems in my head if I can move around blocks or other objects.

Thinking and Learning Styles Inventory Scoring Guide (Level I)

Student Name: _____ Date: _____

Transfer student scores to the grid below. For example, if a student scored the first item with a 3 (Yes! This is just like me!) enter a 3 in the blank. When you have entered all the scores for each question, total each of the five columns.

Item Score	Item Score	Item Score	Item Score	Item Score
1. _____	2. _____	6. _____	3. _____	9. _____
5. _____	4. _____	13. _____	7. _____	12. _____
10. _____	14. _____	15. _____	8. _____	20. _____
11. _____	16. _____	18. _____	19. _____	22. _____
17. _____	23. _____	26. _____	21. _____	24. _____
25. _____	27. _____	30. _____	29. _____	28. _____
TOTAL _____	TOTAL _____	TOTAL _____	TOTAL _____	TOTAL _____
Visual	Auditory	Kinesthetic	Global	Analytic

Learning Style **Thinking Style**

Within the first three columns, the highest total indicates a student's favored learning style (visual, auditory, or kinesthetic). The highest score within the last two columns suggests a student's preferred thinking style (global or analytic).

The lowest score possible for learning or thinking style is 6; this score suggests that students do not feel a particular style describes them. A score of 18, on the other hand, suggests that students strongly prefer a given mode of learning or thinking. A high score of 15 or more is a strong indicator of a student's preferred learning or thinking style. A score of 9 or less is a strong indicator that students are not inclined to a particular style of learning or thinking.

Thinking and Learning Styles Inventory (Level II)

Name: _____ Date: _____

Please read each statement and think about how well it describes you. Use this scoring system:

1 – This never describes me.
2 – This sometimes describes me.
3 – This often describes me.

1. _____ I decorate my written work with pictures and doodles.

2. _____ When making a decision, I talk it over with someone.

3. _____ It is easier to find a new place when I look at a map rather than having someone tell me the directions.

4. _____ I can build things without directions.

5. _____ I need to know the "gist" of a story before reading about it or watching it on TV.

6. _____ I appreciate it when the teacher gives me detailed directions, because I follow them step-by-step.

7. _____ I don't need to take notes in class. I just listen.

8. _____ I can picture information in my head from my papers or book when taking a test.

9. _____ It's easy for me to find a new place when someone tells me how to get there rather than looking at a map.

10. _____ I learn best when I can do something hands on.

11. _____ When I retell a story, I easily explain the main idea or the lessons learned by the main character. I have a hard time remembering the facts.

12. _____ When I take a math test, I start with the problem I want to do first, not necessarily the first problem on the page.

13. _____ When I retell a story, I can easily list the events from beginning to end.

14. _____ I move around when studying or taking a test.

15. _____ I learn best when my teacher uses lots of overheads, PowerPoint presentations, and pictures.

16. _____ I can read with music on but not in front of the television.

17. _____ If given a choice, I'd rather do a class presentation than a written paper.

18. _____ When I take a math test, I always start at the beginning.

19. _____ I need to hear examples of how a rule can be followed or broken in order to really understand it.

20. _____ When trying to decide on the spelling of a word, I write all the possible spellings.

21. _____ I can hear the words in my head while I read.

22. _____ I can understand a rule without examples.

23. _____ When I take notes, they are usually quite messy and difficult for other people to follow.

24. _____ I study better when I can take frequent movement breaks.

25. _____ I learn best when classes have a lot of discussions and guest speakers.

26. _____ I can solve a math problem in my head when I can see the problem written on paper.

Thinking and Learning Styles Inventory (Level II) (continued)

27. _____ I like to squeeze a tennis ball or play with my pencil while sitting in class.

28. _____ I can easily do more than one thing at once.

29. _____ I like to follow step-by-step directions.

30. _____ I need to see "the big picture" in order to really concentrate on what I am supposed to be learning.

31. _____ I understand spelling rules and can apply them.

32. _____ When learning a new computer game, I like it when someone tells me how to use it, rather than shows me how to use it.

33. _____ I prefer to study by myself.

34. _____ I like to solve riddles and logic puzzles.

35. _____ It's difficult for me to listen if I can't see the person's face.

36. _____ I move my hands a lot while talking.

37. _____ I can solve a math problem in my head if I can talk it out.

38. _____ I need to hear all of the facts before I believe something is true.

39. _____ I make decisions based on what feels right in my gut, not necessarily based on facts.

40. _____ If I want to remember something, I have to write it down, but I don't necessarily have to look at it again.

Thinking and Learning Styles Inventory Scoring Guide (Level II)

Student Name: _____ Date: _____

Transfer student scores to the grid below. For example, if a student scored the first item with a 3 (This often describes me.) enter a 3 in the blank. When you have entered all the scores for each question, total each of the five columns.

Item Score	Item Score	Item Score	Item Score	Item Score
1. _____	2. _____	4. _____	5. _____	6. _____
3. _____	7. _____	10. _____	11. _____	13. _____
8. _____	9. _____	14. _____	12. _____	18. _____
15. _____	17. _____	20. _____	19. _____	22. _____
16. _____	21. _____	24. _____	23. _____	29. _____
26. _____	25. _____	27. _____	28. _____	31. _____
33. _____	32. _____	36. _____	30. _____	34. _____
35. _____	37. _____	40. _____	39. _____	38. _____
TOTAL _____	TOTAL _____	TOTAL _____	TOTAL _____	TOTAL _____
Visual	Auditory	Kinesthetic	Global	Analytic

Learning Style

Thinking Style

Within the first three columns, the highest total indicates a student's favored learning style (visual, auditory, or kinesthetic). The highest score within the last two columns suggests a student's preferred thinking style (global or analytic).

The lowest score possible for learning or thinking style is 8; this score suggests that students do not feel a particular style describes them. A score of 24, on the other hand, suggests that students strongly prefer a given mode of learning or thinking. A high score of 18 or more is a strong indicator of a student's preferred learning or thinking style. A score of 10 or less is a strong indicator that students are not inclined to a particular style of learning or thinking.

Parent Checklist

Student Name: _____ Date: _____

As a teacher, I would like to know more about my students and understand the ways they best learn. I hope you will help me by completing this Parent Checklist. Please check the items you believe most accurately describe your child. There are no right or wrong answers. Thank you!

1. _____ Has good balance.
2. _____ Is very interested in math.
3. _____ Remembers songs and melodies.
4. _____ Is highly observant of surroundings.
5. _____ Forms friendships easily.
6. _____ Loves to tell stories and engage in conversations and discussions.
7. _____ Asks questions about fairness; has a strong interest in right and wrong, justice and injustice.
8. _____ Asks questions to seek more information about what she or he observes.
9. _____ Prefers to work independently; is self-directed.
10. _____ Shows mechanical skills; can take things apart and put them back together easily.
11. _____ Spells accurately and easily for his or her age.
12. _____ Is well coordinated and has a good sense of timing.
13. _____ Has leadership abilities; is able to influence others' opinions and actions.
14. _____ Easily computes math problems mentally.
15. _____ Is highly verbal and is able to clearly convey ideas orally.
16. _____ Plays a musical instrument with ease and/or has a good singing voice.
17. _____ Likes making models and three-dimensional figures (for example, LEGO structures).
18. _____ Recognizes and understands her or his personal strengths and limitations.
19. _____ Likes to move around and stay active.
20. _____ Draws and sketches accurately and with detail.
21. _____ Improvises vocal or instrumental music and/or composes music.
22. _____ Is able to adapt and adjust to changing circumstances; is flexible.
23. _____ Develops physical skills quickly and easily.
24. _____ Often sings or hums.
25. _____ Is sensitive to the feelings, thoughts, and motivations of others.
26. _____ Prefers things to be orderly and logical.
27. _____ Enjoys acting out things, doing skits and plays; is dramatic.
28. _____ Excels in sports or other physical activities (dancing, martial arts, creative movement).
29. _____ Likes to sketch out ideas or represent them visually.
30. _____ Enjoys puzzles, mazes, and other visual challenges.
31. _____ Can easily identify, categorize, and classify objects, information, and ideas.

CONTINUED ➤

Parent Checklist (continued)

32. _____ Prefers to work and learn with others.

33. _____ Shows a strong sense of rhythm in movement and speech.

34. _____ Understands cause and effect, actions and consequences.

35. _____ Has a strong will.

36. _____ Shows a strong interest in music.

37. _____ Accurately identifies and conveys feelings.

38. _____ Interacts comfortably and confidently with others.

39. _____ Learns best by seeing and observing; recalls information through images and pictures.

40. _____ Is able to organize and motivate others.

41. _____ Easily conveys thoughts and ideas in writing.

42. _____ Is interested in and sensitive to nature.

43. _____ Has a good vocabulary in comparison to age peers.

44. _____ Likes to read and do research to find out about topics of interest.

45. _____ Is fascinated with numbers and statistics (for example, baseball averages); has an excellent memory for such figures.

46. _____ Enjoys books and/or TV shows about nature and animals.

Parent Checklist Scoring Guide

Student Name: _____ Date: _____

Transfer the checks the parents gave next to each item below. When you have entered all the checks, total the number of checks in each of the eight columns. Some items are listed twice because the statements on the checklist are related to two intelligences. The highest number of checks indicates the parents' perception of their child's strongest multiple intelligence.

Item	Item	Item	Item	Item	Item	Item	Item
6. _____	1. _____	7. _____	2. _____	3. _____	4. _____	10. _____	5. _____
11. _____	12. _____	9. _____	10. _____	16. _____	8. _____	17. _____	7. _____
15. _____	19. _____	18. _____	14. _____	21. _____	22. _____	20. _____	13. _____
41. _____	23. _____	25. _____	26. _____	24. _____	31. _____	29. _____	32.
43. _____	27. _____	35. _____	34. _____	33. _____	42. _____	30. _____	38.
44. _____	28. _____	37. _____	45. _____	36. _____	46. _____	39. _____	40. _____
Verbal/ Linguistic TOTAL _____	Bodily/ Kinesthetic TOTAL _____	Intra-personal TOTAL _____	Logical/ Mathema-tical TOTAL _____	Musical/ Rhythmic TOTAL _____	Naturalist TOTAL _____	Visual/ Spatial TOTAL _____	Inter-personal TOTAL _____

Note: Numbers 7 and 10 appear twice because the statements apply to more than one intelligence.

Multiple Intelligences Teacher Observation Form

Student Name	A	B	C	D	E	F	G	H	I	J
Logical/Mathematical										
Bodily/Kinesthetic										
Interpersonal										
Intrapersonal										
Naturalist										
Musical/Rhythmic										
Visual/Spatial										
Verbal/Linguistic										
Logical/Mathematical										
Bodily/Kinesthetic										
Interpersonal										
Intrapersonal										
Naturalist										
Musical/Rhythmic										
Visual/Spatial										
Verbal/Linguistic										

CONTINUED →

Multiple Intelligences Teacher Observation Form (continued)

Logical/Mathematical Intelligence

A. Is very interested in math.

B. Loves to chart, graph, map, and organize information.

C. Easily computes math problems mentally.

D. Enjoys working on logic puzzles or brainteasers.

E. Understands abstract ideas.

F. Is fascinated and challenged by computers; easily uses computers for more than playing simple games.

G. Usually prefers things to be orderly and logical.

H. Understands cause and effect, actions and consequences.

I. Is fascinated with numbers and statistics; has an excellent memory for such figures.

J. Enjoys chess, checkers, and other strategy games.

Bodily/Kinesthetic Intelligence

A. Demonstrates balance, small- and large-motor dexterity, and precision in physical tasks.

B. Is well coordinated and has a good sense of timing.

C. Likes to move around and stay active.

D. Develops physical skills quickly and easily.

E. Enjoys acting out things, doing skits and plays; is dramatic.

F. Can mimic others' gestures or mannerisms.

G. Prefers to do things rather than hear or read about them.

Interpersonal Intelligence

A. Has leadership abilities; is able to influence others' opinions and actions.

B. Is sensitive to the feelings, thoughts, and motivations of others.

C. Prefers to work and learn with others.

D. Interacts comfortably and confidently with others.

E. Is able to organize and motivate others.

F. Forms friendships easily.

Intrapersonal Intelligence

A. Asks questions about fairness; has a strong interest in right and wrong, justice and injustice.

B. Prefers to work independently; is self-directed.

C. Has a strong will.

D. Accurately identifies and conveys feelings.

E. Is comfortable with his or her individuality, regardless of peer pressure.

F. Has a strong sense of self.

G. Reflects on and ponders situations.

H. Clearly recognizes and understands her or his personal strengths and limitations.

CONTINUED

Multiple Intelligences Teacher Observation Form (continued)

Naturalist Intelligence

A. Is highly observant of surroundings.

B. Asks questions to seek more information about what he or she observes.

C. Is able to adapt and adjust to changing circumstances; is flexible.

D. Is "street smart"; understands how systems work and may use them to personal advantage.

E. Is interested in and sensitive to nature.

F. Can easily identify, categorize, and classify objects, information, and ideas.

Musical/Rhythmic Intelligence

A. Remembers melodies.

B. Plays a musical instrument with ease and/or has a good singing voice.

C. Improvises vocal or instrumental music and/or composes music.

D. Shows a strong interest in music.

E. Shows a strong sense of rhythm in movement and speech.

F. Often sings or hums.

Visual/Spatial Intelligence

A. Shows mechanical skill; can take things apart and put them back together easily.

B. Draws and sketches accurately and in detail.

C. Likes to sketch out ideas or represent them visually.

D. Learns best by seeing and observing; recalls information through images and pictures.

E. Enjoys puzzles, mazes, and other visual challenges.

F. Likes making models and three-dimensional figures.

Verbal/Linguistic Intelligence

A. Loves to tell stories and engage in conversation and discussion.

B. Spells accurately and easily.

C. Is highly verbal and is able to clearly convey ideas.

D. Has a good memory for names, places, dates, and other facts.

E. Enjoys word games such as crossword puzzles, Scrabble, and acrostics.

F. Easily conveys thoughts and ideas in writing.

G. Has a good vocabulary in comparison to age peers.

H. Likes to read and do research to find out about topics of interest.

Chapter 4

Academic Assessment

Along with personalized learner assessment, Response to Intervention calls for ongoing, comprehensive, and student-centered academic evaluation. This type of sustained evaluation allows teachers to identify academic challenges as they arise and implement early intervention strategies to resolve learning problems before they become severe, prolonged difficulties.

This chapter offers a variety of assessment techniques and tools you can use to gauge academic performance on a regular basis. The four primary types of evaluation—screening, diagnostic evaluation, progress monitoring, and outcome assessment—play distinct roles within the RTI process. These assessment methods help you gain clearer insight into students' skills, make sound decisions for instruction, and monitor academic growth over time.

Screening

Screening is a quick assessment of student understanding and gauges learners' knowledge and critical abilities (such as basic reading or math skills). It can help answer the question: Which of my students need extra assistance or further evaluation in this area? By systematically screening all learners, teachers can identify those who might benefit from further diagnostic evaluation.

Some wonder how certain screening tools, which can be performed in a matter of minutes, can possibly provide any information that would drive instruction. Consider a typical screening tool: Most of these tests look at key indicators that provide insight into skills that are the focus of instruction. For example, looking at the number of words a student can correctly read per minute provides insight into overall reading proficiency (since students who read at a rapid rate typically are proficient readers).* Figure 4.1 lists some of these critical indicators that can be used to gauge student performance.

---

*Good, Simmons, and Kame'enui (2001) and Klauda and Guthrie (2008).

Fundamental RTI practice dictates that screening be conducted with students a minimum of three times per year. When all students are screened, the process is referred to as "universal screening." Universal screening is key to the RTI process because of the emphasis on early identification—the need to detect as many students who might be at risk for academic failure as possible.

Screening of critical indicators follows the same logic that medical professionals use when they take a patient's temperature. A high temperature may indicate illness, but it does not reveal what health problem is at play. Additionally, the assessment is not completely reliable. For example, has a patient recently had a cup of hot coffee that skewed the thermometer's reading? Was the person working out prior to the appointment? Is another factor responsible for the high temperature? Despite these limitations, a person's temperature will always be taken because it is a quick, minimally invasive assessment that can provide relevant data about a person's health condition.

Similarly, screening tests can have a high rate of false positives. Students may be identified as at risk when they are in fact performing at grade level. While not ideal, this situation is preferred to the alternative (false negatives resulting in students with problems being overlooked). No test is accurate 100 percent of the time, and screening results can be especially volatile since they are not as comprehensive as other assessments. Screening is a starting point—one tool that can potentially identify students at risk of academic failure. The other assessments in this section (and in Chapter 3) provide additional information on learners' struggles and how you might best address them. In your school's RTI program, multiple measures of student performance will help you make sound decisions about instruction and intervention.

Examples of Screening Indicators   FIGURE 4.1

Early literacy: Rapid letter naming, phoneme segmentation, initial sound fluency

Overall reading proficiency: Number of words read correctly per minute

Reading decoding: Nonsense word fluency

Reading comprehension: Number of words correctly restored (also referred to as the Maze Technique)

Written expression: Number of word sequences

Spelling: Number of letter sequences

Math computation: Number of math facts (addition, subtraction, multiplication, and division) solved per minute

Early numeration: Missing numbers, number identification, quantity array, quantity discrimination

Examples of Screening Tools

FIGURE 4.2

Tool	Description	Skill Areas	Grade Levels
Dynamic Indicators of Basic Early Literacy Skills (DIBELS)	A standardized, individually administered screening assessment of early literacy skills.	Initial Sound Fluency Nonsense Word Fluency Phoneme Segmentation Fluency Oral Reading Fluency	K–2 Oral reading fluency probes are available through grade 6
Running Records	Administered one-on-one. The observation of reading is designed to capture what the reader said and did while reading and assess understanding of the text.	Oral Reading Accuracy Oral Reading Fluency	K–12
Gates-MacGinitie Reading Tests (GMRT)	A group-administered assessment that surveys the level of reading achievement for individual students. Pencil and paper and online versions are available.	General Reading Achievement	PreK–12
Slosson–Diagnostic Math Screener (S-DMS)	A math assessment that can be administered to groups or individuals.	Math Conceptual Development Math Problem-Solving Math Computation	1–8
STAR Math and STAR Reading	Computer-based assessments that can be administered to individuals or groups.	Math Computation Basic Math Concepts and Application General Reading Achievement Reading Comprehension	K–12

Note: Please see "References and Resources" (beginning on page 225) for publisher information on these and additional screening tools for diverse subject areas and grade levels.

RTI in Action

Screening Using Running Records

Mrs. Veltman conducts screening in her second-grade classroom using running records, an evaluation method that records students' reading and retelling abilities to assess word recognition, fluency, and comprehension. While students read aloud for two-minute intervals, Mrs. Veltman records accuracy, self-corrections, and miscues (classifying them by substitutions, omissions, insertions, and repetitions toward identifying skill strengths and needs). In late September, Mrs. Veltman meets one-on-one with every student. She asks each learner to read the book *Frog and Toad Are Friends* by Arnold Lobel (written at the beginning second-grade level, or level K, according to the Fountas and Pinnell Leveling System).

When Mrs. Veltman meets with Alex, she finds that he reads *Frog and Toad Are Friends* with 87% accuracy. This concerns her because an accuracy rate of 89% or below indicates that this level is too hard. She would prefer Alex be at the instructional level (90–94%) or the independent level (95–100%). She is pleased that his self-correction rate is at 1:2 (meaning he is correcting one out of every two mistakes he makes while reading). This is an indication that he is self-monitoring and noticing when he makes mistakes.

Mrs. Veltman documents Alex's scores on a spreadsheet and notices he is one of six students not reading independently or instructionally at level K, the benchmark for this time of year. She takes a closer look at the data she has collected on the running records for these six students in conjunction with DIBELS data (see Figure 4.2) collected at the beginning of the year. DIBELS results suggest her concerns about Alex and the other five students are well founded. Through examination of this data, she identifies two other students who may benefit from additional assessment.

Diagnostic Evaluation

Screening helps you identify students not achieving grade-level benchmarks, but it does not provide a full picture of learners' abilities. These assessments really only indicate that there is a problem of some kind; they're less useful toward revealing the specific skills that have yet to be mastered. Diagnostic evaluation, on the other hand, can provide you with the particular challenges a student faces. In essence, this form of assessment is designed to answer the question: What are the student's specific strengths and needs?

Many assessments for diagnostic evaluation—such as formal achievement tests, informal reading or math inventories, classroom observations, and student work samples can shed light on a given student's learning needs and many of them educators already use on a regular basis. Another good source of information often overlooked by educators is data collected in a student's school file. Background information on student health, attendance, and family life can all provide insight into why a student is struggling in a particular area. The "Educational Profile" on pages 118–134 is a helpful tool for compiling this information for diagnostic evaluation.

Diagnostic evaluation helps educators pinpoint skills from the curriculum that should be targeted for intervention. Figure 4.3 lists some of these common academic difficulties that can be tracked with progress monitoring assessments. Reference the "What to Try When" charts in Chapter 6 to find appropriate research-based strategies and programs designed to meet specific student learning needs. Careful evaluation can lead to targeted and specific intervention, eliminating the inefficient situation of trial and error in coming up with the right instructional approach.

 Spotlight

Documenting Student Observations

Anecdotal information or checklists about students can be very helpful when diagnosing both academic and behavioral difficulties. These observations, collected over time, can illuminate trends in a student's life at school and serve as clues for addressing challenges. Being conscious of how you record these observations can ensure that they provide as much relevant data as possible. Student observations should be written clearly (as if you were explaining what you observed to another person or group of people) and objectively. Record the date, time, place, and full description of events as they occurred. Following is an example:

- Tuesday, November 7: At 2:50 p.m., Jason wrote three large Xs over his math paper (long division worksheet) and left the classroom to use the bathroom. He was gone for about ten minutes. When he returned, the bell rang and it was time to go home.

Here are some additional techniques you can use to document student observations:

- Write the observation on a sticky-note. After class, stick the note on a page specially designed for each student. Keep all the pages in a class binder.

- Write the observation on an index card and file it in a recipe box. Use tabbed dividers to create separate sections for each student in your class. Add index cards to the section after each observation.

- Use a computer or PDA to record your observations.

- Fill out an academic/behavior log and add it to the student's section in a class binder.

If you are conscientious in your collection, careful examination and analysis of these student behavioral aspects can aid significantly in full diagnosis of academic difficulties as well as behavioral concerns. Consider using the "Student Observation Log" (part of the "Educational Profile") on page 126 to document difficulties.

Diagnostic Evaluation of Academic Skills (Common Areas of Difficulty)

FIGURE 4.3

Reading Decoding and Word Recognition

Student:

- has difficulty hearing and/or manipulating sounds in words
- cannot rhyme
- has difficulty with letter-sound correspondence
- tries to sound out words letter by letter
- cannot generalize reading of known words to read new words
- guesses at unknown words, using no visual cues
- over relies on phonics to read words
- guesses at words using only the first letter

Reading Fluency

Student:

- reads quickly, but inaccurately
- reads quickly and accurately, but with little prosody (for example, struggles with expression and proper phrasing)
- reads with such limited fluency that comprehension is lost
- stops at every unfamiliar word
- lacks confidence when reading aloud

Reading Comprehension

Student:

- has difficulty focusing during reading
- struggles to remember what was read
- cannot make inferences
- cannot summarize or retell
- does not understand the key elements of a story (setting, characters, problem, solution, theme) or story structure
- cannot draw conclusions after reading an informational piece
- cannot determine what is important in informational text
- has limited vocabulary
- has difficulty choosing appropriate books for his or her reading level

Written Expression

Student:

- has difficulty coming up with topics on which to write
- has difficulty writing stories
- has difficulty writing an informational piece
- cannot or does not edit papers
- writes in dull or dry way
- lacks structure in writing

Math Computation

Student:

- has trouble with basic math skills (counting, adding, subtracting, multiplying, and/or dividing)
- does not follow the math operations sign
- has difficulty memorizing math facts
- does not know or follow the appropriate steps to complete a math problem
- has difficulty spatially organizing multi-digit math problems

Math Reasoning

Student:

- has difficulty understanding the meaning of numbers (number sense)
- has trouble recognizing groups and patterns
- cannot identify critical information needed to solve equations and complex problems
- has difficulty with mental math (i.e., solving math problems in his/her head)
- has difficulty comprehending story problems
- cannot decide on the mathematical operation for a story problem
- has problems with fractions
- has trouble with estimation
- does not understand the purpose of math outside of school

The goal of the diagnostic evaluation, regardless of the specific tools used, is to determine students' capabilities and specific areas of need. Use this information to guide instruction across the three tiers to remediate specific skill deficits. Diagnostic evaluation is especially useful in Tiers II and III where it generally occurs within the context of the problem-solving process detailed in Chapter 2. Members of Grade Level and Support Teams provide multiple perspectives to help make the best decisions for student instruction. Specialists and support personnel, such as school psychologists and literacy specialists, often prove invaluable in these meetings.

Examples of Diagnostic Evaluation Tools

FIGURE 4.4

Tool	Description	Skill Areas	Grade Levels
Wechsler Fundamentals: Academic Skills	An empirically based achievement test that can be administered to individuals or groups.	Spelling / Reading Comprehension / Word Reading / Numerical Operations	K–12
Woodcock-Johnson III NU Tests of Achievement (WJ III NU)	Tests individually administered and designed to diagnose a student's achievement level.	Oral Expression / Written Expression / Listening Comprehension / Reading Decoding / Reading Comprehension / Reading Fluency / Math Calculations / Math Reasoning	PreK–Adult
Process Assessment of the Learner (PAL-2)—Math	Used to diagnosis math problem areas; it can also be used as a progress monitoring tool. A Reading and Writing version of PAL-2 is also available.	Multiple subtests in the areas of conceptual development, problem-solving, and computation	K–6
KeyMath-3: A Diagnostic Inventory of Essential Mathematics (KM-III)	An individually administered test designed to diagnose a student's level of math achievement.	Multiple subtests in the areas of basic concepts, operations, and applications	K–12

Note: The "References and Resources" section (beginning on page 225) features publisher information on these and additional diagnostic evaluation tools for diverse subject areas and grade levels. As previously mentioned, informal assessments such as documented observations, work samples, or reading inventories can also be analyzed as part of the diagnostic evaluation.

RTI in Action

Using Diagnostic Evaluation to Guide Instruction

Mrs. Veltman examined the running record she took for Alex. Based on her analysis of his miscues while reading *Frog and Toad Are Friends,* she noticed that Alex primarily uses meaning and structural cues when reading. Words need to make sense and sound right to him. Whether they look right is a secondhand concern. Alex is able to self-monitor while he reads (as indicated by his 1:2 self-correction rate) and he uses a combination of meaning, structural, and visual cues to correct mistakes. Alex's use of appropriate expression while reading indicates he comprehends what he reads, which is notable given his lack of reading accuracy at the level. His oral retelling of the story confirms this observation.

Mrs. Veltman looked at the file Alex's first-grade teacher passed along to her. The documents in the file supported her initial evaluation, but she wanted to discuss Alex's reading skills with her Grade Level Team just to be certain she was on the right track. At a Grade Level meeting, the team concluded that Alex would benefit from additional instruction with books written at his instructional level to improve his accuracy, phrasing, and ability to read smoothly (without repetitions and hesitations). Mrs. Veltman will work with Alex on using visual cues to read unknown words and give him tips to help draw his attention to the words on the page (such as tracking the text with his finger). Since this learning challenge is relatively minor, the intervention will take place within the classroom at Tier I.

Mrs. Veltman will also focus on Alex's strengths, reading with expression and comprehension, to help him increase his reading accuracy. She will set him up with the Readers' Theatre Troupe, a group of students who practice and act out scenes from their favorite books. This will provide Alex with the opportunity to repeatedly read text, a proven strategy for building reading fluency and accuracy, as he practices for his Readers' Theatre performances. She will ensure the scripts the troupe selects are close to Alex's independent reading level. She will continue to monitor Alex's progress by having him read to her once every other week throughout the next marking period. He will continue to participate in the routine classroom assessments as well. If he does not make progress, she will seek out the Support Team to help with further evaluation, such as administration of a comprehensive reading achievement test (for example the reading portion of the Woodcock-Johnson III).

Parents are also important allies in making determinations about student learning needs. While guardian consent technically may not be required to carry out diagnostic evaluation as described here (because it is comprised of general education assessments and not intended to determine if a disability exists), adults at home possess a unique depth and breadth of information about students; they should have the opportunity to share that knowledge with school staff (such as with the learning inventories in "Chapter 3: Personalized Learner Assessment"). A "Parent Contact Log" is provided on page 134 for documenting communication with adults at home.

Progress Monitoring

After diagnostic assessments are used to determine learners' specific skill deficits, progress monitoring gauges the effectiveness of the academic interventions. Progress monitoring is essential to successful RTI programs. This form of assessment is important because it alerts educators when changes to the educational program are needed because learning is not occurring.

Progress monitoring emphasizes the need to assess student performance on a regular and frequent basis to determine whether learners are advancing. Progress monitoring should occur using a consistent set of administration and scoring procedures that are followed every time they are used so that educators can reliably measure growth. Monitoring students' responsiveness to intervention can help identify students who need additional or more intensive instruction. This form of assessment answers the question: Is learning happening?

It's important to note that these assessments are not one size fits all. The intensity of the assessment program will match the scope and severity of a learner's academic difficulties. Some students, for example, may be monitored on a monthly basis while others with more severe, prolonged difficulties might be assessed once or twice a week.

Curriculum-Based Measurement

Curriculum-based measurement (CBM) is a well-known progress monitoring technique developed by Stan Deno and Phyllis Mirkin in the late 1970s at the Minnesota Institute for Research on Learning Disabilities. CBM has been widely researched with over a hundred studies proving its reliability and validity as an assessment.* This form of assessment is popular because it not only indicates whether learning is happening, but also the rate at which students are building academic skills. In essence, CBM serves as a barometer of the effectiveness of an intervention or instruction.

Similar to screening assessments, CBM allows teachers to assess skills by tracking how students perform on key indicators (see Figure 4.1). The indicators assessed must be closely related to the content covered in the curriculum. For example, if a student is learning to add two-digit numbers with regrouping, the CBM would be made up of two-digit addition problems.

CBM is effective for monitoring academic progress because it is highly standardized—a standard set of directions, standards for evaluating performance, and a standard amount of time given for administration. The time element is important because a student's ability to perform a task helps indicate whether the student has mastered the skill.**

CBMs can be administered in six easy steps:

Step 1: Select the appropriate indicator for the skills to be measured. Table 4.1 provides a list of skills with corresponding indicators that may be chosen

---

*Hosp, Hosp, and Howell (2007).
**Fewster and MacMillan (2002), Gurganas (2007), and Jiban and Deno (2007).

as the focus for CBM. For example, measuring the number of words read correctly per minute can shed light on overall reading proficiency.

Step 2: Locate or create assessment probes. Assessment probes, or quick tests of student knowledge, are the basis upon which student skill will be measured. These probes are comprised of multiple forms that measure performance based on a specific indicator. Many probes are available online at teacher sites. Type in the subject area you are looking for and the word *probe* into any search engine. The "References and Resources" section (page 225) has additional sites you can visit. Probes can also easily be created on your own.

Step 3: Establish baseline of performance. The next step is to determine a given learner's academic baseline in a particular area. Teachers assess students on three separate occasions over the course of a week. An average of these scores is then determined and recorded as the baseline score.

Step 4: Establish a timeline and learning goals. When a baseline has been determined, the RTI team works to determine goal scores and the length of the assessment period. In determining the CBM timeline—or any progress monitoring timeline for that matter—it's important to keep in mind that students at Tier II should be monitored at least biweekly. Students at Tier III should be monitored more frequently due to the severity of their academic challenges; a minimum of once a week is recommended. Following are some standards by which to establish learning goals.* Learning goals should be achievable, yet challenging enough that the student is able to eventually catch up to peers.

> **Progress monitoring emphasizes the need to assess student performance on a regular and frequent basis to determine whether learners are advancing.**

- Norms: Establish performance objectives by looking at researched norms collected over numerous years and from numerous sources. After looking at the norms, determine a reasonable goal line by comparing the norm and the student's baseline score. You can also establish norms for your particular setting by screening all students three times a year (in the fall, winter, and spring) and averaging scores to establish the norms for your class or school.

- Exemplary Sampling: Take a sample of students who you know to be proficient with the specific skills that CBM is measuring. Test the students using a standard set of probes and use their scores to establish the criteria on which other performance objectives will be based.

- Growth Rate Chart: Researchers have investigated how much progress we can expect a typical student to make given standard instruction. If growth rate charts have been researched for the skills you are measuring, you can take your student's baseline score and add the expected

*Hosp, Hosp, and Howell (2007).

RTI in Action

Progress Monitoring with Running Records

Teachers from Mrs. Veltman's Grade Level Team suggested she use running records with leveled books to determine Alex's reading level. Mrs. Veltman subscribes to Reading A–Z, a Web site that provides leveled, downloadable books that can be printed and used to take running records. Mrs. Veltman sat down with Alex during independent reading time to take the additional running records. It turned out that Alex was reading at level F independently (99% accuracy) and his instructional level was G (92%). Over the next months, Mrs. Veltman recorded the following scores for Alex:

9/30 Level G – accuracy rate: 92%
10/13 Level G – accuracy rate: 99%
10/27 Level H – accuracy rate: 95%
11/10 Level I – accuracy rate: 99%
11/24 Level J – accuracy rate: 89%
12/07 Level J – accuracy rate: 98%

rate of growth to develop the goal line. Page 231 features resources helpful for identifying norms and growth rate charts appropriate for your setting.

Step 5: Plot the baseline and goal line on a graph. Once the timeline and goals are established, plot the goal line on a graph starting from the baseline. (A sample graph is on page 111.) Visual representation of academic progress can make it easier to share assessment results with colleagues in RTI settings. Additionally, involving students in graphing scores can be powerful motivation; documenting their scores gives them concrete feedback on their rate of learning.

Step 6: Assess students by their progress against the goal line. As the checkpoint scores are recorded, evaluate whether the student is on track to meet established learning goals. If scores fall short of the goal line for three checkpoints in a row, discuss with the RTI team whether a new research-based intervention should be implemented or if the goals or timelines were unreasonable.

Additional Progress Monitoring Tools

CBM is a valuable form of progress monitoring but by no means the only way. Students' classroom work samples can be collected in a portfolio and evaluated to determine if progress is being made according to a hierarchy of skills. Running records of a student's reading performance might be taken. A number of commercially produced tools (see "Examples of Progress Monitoring Tools" on page 105 and "References and Resources" starting on page 225) can be used to show progress over time. You might also document your observations or use a rubric to evaluate academic performance—the possibilities are many. Simply ask the following questions to determine if an assessment can be used for progress monitoring:

- Does it provide information regarding students' academic performance?
- Does it evaluate the effectiveness of instruction?
- Are there enough alternate versions or forms so that it can be used on a frequent and regular basis (weekly or monthly)?
- Can it be administered in a standardized fashion?
- Is the tool reliable and valid?

If the answer is "yes" to all of the questions, the assessment may be used as a progress monitoring tool. When developing your own progress monitoring tools, just be certain they are carefully crafted to reflect a student's grasp of skills and academic growth. Such informal progress monitoring tools can be used in combination with CBM, running records, or other more structured

Examples of Progress Monitoring Tools

FIGURE 4.5

Tool	Description	Skill Areas	Grade Levels
AIMSweb	A Web-based formative assessment system that uses CBM probes that can be taken in increments of between one and three minutes.	Early Literacy Reading Fluency Reading Comprehension Spelling Early Numeracy Math Computation Written Expression	K–8
EdCheckup	Uses CBM to monitor student progress in reading, writing, and math.	Early Literacy Reading Fluency Reading Comprehension Written Expression Math Computation Written Expression	K–8
Accelerated Math	A computerized progress monitoring tool that generates individualized quizzes and provides immediate feedback.	Multiple areas of math computation and problem solving	1–7
Developmental Reading Assessment	A set of individually administered, criterion-referenced reading.	Oral Reading Reading	K–8
Reading A–Z Assessments	A Web site that contains various forms of progress monitoring tools such as running records, comprehension quick checks, and rubrics.	Oral Reading Phonics Reading Fluency Reading Comprehension	K–12

Note: Please see "References and Resources" (beginning on page 225) for publisher information on these and additional progress monitoring tools for diverse subject areas and grade levels.

assessments. In fact, a comprehensive assessment program—one that incorporates a full battery of assessments—generally results in the best instructional decision-making and, ultimately, greatest student progress.

Outcome Assessment

Outcome assessment can be used to document or gauge the overall effectiveness of instruction. This type of evaluation differs from progress monitoring in that it is summative, given at the end of unit instruction to determine whether learners have met academic objectives. Outcome assessment demonstrates student proficiency or growth over an extended period, particularly in relation to a desired objective. This form of evaluation serves to answer the questions: Did the student meet the goal or desired outcome? Is the student ready to move on?

Outcome assessment can be given to individual students or an entire class. Examples of this type of evaluation are many, diverse, and often already staples of the regular curriculum. Projects or tests administered at the end of a unit of study, for example, constitute outcome assessment. These tools for evaluating student skills may be part of Tier I research-based curricular materials in place (an end of the unit math test, for example) or teacher-created (such as a capstone project designed to measure comprehension of a chapter book). Examination of pre- and post-test CBM data to assess overall growth can also constitute outcome assessment. (This process is referred to as curriculum-based assessment, or CBA, instead of CBM due to the shift from formative assessment to summative evaluation.)

Outcome assessments have limited value in making day-to-day decisions regarding instruction or intervention. That is the purpose of progress monitoring. This type of assessment, however, can prove very helpful when making decisions regarding movement among the tiers. RTI teams, within the scope of their meetings, can examine both summative and formative data to make decisions regarding which tier of instruction is most appropriate for each student.

RTI in Action

Using Outcome Assessment to Determine Instruction

In December, Mrs. Veltman examined progress monitoring data for Alex and estimated that he was reading at level K instructionally (the benchmark for the beginning of the year). She wanted to be sure of this determination, however, and gathered books at levels J, K, and L. Mrs. Veltman then sat with Alex again to find his independent and instructional levels by taking running records. She found that Alex was reading instructionally at level K (92%). Pleased with his progress over the last three months, she shared this result with Alex and his parents. She also remained concerned, however, that Alex was not catching up to his peers and might not meet the January benchmark (reading instructionally at level M). Mrs. Veltman reviewed the comprehension assessments she gave periodically and her observation notes, deciding to discuss the situation with his parents and the Grade Level and Support Teams to determine how to best meet Alex's needs.

RTI Assessment

FIGURE 4.6

Assessment Type	What is it?	What decisions does it help educators make?	When is it used?
Screening	A method of assessing all students with brief checks of critical indicators.	It informs the educator as to which students may need extra assistance or additional diagnostic evaluation. The data from screening assessments can also be used to establish classroom or school norms.	All students are screened a minimum of three times per year (fall, winter, and spring).
Diagnostic Evaluation	Assessment aimed at pinpointing specific information regarding a student's strengths and needs.	It helps educators target instruction to build on existing strengths and remediate needs.	Diagnostic evaluation is used any time an educator needs clarification on a starting point for instruction or specific skills on which to focus intervention.
Progress Monitoring	Formative assessment of student performance on a regular and frequent basis using standard procedures.	It tells educators if individual students are making progress or if they need a change in educational programming.	Progress monitoring is used throughout the tiers on a monthly, weekly, or daily basis depending on the intensity of the problem.
Outcome Assessment	Summative assessments that are given at the end of a unit or after a longer period of instruction.	It documents the overall effectiveness of instruction and tells the teacher if the student has met a desired goal or outcome.	Outcome assessments are given at the end of units of instruction or before major educational decisions are made regarding a student's educational program.
Personalized Learner Assessment (see Chapter 3)	Assessment of a student's personal interests, learning styles, and multiple intelligences.	It helps the educator get to know the student on a personal level and how to differentiate instruction by tapping into interests and learning strengths.	It is ongoing, but should be heavily focused at the beginning of the year (or at the first introduction of a student).

Finding Time to Assess

With so much emphasis on assessment within the RTI model, some educators have wondered how they will find time to teach. Assessment can feel overwhelming and many teachers have worried these practices will affect their ability to get through the curriculum. This concern is certainly valid; education isn't about measuring academic achievement, after all. But, it is not really about teaching either. It is about learning. An emphasis on teaching places the focus on what the teacher is doing; an emphasis on learning, however, makes student needs the focus of instruction. This "responsiveness" to learners is a hallmark of RTI.

> **An emphasis on teaching places the focus on what the teacher is doing; an emphasis on learning, however, makes student needs the focus of instruction. This "responsiveness" to learners is a hallmark of RTI.**

The question remains: How can we as educators conduct this assessment within the context of an already busy school day? It's important to first remember that the full burden of assessment should not fall on the shoulders of classroom teachers. Support staff including aides, reading specialists, special educators, and school psychologists all have an active role in the assessment process. These professionals can be helpful in administering assessments and reporting results to Grade Level Teams and other RTI groups. In assessment, as in the problem-solving process, we are all collaborative partners in the education of children.

Schools have also begun to use some creative methods for evaluating learners. Some with shortages of support staff have employed education students from nearby colleges and universities to conduct screening (a school psychologist might coordinate schedules and oversee compilation of data). Parents, as explained in the last chapter, may be called on to support your efforts. Older students from the district might also be asked to help in classrooms where younger students are being assessed. Administrators and other members of the Navigation Team can examine school procedures in place and strategize the most efficient ways to conduct screening.

When assessment might seem like a burden, it can help to remember that it is instrumental toward effective instruction. Consider the lost opportunities of one-size-fits-all instruction over time. What potential is lost when students, their specific learning needs unmet, languish behind peers for months? What kind of resources, financial and otherwise, must ultimately be used to bring these students to grade level? Viewed from the perspective of a long-term benefit, a comprehensive assessment program emerges as an important aspect of effective schools.

Using Assessment to Determine Movement Across RTI Tiers

A comprehensive assessment program begins at Tier I with personalized learner assessment. This form of evaluation, which identifies student interests and learning strengths, helps you get to know students on a personal level and differentiate instruction accordingly. You can use surveys, interviews, and class activities, including those in Chapter 3, to gather this information about students. Academic achievement data at Tier I should be collected from universally administered screening tests. These assessments can be used to develop school or classroom norms and to identify students who are at risk. In many schools, a first line of screening consists of state- and district-required testing.

After initial screening, assessment programs will vary from student to student. In the day-to-day workings of a differentiated classroom, student work will be assessed in different ways. One student, for example, may write a report on a biography of Abraham Lincoln while another might give a presentation recounting key events from his life. The frequency of progress monitoring for students will also differ depending on their respective skill levels. In essence, assessment methods are informed by one basic question: What information do I need to guide my instruction and maximize learning for each student?

Assessment data is vital toward the selection of interventions that have the best chance of helping students succeed. But how is it used in determining movement between the RTI tiers? Chapter 2 details a problem-solving process RTI groups can use to make instructional decisions about students. The Navigation Team at your school will make decisions about the specifics of this process, including screening measures to be put in place. While these and other RTI procedures will to some extent be unique to your school, here are some general guidelines to keep in mind when it comes to analyzing assessment data to guide instruction.

Note: The "Educational Profile" (beginning on page 118) can serve as a one-stop source of information for educators deliberating on student movement between the tiers. This compilation of student data can be helpful during RTI meetings.

Movement from Tier I to Tier II

While screening data can help identify struggling students, it is not generally an exclusive determining factor for Tier II intervention. Instead, diagnostic evaluation by a collective of educators (including members from Grade Level and Support Teams) should be conducted before students are given more intensive interventions. This evaluation may involve administering additional assessments, though oftentimes sufficient diagnostic data will be available in a student's school record. Individualized learner information is analyzed toward establishing students' respective strengths and areas of need.

RTI team members closely examine classroom performance and teacher observations. If it is determined that a student's needs cannot be met in Tier I, the diagnostic evaluation should result in RTI team members highlighting specific skills that will be worked on with the learner. This will include a starting point for instruction at this Tier II intervention. A method for monitoring progress will be established along with baseline information that can in turn be used to help determine whether a given intervention is successful.

RTI in Action

Tier II Referral

After the fourth week of school Mr. Rodriguez, a fifth-grade teacher at Youngstown Elementary, met with his Grade Level Team to discuss the needs of students in his classroom. Universal screening assessments conducted the previous week identified seven students who were at risk of failing in math. Mr. Rodriguez looked at the Educational Profiles prepared the previous year by fourth-grade teachers, making some updates (including the screening data) prior to the meeting with his Grade Level Team. The team discussed the seven at-risk students and helped Mr. Rodriguez identify next steps for instruction. Four students would be provided with Tier II intervention based on their specific areas of difficulty. Mr. Rodriquez would establish a baseline and monitor progress twice a month using CBM. Two students would be further assessed, since their areas of need were not evident based on the existing data. The team would follow-up with these students in two weeks. One student would remain in Tier I without any additional support since classroom work and previous math scores made the team feel that wasn't needed (although Mr. Rodriguez will closely monitor this student).

Guiding Questions:

- What are a student's strengths and specific areas of need?

- Can these areas of need be addressed in Tier I? Why or why not?

- Are external factors influencing the student's pace of academic growth? If so, how will these factors be addressed?

- Was Tier I instruction differentiated based on the student's academic readiness, learning strengths, and interests?

- Is Tier I instruction based on research-based teaching practices?

Movement from Tier II to Tier III

Determining whether to move students into Tier III instruction involves multiple factors. First, RTI team members should consider the academic growth students have shown since inception of Tier II interventions. Second, it's important to look at the remaining achievement difference between a student and the rest of the class. If the rate of progress is insufficient and the goals have not been met, the intensity or type of intervention must be changed. Decisions made on whether to try another Tier II intervention or institute Tier III instruction (generally determined by the Grade Level Team in conjunction with the Evaluation Team) will vary based on the progress monitoring tools used at each respective grade level.

Guiding Questions:

- Is the student consistently scoring below the predetermined goal line according to the data from CBM (6–8 data points)?

- Did the student receive Tier II level intervention long enough to demonstrate progress (6–10 weeks)?

- Would the student benefit from another round of Tier II?

- Was the intervention implemented correctly?

 RTI in Action

Tier III Referral

Mrs. Murphy, a third-grade teacher at Jefferson Elementary, met with members of her Grade Level and Support Teams to discuss a student named Joy. Joy was not making sufficient reading progress after eight weeks of Tier II level support. The team looked at the graph Mrs. Murphy had been keeping that showed Joy's Maze scores; it revealed she consistently scored significantly below grade-level benchmarks. Members from the team also reviewed Joy's Educational Profile, which identified reading comprehension as an area of past weakness. The group determined that more intense instruction was needed. It discussed the type and frequency of Tier III interventions for Joy, as well as how implementation would be monitored.

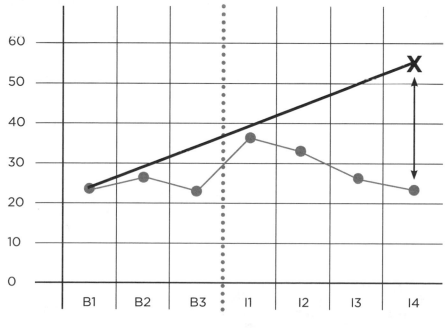

•••• Intervention

X Benchmark goal

— Aimline

● Joy's reading comprehension scores

Benchmark Scores   **Post-Intervention Scores**

RTI in Action

Making Progress at Tier III

Brady, a first grader at Valley View Elementary, has been receiving Tier III level support for six weeks in the area of phonological awareness and phonics. He has made remarkable gains and is now reading at grade level. Brady's teacher and parents, along with Grade Level and Support Teams, determine that he should continue to receive Tier II level intervention, but that his gains are sufficient to start pulling back Tier III support. Brady's teacher will continue to monitor his progress to ensure that he continues to make reading gains.

Movement from Tier III back to Tier II or I

When assessment is used to carefully guide instruction, students can thrive. It should be celebrated when students meet their individual goals and this acknowledgment of success can be instrumental toward fostering student motivation. It's also important to monitor student scores after transitions between tiers so that learners do not lose gains they made.

Guiding Questions:

- Is the student consistently meeting or exceeding the goal line (based on progress monitoring data)?
- Has enough gain been made so that the student will eventually catch up with peers?
- Is the academic progress stable enough to pull away the extra support provided in Tier II or Tier III?

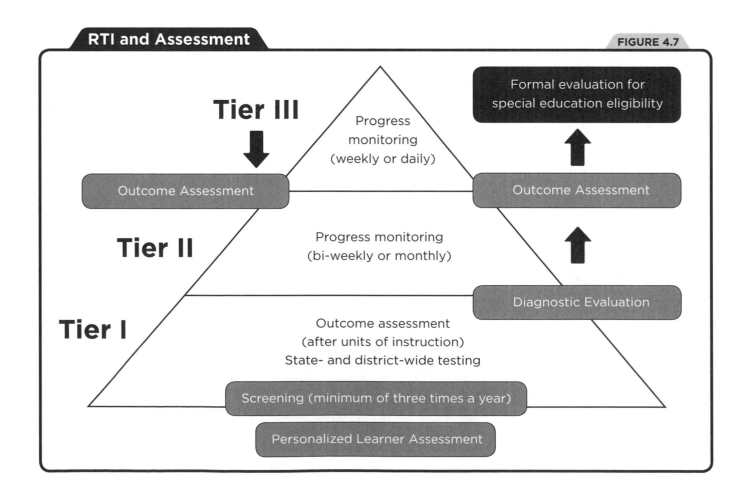

RTI and Assessment   FIGURE 4.7

Eligibility for Special Education Services

It is the school's responsibility under the Individuals with Disabilities Education Act (IDEA) to identify students with a suspected disability in a timely manner. A referral can be made at any time, regardless of the level of intervention in the multi-tiered model. If the RTI team suspects a disability, a referral must be made and parent or guardian consent obtained prior to initiation of a special education evaluation. (Parents continue to have the right to request a referral for special education evaluation at any time.) Parents should be given a copy of the procedural safeguards and the due process timeline (which begins at the time of the parent's consent).

Legal basis for using RTI to determine learning disability eligibility is found in the 2004 reauthorization of IDEA. The law states:

> "In determining whether a child has a specific learning disability, a local educational agency may use a process that determines if the child responds to scientific research-based intervention as a part of the evaluation procedures described in paragraphs (2) and (3)."*

The implication of this language is that schools are allowed to use the results of assessments demonstrating student responsiveness to interventions in eligibility decisions. While the law allows for this flexibility, careful consideration should be made before qualifying a student for special education services. Some states have developed formal policies for making special education determinations within the RTI framework. In places where this is not the case, a school or district should develop guidelines of its own for making decisions related to special education. As outlined in Chapter 2, this is the responsibility of the RTI Navigation Team (or another corresponding group) in your school.

IDEA 2004 outlines criteria that should be used as guidelines for learning disability determination. The legislation states that a student "exhibits a pattern of strengths and weakness in performance, achievement, or both, relative to age, state-approved grade-level standards, or intellectual development, that is determined by a group to be relevant to the identification of a learning disability, using appropriate assessments."** This evaluation must be consistent with all of the following requirements:

> Schools are allowed to use the results of assessments demonstrating student responsiveness to interventions in eligibility decisions. While the law allows for this flexibility, careful consideration should be made before qualifying a student for special education services.

- A variety of assessment tools and strategies are used to gather relevant functional, developmental, and academic information about the child, including information from the parent

---

*IDEA 2004, U.S.C. 1414(b)(6)(B).
**IDEA 2004, §300.309(a)(2)(ii).

- No single measure is used as a sole criterion

- Technically sound instruments that assess the relative contribution of cognitive and behavior factors, as well as physical or developmental factors are used

- Assessments are nondiscriminatory on racial or cultural basis

- Assessments are administered in native language/mode of communication to yield accurate information

- Assessments are valid and reliable

- Administration is done by trained/knowledgeable personnel

- Assessments are tailored for specific areas

- Assessments are selected to measure aptitude rather than other limitations

- The child is assessed in all areas related to the suspected disability, including, if appropriate, vision, hearing, social and emotional status, general intelligence, academic performance, communicative status, and motor abilities

- Assessment tools and strategies are provided that present relevant information to directly assist persons in determining the educational needs of the child*

Definition of a Specific Learning Disability   FIGURE 4.8

"Specific learning disability" means a disorder in one or more of the basic psychological processes involved in understanding or in using language, spoken or written, that may manifest itself in an imperfect ability to listen, think, speak, read, write, spell, or do mathematical calculations. The term includes such conditions as perceptual impairments, brain injury, minimal brain dysfunction, dyslexia, and developmental aphasia. The term does not include children who have learning problems that are primarily the result of a visual, hearing, or motor impairment; of a cognitive impairment; of an emotional impairment; of an autism spectrum disorder; or of environmental, cultural, or economic disadvantage.**

It's important that teams making decisions on special education eligibility be made up of a cross section of education professionals. This group should examine multiple sources of relevant data, including all academic achievement measures, medical information, and behavioral factors. Students should be evaluated on an individual basis in the seven domains—listening, speaking, reading, writing, spelling, and mathematical calculation—outlined in the definition of a learning disability.

If RTI has not yet been fully implemented in your school, data that has been collected can be used in conjunction with the discrepancy model. In this scenario, achievement and aptitude tests are administered to determine whether a discrepancy exists between ability and achievement prior to the determination of eligibility for special education services.

---

*IDEA 2004, 300.304 as cited in MAASE (2006).
**IDEA 2004, R340.17.

The Educational Profile

RTI calls for a significant amount of documentation on the part of educators. Screening, diagnostic information, outcome testing, and progress monitoring data must all be recorded for evaluating student performance. Personalized learner information also must be considered alongside these results to determine interventions that are most appropriate for students. The ultimate success or failure of these academic strategies must also be recorded, including legal documentation related to special education eligibility.

The "Educational Profile" (see pages 118–134) serves as a single place where all information about a student can be kept. You might think of the assessment process as an attempt to put together a puzzle—as more pieces of the puzzle come together, a clearer picture of a student's needs emerges. Having this information compiled in a single document serves as an ever-growing source of information in RTI meetings that can improve the accuracy and efficiency of your instructional decision-making. It can also help you standardize RTI procedures at your school. Documentation of assessment measures and student responsiveness to research-based strategies are important aspects of evaluation.

> **Documentation of assessment measures and student responsiveness to research-based strategies are important aspects of evaluation.**

A single person is generally responsible for filling in data on the "Educational Profile." This is often a student's general education teacher, though RTI teams may decide on another method. Existing data can come from a review of the student's file with new information on achievement scores and other data being added over time. The multi-part form that follows can be used to record diverse learner information collected over time. You might also choose to customize the "Educational Profile" (using the forms on the included CD-ROM) based on common assessments already conducted in your building.

Data sources for the "Educational Profile" include:

- interest inventories
- thinking and learning styles assessments
- multiple intelligence assessments
- classroom observations
- screening tests
- standardized state-wide tests
- achievement tests
- aptitude tests
- work samples
- curriculum-based measurements
- running records
- informal reading inventories
- teacher-made tests
- parent checklists and interviews
- student interviews
- behavior logs
- attendance records
- previous report cards

Elements of the "Educational Profile"

You will find the reproducible "Educational Profile" on pages 118–134. It enables you to collect student data in these areas:

Background Information (pages 118–119). Issues outside of school settings can dramatically affect how a student performs in the classroom. The RTI team should consider such factors as attendance, health conditions, and familial support. This information is recorded in the first section of the profile.

Academic Assessment Data (pages 120–123). Results from achievement tests, aptitude tests, and state or district assessments are recorded in this section. While these measures are not required for determining special education eligibility (as in the discrepancy model), RTI and these assessments can be used concurrently to identify a student as learning disabled. If available, these tests can provide important perspective on student learning.

Personalized Learner Data (pages 124–126). Student interests, learning preferences, and thinking styles are important factors in determining instruction. This portion of the profile compiles information gathered through assessments and activities from Chapter 3. You can also use the "Student Observation Log" to document additional events or occurrences you witness (such as behavior difficulties).

Screening Results (page 127). Compile academic information you gather on screening assessments on this form. You might use a single form for each subject area, including multiple forms within a learner's profile.

> The "Educational Profile" acts as a living document that details all the information about a student— performance, preferences, and interventions. It can be helpful in drawing up individualized education programs (IEPs) and sharing information with parents at conferences.

Intervention Plan Form (page 128). For those learners who do demonstrate difficulties in the classroom, academic interventions will be necessary. Fill out this portion of the "Educational Profile" after your RTI group has completed the problem-solving process to determine next steps in instruction.

Progress Monitoring Data (pages 129–130). Progress monitoring allows you to gauge the effectiveness of academic interventions. Track student progress over time, charting results on the graph. Visual representation of student progress can be especially helpful in RTI meetings.

Diagnostic Evaluation Results (page 131). The profile includes an area where you can record the analysis of the student's areas of strength and academic needs based on your comprehensive assessment battery. Having this information included among other academic and personal data can be helpful in full analysis of learning difficulties.

Research-Based Interventions (pages 132–133). It's important within the RTI framework that the interventions be recorded and referenced over time. The profile includes room where this can be done along with an "Observation of Fidelity" form to document that the intervention was implemented properly.

Parent Contact Log (page 134). Communication with parents (or other home adults) is important within the RTI model. Record communications with learners' parents in this section.

The "Educational Profile" acts as a living document that details all the information about a student—performance, preferences, and interventions. It can be helpful in drawing up individualized education programs (IEPs) and sharing information with parents at conferences. Profiles may also be shared with learners (provided a given student is mature enough) toward updating background information, interests, and learning preferences.

Spotlight

Considering Student Behavior

It is important to consider behavior when analyzing student performance and participation at school—particularly if undesirable behaviors are adding to the student's challenges in the classroom. While it's difficult to determine with certainty why a student may be misbehaving, getting to the root cause of these issues can lead to academic breakthroughs. Consider the following questions:

- Does the student lack the academic skills needed to feel successful?
- Is the student misbehaving in order to seek attention from adults or peers?
- Is the student misbehaving to avoid work?

- Is the student bored or under-challenged?
- Is the student misbehaving to escape an overstimulating environment?
- Is the student's behavior a result of teasing or bullying?
- Is the student misbehaving as an attempt to feel in control in the school setting?

You might involve parents and other school staff in considering these questions, recording any trends that emerge in the "Personalized Learner Data" portion of the "Educational Profile." You can also keep tabs on behavior using the "Student Observation Log."

Educational Profile: Background Information

Student name: _____ Date of birth:_____ Sex: M F

Parent/guardian name: _____

Home phone: _____ Work/cell phone:_____

Address: _____

City, state, zip code: _____

Parent/guardian name: _____

Home phone: _____ Work/cell phone:_____

Address: _____

City, state, zip code: _____

With whom does the student reside? _____Relationship:_____

Position of the student in the family:

Only child _____ Oldest of _____ Youngest of _____ Middle of _____

Language spoken at home: _____ Hand preference: Right Left Both

Have there been previous evaluations (academic, psychological, developmental) of the student?
If so, please provide results below or attach reports.

_____

_____

_____

_____

Has the student experienced any developmental delays? Explain.

_____

_____

_____

Educational Profile: Background Information (continued)

Has the student had major illnesses and/or injuries? Explain.

_____

_____

_____

_____

Does the student have any chronic medical conditions such as disease or allergies? Explain.

_____

_____

_____

_____

What is the student's attendance record? Provide a summary.

_____

_____

_____

_____

Is there any other pertinent family, health, or background information that might be helpful to understand the student's needs (illness of a family member, student has vision or hearing problems, student was premature at birth, student is on medication, etc.)?

_____

_____

_____

_____

Educational Profile: Academic Assessment Data (Achievement Test)

Student name: _____

Name of test: _____

Date of administration: _____ Age at administration: _____

Area	Standard Score	Percentile	Notes
Reading Overall _____ (subtest) _____ (subtest) _____ (subtest)			
Written Expression Overall _____ (subtest) _____ (subtest) _____ (subtest)			
Mathematics Overall _____ (subtest) _____ (subtest) _____ (subtest)			

CONTINUED ➤

Educational Profile: Academic Assessment Data (Achievement Test) (continued)

Area	Standard Score	Percentile	Notes
Subject _____ _____ (subtest) _____ (subtest) _____ (subtest)			
Subject _____ _____ (subtest) _____ (subtest) _____ (subtest)			
Subject _____ _____ (subtest) _____ (subtest) _____ (subtest)			

Educational Profile: Academic Assessment Data (Aptitude Test)

Student name: _____

Name of test: _____

Date of administration: _____ Age at administration: _____

Area	Standard Score	Percentile	Notes

Educational Profile: Academic Assessment Data (State- or District-Wide Test)

Student name: _____

Name of test: _____

Date of administration: _____   Age at administration: _____

Area	_____ (Indicator)	_____ (Indicator)	Notes

Educational Profile: Personalized Learner Data

Student name: _____

Interests, activities, familial issues, points of pride, feelings regarding school

Source: _____

Summary: _____

_____

_____

_____

_____

_____

_____

_____

Learning and thinking style preferences (visual, auditory, kinesthetic, global, analytical)

Source: _____

Summary: _____

_____

_____

_____

_____

_____

_____

_____

CONTINUED

Educational Profile: Personalized Learner Data *(continued)*

Multiple intelligences preferences (verbal/linguistic, visual/spatial, bodily/kinesthetic, logical/mathematical, musical/rhythmic, naturalist, interpersonal, intrapersonal)

Source: _____

Summary: _____

_____

_____

_____

_____

_____

Social and behavioral considerations

Source: _____

Summary: _____

_____

_____

_____

_____

_____

_____

Educational Profile: Personalized Learner Data (Student Observation Log)

Student name: _____

Date and Time	Event

Educational Profile: Screening Results

Student name: _____

Name of test: _____

Date: _____ Benchmark or desired scores: _____

_____

_____

_____

_____

_____

Name of test: _____

Date: _____ Benchmark or desired scores: _____

_____

_____

_____

_____

_____

Name of test: _____

Date: _____ Benchmark or desired scores: _____

_____

_____

_____

_____

_____

Educational Profile: Intervention Plan Form

Student name: _____

Goal: _____

_____

_____

Intervention Plan

Title of intervention _____

Tier _____ Intervention setting _____

Planned start date _____ Frequency of implementation _____

Person(s) responsible for implementing the intervention _____

_____

How will progress be monitored? _____

_____

_____

_____

_____

_____

How will fidelity of implementation be monitored? _____

_____

_____

_____

_____

Educational Profile: Progress Monitoring Data

Student name: _____

Area _____ Baseline _____ Date _____ Score _____

Checkpoint 1: Date _____ Goal _____ Actual Score _____

Checkpoint 2: Date _____ Goal _____ Actual Score _____

Checkpoint 3: Date _____ Goal _____ Actual Score _____

Checkpoint 4: Date _____ Goal _____ Actual Score _____

Checkpoint 5: Date _____ Goal _____ Actual Score _____

Checkpoint 6: Date _____ Goal _____ Actual Score _____

Area _____ Baseline _____ Date _____ Score _____

Checkpoint 1: Date _____ Goal _____ Actual Score _____

Checkpoint 2: Date _____ Goal _____ Actual Score _____

Checkpoint 3: Date _____ Goal _____ Actual Score _____

Checkpoint 4: Date _____ Goal _____ Actual Score _____

Checkpoint 5: Date _____ Goal _____ Actual Score _____

Checkpoint 6: Date _____ Goal _____ Actual Score _____

Area _____ Baseline _____ Date _____ Score _____

Checkpoint 1: Date _____ Goal _____ Actual Score _____

Checkpoint 2: Date _____ Goal _____ Actual Score _____

Checkpoint 3: Date _____ Goal _____ Actual Score _____

Checkpoint 4: Date _____ Goal _____ Actual Score _____

Checkpoint 5: Date _____ Goal _____ Actual Score _____

Checkpoint 6: Date _____ Goal _____ Actual Score _____

Educational Profile:
Progress Monitoring Data (Graph)

Student name: _____

Area monitored: _____

	Baseline Date	Checkpoint Date	Checkpoint Date	Checkpoint Date	Checkpoint Date	Checkpoint Date

Educational Profile: Diagnostic Evaluation Results

Student name: _____

Summary

_____

_____

_____

_____

_____

_____

_____

_____

_____

_____

_____

Diagnostic Evaluation Team Members

Name: _____   Title: _____

Name: _____   Title: _____

Name: _____   Title: _____

Name: _____   Title: _____

Name: _____   Title: _____

Educational Profile: Documentation of Research-Based Interventions

Student name: _____ Tier: _____

Title of intervention: _____

Start date: _____ End date: _____ Time allotted: _____

Outcome _____

_____

_____

_____

_____

Action to be taken _____

_____

_____

_____

_____

_____

Notes _____

_____

_____

_____

_____

_____

Educational Profile: Research-Based Interventions (Observation of Fidelity)

Reminder to the observer: The goal of the observation is not to judge or evaluate the teacher; it is to evaluate the degree to which the intervention is being implemented effectively and as designed.

Student name: _____ Date: _____ Time: _____

Interventionist: _____ Observer: _____

Does the observer have the necessary background knowledge and qualifications to evaluate the effectiveness and fidelity of this particular intervention?   Yes   No

Goal _____

_____

_____

Observation of Research-Based Intervention

Title of intervention: _____

Notes _____

_____

Was the intervention implemented as it was designed? Explain. _____

_____

_____

_____

What was the student's level of engagement during the lesson? _____

_____

_____

Signature of the observer: _____ Date: _____

Signature of the interventionist: _____ Date: _____

Educational Profile: Parent Contact Log

Student name: _____

One of the hallmarks of effective home-school collaboration is open communication with parents and guardians. Documentation of your contacts can serve as a way of monitoring your level of communication throughout all stages of each student's learning process.

Date/Contact	Notes
Date: Contacted by:	
Date: Contacted by:	
Date: Contacted by:	
Date: Contacted by:	

Part III

Instruction

School success would be much more straightforward if learners responded in the same way to teaching methods. Instead, what students take away from lessons and specific instructional strategies can vary significantly depending upon their areas of strength and interest. Response to Intervention is about finding what works with individual learners. This can be more art than science and require multiple attempts before a technique proves effective.

Part III of this book features educational techniques to support you in these efforts. Chapter 5 includes grouping strategies for differentiating instruction in mixed-ability classrooms. These methods allow you to remediate specific skill deficits in struggling learners without diminishing the overall effectiveness of classroom instruction. Chapter 6 features hundreds of proven instructional techniques to use with students. You might already use many of these techniques in your teaching while others may represent opportunities for you to expand your base of strategies. These instructional methods can be selected based on students' specific areas of need and strength.

The grouping and instructional strategies in this section can be especially helpful to classroom teachers, special educators, literacy specialists, and other members of Support Teams working directly with students. Administrators and other school leaders, however, will also find the information helpful—particularly those who are members of RTI teams and involved in identifying appropriate instructional methods for learners.

Chapter 5

Purposeful Grouping

Today's classrooms are incredibly diverse. As the personalized learner assessments from Chapter 3 reveal, students come to school with a wide range of abilities and interests. A comprehensive assessment program, detailed in Chapter 4, will continually identify different areas of need among students. Effective instruction accounts for students' unique academic challenges and strengths, but how can teaching be individualized in classrooms where learners differ from one another in so many ways?

Purposeful grouping allows you to provide personalized instruction in the general education setting. It can help you design lesson plans that set up all students for success, including those struggling with particular skills from the curriculum. In fact, grouping can be one of the most powerful support tools in your RTI efforts. You can provide intensive academic interventions— even with limited time and resources—without diminishing the potency of instruction for the greater student population.

Grouping students effectively relies on a thorough working knowledge of students' strengths, interests, thinking and learning styles, multiple intelligences preferences, and academic needs. The assessment methods discussed in this book can help you collect this information. Grouping strategies in this chapter build on the student information compiled in earlier RTI stages.

How Do I Group Students?

The primary motivation for grouping students is to differentiate instruction for diverse learning needs. Differentiating instruction involves adjusting the pace, level, or type of teaching to address unique academic challenges and instruct students in the ways they learn best. When you divide students into groups, you can reach diverse learners in the classroom, even as you provide more intensive instruction in challenge areas for struggling learners.

The learning groups that you create will not be fixed or permanent. Instead, they will be flexible and change often over time. This practice of flexible grouping allows you to routinely adapt your instruction; you can consistently arrange students to meet specific learning objectives within subject areas. When you analyze screening results, progress monitoring data, and other assessments, you can identify evolving student needs and ensure your teaching is responsive to those needs.

It's important to be thoughtful in grouping practices. How many students will you include within each group? Will you group learners homogenously (by shared traits) or heterogeneously (based on student differences)? What kind of teaching strategies will you use within group structures? The answers to these and other questions will be determined by your specific circumstances. Perhaps during math instruction some students require remediation in a particular multiplication skill. You might set up heterogeneous pairs in which a student who excels in the given skill area can help another who struggles with it. (See "Using Peer and Cross-Age Tutoring" on page 141 for more on this grouping strategy.)

> **Purposeful grouping allows you to provide personalized instruction in the general education setting. It can help you design lesson plans that set up all students for success, including those struggling with particular skills from the curriculum.**

In another situation, a different type of grouping might be more effective. For example, in teaching a unit on the Revolutionary War you might group students based upon preferred learning styles. In this scenario, a quality shared among students determines their grouping and how they will demonstrate knowledge of the topic. A group of visual learners might focus on presenting information about the Revolutionary War on a poster, brochure, bulletin board, or Web site. The auditory learning group might prepare a speech, a rap, or another performance incorporating information from the unit. Finally, students favoring kinesthetic learning might create a play or reenact a key battle for the class.

The "Class Profile" (page 149) can help you make grouping decisions. This table incorporates student data collected in "Educational Profiles" (pages 118–134). By referencing learner qualities during your academic planning, you can design lesson plans that address academic deficits while focusing on strength and interest areas. The result: personalized instruction for meeting student needs at any tier within the RTI framework.

Example of "Class Profile"

FIGURE 5.1

Class Profile

Student Name	Relative Academic Strengths	Relative Academic Needs	Accommodations and Modifications	Multiple Intelligence Preferences	Learning and Thinking Styles	Documented Disabilities	Special Interests
Davis, John	Reading comprehension	Spelling, Science	Reduced spelling lists	Verbal/Linguistic Logical/Mathematical	Visual, Global		Basketball, Computers
Ecker, Steve	Reading fluency	Math computation		Bodily/Kinesthetic Interpersonal	Auditory, Analytic	Cognitive impairment	Soccer
Franklin, Laticia	Math reasoning, Math computation	Reading fluency, comprehension	Taped reading materials	Bodily/Kinesthetic Naturalist Intrapersonal	Kinesthetic, Global		Swimming, Hiking
Johnson, Harold	Reading fluency, comprehension	Math reasoning, Math computation	Peer tutor, Extend math time	Bodily/Kinesthetic Musical/Rhythmic	Kinesthetic, Global		Scrapbooking
Klein, Pam	Spelling, Reading comprehension, Social studies	Basic math facts		Musical/Rhythmic Naturalist	Visual, Global		Animals, Soccer
Lozer, Patrice	Math computation	Reading comprehension	Spell checker	Visual/Spatial Intrapersonal	Kinesthetic, Global	Learning disability	Computers
Manas, Roberta	Reading comprehension	Math computation		Bodily/Kinesthetic Interpersonal	Auditory, Analytic		Sewing, Knitting
Rogers, Kristin	Basic math facts	Reading comprehension	Extended reading time	Logical/Mathematical Visual/Spatial	Auditory, Analytic		Computers
Sampson, Ben	Listening, Basic math facts	Reading comprehension	Behavior management plan	Bodily/Kinesthetic	Kinesthetic, Global		Football, Video games
Stein, Will	Reading fluency	Reading comprehension		Naturalist Visual/Spatial	Visual, Global		Hunting and fishing
Tao, Jing	Reading comprehension	Basic math facts		Verbal/Linguistic Interpersonal	Kinesthetic, Analytic		Writing, Computers
Wendell, Terrell	Math computation	Reading comprehension		Visual/Spatial Logical/Mathematical	Kinesthetic, Global		Skateboarding, Video games

Reproducible form on page 149.

The "Class Profile" gives you at-a-glance information on academic deficits, learning strengths, and personal interests. These learner attributes allow you to easily group students for virtually any instructional purpose. You can also feel free to add other categories of your own—including open lesson periods when you are not targeting specific learning objectives in a given subject area. For these situations you might divide students based on physical features (such as eye or hair color) or personal preferences (like a favorite food or sport).

Classroom Grouping Strategies

After you have set up student groups, you can begin to concentrate on how you will monitor students during your lesson time. Because these structures are flexible and based on instructional needs for various subject areas, you will probably have a number of groupings prepared for different times of the day or week. You might, for example, have evolving groupings of homogenous learners for

English and math blocks when it's important you focus on building basic skills. You might mix things up from time to time in the math block with peer-tutoring sessions, checking in with student pairs as they work together. You might also have groups for science and social studies periods that have been determined by multiple intelligences preferences or thinking and learning styles.

Regardless of the number or type of groups you might have, this section can provide you with ideas for overseeing students and making smooth transitions within the school day.

Clock Grouping

Grouping students often is directly tied to teaching specific units or subjects. Clock grouping is one method that is simple and appropriate for all age groups. It allows the teacher to easily manage the grouping of students in up to twelve different ways. Teachers can effectively transition from group to group by calling out the time of the group they want students to form. (These groupings are not related to actual time.) Many create a clock prop for the classroom, turning its hands to the appropriate group time at transition times.

1. Use your "Class Profile" to determine groupings. Groups should account for student interests and attributes as well as any specific learning needs that might be present.

2. Create the clock visual aid that you will use to indicate changes in groupings. You might add your school name or mascot in the center of the clock (or involve students in its decoration). Place the clock in an area where it will be visible to all students (such as on a bulletin board).

3. Add student grouping structures to the clock. You can make additions to or rearrange groups as necessary throughout the school year as points of instructional emphasis change.

4. During instruction, identify transition times by drawing attention to the clock and asking students to assemble in appropriate groups. An alternative to creating a large clock in the classroom is to provide a clock visual on handouts for respective students or groups.

In Figure 5.2, a teacher has used the "Class Profile" to create 12, 3, 6, and 9 o'clock groups.

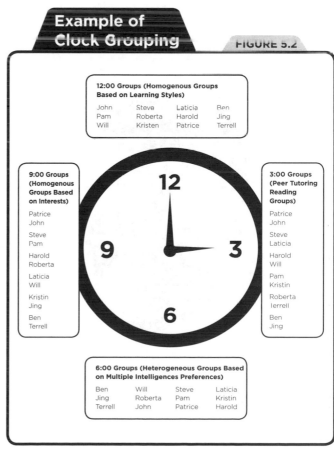

Example of Clock Grouping — FIGURE 5.2

12:00 Groups (Homogenous Groups Based on Learning Styles)

John	Steve	Laticia	Ben
Pam	Roberta	Harold	Jing
Will	Kristen	Patrice	Terrell

9:00 Groups (Homogenous Groups Based on Interests)

Patrice
John
Steve
Pam
Harold
Roberta
Laticia
Will
Kristin
Jing
Ben
Terrell

3:00 Groups (Peer Tutoring Reading Groups)

Patrice
John
Steve
Laticia
Harold
Will
Pam
Kristin
Roberta
Terrell
Ben
Jing

6:00 Groups (Heterogeneous Groups Based on Multiple Intelligences Preferences)

Ben	Will	Steve	Laticia
Jing	Roberta	Pam	Kristin
Terrell	John	Patrice	Harold

Pocket Chart Grouping

A second simple approach to grouping is through the use of pocket charts. With this method, student names are placed into groups and posted on a visual display. The pocket chart, which can be hung on any wall or bulletin board, shows the rotation order to be followed during small group work time. Following are steps for setting up pocket charts in your classroom.

1. Begin by buying or creating a pocket chart for the classroom. Common materials for charts include clear pockets, index cards, construction paper, and other art supplies. You might also incorporate different curriculum themes within the display.

2. Use the "Class Profile" to organize students into groups based on your teaching objectives.

3. Post student names in groups, putting them in the pocket under the appropriate subject area or specific teaching time. The names of student groups can be based on information taught within the teaching unit. For example, if you are teaching a science unit on insects, groups might be identified by bug names.

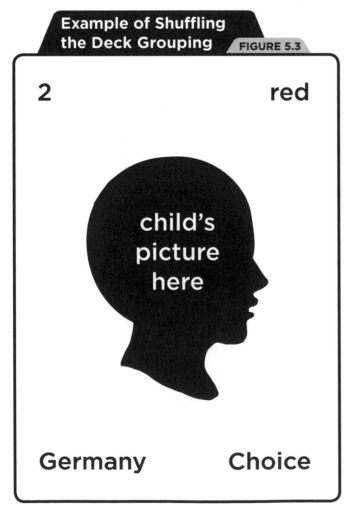

Example of Shuffling the Deck Grouping FIGURE 5.3

Shuffling the Deck Grouping

This grouping method allows you to create groups of varying size for different lessons. Each student is featured on a card along with identifying categories that can be used to form groups. Before a session of small group work, take out the deck of cards and identify the factor that will determine groups (making your selection based on the number of students you'd like in groups). Following are directions for this grouping method:

1. Obtain a pack of 3" x 5" index cards and create a card for each student in your classroom. (You may also create cards digitally.) Student names or pictures can be placed in the middle of cards. Various grouping criteria will appear in the card's four corners.

2. Determine how many students you want in the first group and how you want them to be grouped. This will be your largest grouping; if you have 24 students and want three groups of eight then you will use numbers 1–3. Place the appropriate number (1–3) in the top left corner of each student's card.

3. In the top right of each card, write one of eight colors. In a classroom of 24 students, each color group will be composed of three students.

4. In the bottom left corner of each card, list one of twelve countries. This creates twelve student pairs.

5. In the bottom right corner of each card, write "Choice." This is a grouping you can use to reward students by letting them work with others of their choosing during fun activities or free periods.

6. Set up with determining factors that include countries, colors, and numbers, this grouping method is less about grouping by achievement level and more about the number of students you would like for groups. For example, if you wanted to set up a peer-tutoring session, you could make the country the determining factor in group selection. You can replace these grouping characteristics with others (such as multiple intelligences preferences or thinking and learning styles) that are more directly tied to instructional goals.

 Spotlight

Using Peer and Cross-Age Tutoring

Peer and cross-age tutoring are teaching strategies that involve pairing students together as they learn new information or practice academic skills. Pairing students of the same age is peer tutoring; cross-age tutoring consists of partnering those who differ in age by two or more years. Peer and cross-age tutoring allow you to accommodate a classroom of diverse learners.

When using these methods, of course, it's important that students are quality tutors. Learners should know how to give positive feedback and identify when a partner needs help. It's also important they be able to provide explanations about the material and work with partners to find solutions (rather than just providing answers). Finally, students should be able to identify when to seek out the teacher for assistance.

You can train student tutors by role-playing with your class and helping learners develop a list of prompts and praises. How you implement peer or cross-age tutoring will depend on your specific setting and students, but here are some general guidelines for the process:

1. Teach students how to tutor and review expectations for tutor/tutee roles.

2. Assign partners and hand out necessary materials.

3. Ask that students follow a highly structured tutoring routine; tutors should present material previously covered by the teacher and provide feedback to the tutee.

4. Monitor pairs by circulating around the room; provide feedback as necessary.

Grouping Guidelines

Grouping students effectively can help them learn and demonstrate their knowledge in ways that set them up for success. Grouping also gives you flexibility in your instruction to address unique academic deficits, learning strengths and interests, thinking styles, and multiple intelligences preferences. Research suggests that the most effective small groups have three to four students.* Using group sizes any larger should be reserved for select activities where community building (rather than skill remediation) is the primary focus.

Grouping students allows you to directly address areas of student need, but it can also do something else. When you group students, you allow them to become partners in one another's learning. Grouping methods such as peer and cross-age tutoring have been shown to improve on-task behavior, promote stronger student-to-student relationships, and increase academic growth for both the tutor and the tutee.** Chapter 6 includes information on some techniques you can use to help create productive learning relationships.

> Grouping students effectively can help them learn and demonstrate their knowledge in ways that set them up for success. It's important that groups are not static. Rather, they should be changed frequently and continually formed based on regular assessment of student strengths and needs.

It's important that groups are not static. Rather, they should be changed frequently and continually formed based on regular assessment of student strengths and needs. Additionally, research has consistently shown that grouping by ability level should be done sparingly, if at all.† Students with low academic achievement perform more poorly when they are grouped by ability with similarly performing peers.†† Ability grouping has also been identified as a source of lowered self-esteem and motivation among struggling students.†††

Grouping within RTI will often mean placing together students who are achieving at similar levels in specific academic areas. This is not the same as ability grouping, which separates learners into groups of high, average, or low general ability. Instead, students are grouped based on specific skill deficits with the intention of improving performance in those areas. As learning needs change, so do groupings. Groups are thus in constant flux as student needs vary over time, across subject areas, and in accordance with particular learning strengths and interests.

*Lou, et al. (1996).
**Marzano, Pickering, and Pollock (2001).
†Cohen, Kulik, and Kulik (1982).
††Lou, et al. (1996).
†††Pierangelo and Giuliani (2006).

Spotlight

Reasons to Avoid Ability Grouping

It's important that your grouping be varied and constantly evolving. Stagnant ability grouping can have a negative social-emotional impact on students. When learners perceive they are consistently being placed in groups of low-achieving students, their self-esteem can be severely damaged. There may be times when grouping students based on specific skill strengths and deficits is in order to provide targeted instruction; however, it is important to vary your grouping styles enough to camouflage grouping by academic means. Following are reasons to avoid ability grouping.

- It doesn't work well. Kids can learn more if their diverse needs are being met using other techniques.

- It has a negative effect on students' self-esteem, and kids know who's in the low-achieving group.
- Parents have legitimate concerns about the social stigma of their child's perceived lower status.
- Students of similar economic backgrounds are often placed in the same group—displaying possible discrimination.

Adapted from "Is the Bluebird Really a Phoenix?" by Bruce Hansen (*Reading Today,* 25(6), 19, 2008). Reprinted with permission of the International Reading Association (www.reading.org).

Grouping Students Within RTI Tiers

Purposeful grouping is an important tool for differentiating instruction to meet unique student needs. But how do these groups function within the RTI framework?

Tier I

Tier I instruction is the universal level of teaching in the classroom. Schools often designate specific research-based education programs for core subject areas. These programs offer teachers curriculum that is explicit and structured in its approach. Even with stringent guidelines for teaching in core subject areas, however, grouping comes to play a vital role in teaching. Students, after all, have mixed abilities and will respond to the curriculum in varying degrees. Additionally, they'll respond best to instruction methods that account for their particular learning strengths and interests.

The best teaching at Tier I generally features a combination of whole class and small group instruction. There are two primary ways to group students at this level—peer pairs and heterogeneous groups. Teachers often use heterogeneous groups to carefully observe, assess, and monitor each student's abilities. Peer pairing helps students learn from one another during Tier I instruction (as does heterogeneous grouping). Both methods reduce the student-teacher ratio while still allowing mixed ability students to work together. Both also allow you to carry out individual assessment, instruction, and progress monitoring. Group goals can be set to ensure student learning.

As your class works in peer pairs or heterogeneous groups, you can monitor groups to ensure students are achieving benchmarks. This close monitoring of progress can help you make ongoing decisions regarding the need for Tier II intervention.

 RTI in Action

Reading Groups at Tier I

The primary focus of third-grade teacher Ms. Ciaccio's reading instruction is teaching students how to effectively use comprehension strategies. Most recently, she has been teaching the importance of visualization and predictions in the reading process. While her students must ultimately learn multiple comprehension strategies, Ms. Ciaccio has found it is most beneficial to focus on just one or two techniques at a time. She is now teaching students how to make predictions before and during reading using the Directed Reading-Thinking Activity, a reading comprehension strategy (see page 184).

In the full class group, Ms. Ciaccio asks students to make predictions about the story they are going to read. She encourages them to draw upon their prior knowledge to make predictions, asking students to write predictions on a whiteboard. There is then a class discussion that covers why predictions have been made and how they can help with comprehension. Following the group discussion, students partner with reading buddies. These pairings have been determined by Ms. Ciaccio based on information gathered in students' Educational Profiles.

The reading buddies are one of four groupings established through clock grouping:

- The 12:00 grouping consists of twelve pairs of students with similar thinking and learning styles.

- The 3:00 grouping consists of four groups of six children who share similar areas of interest.

- The 6:00 grouping consists of six homogeneous groups of four students organized by reading strengths and deficits.

- The 9:00 grouping is made up of four groups of six students (heterogeneously grouped in four groups so not to disturb the 12:00 grouping of peer pairs).

After the whole group reading instruction, Ms. Ciaccio works with one reading group of six (9:00 grouping). The remaining students are in 12:00 groupings; along with their reading buddies, they continue to make predictions as they read. Ms. Ciaccio has found that pairing students with reading buddies gives each student more practice than reading in small groups of three or four. She has also found that it is more efficient to model the reading comprehension strategy with the whole group, and then transferring the work to the students to practice with their peers. Ms. Ciaccio plans to extend this by encouraging students to make predictions during their independent reading.

RTI in Action

Science Groups at Tier I

Mr. Campbell, an eighth-grade science teacher, frequently uses differentiated instruction in his class by varying the complexity of the content and the techniques he uses to introduce and reinforce content. He also offers students choices for how they can demonstrate their learning. In a lesson on plants, Mr. Campbell decided that the problem-solving activity he had in mind would work best with heterogeneous groups based on learning and thinking styles. The students would be testing whether water can travel through plant stems. First, students would be working in pairs (one student who is strong in comprehension paired with a student who struggles in this area) to review information about plant parts in their textbook using the THIEVES strategy (see page 190). Mr. Campbell instructed the pairs to pay special attention to the terms *xylem* and *phloem.*

In order to carry out the experiment in cooperative groups, he selected one student from each grouping who demonstrated each of the following strengths: verbal, auditory, kinesthetic, global, and analytical. He gave the student who demonstrated strength in auditory skills the job of "note taker." This student was assigned to listen to the discussion and take notes on the experiment. The students who were highly kinesthetic and highly analytic were in charge of following the step-by-step instructions that needed to be carried out. The students who were highly global and highly verbal were in charge of communicating the results to the rest of the class.

Tier II

Though there are fewer students receiving Tier II level support, it generally is still not practical or possible to provide individualized instruction for each student. Purposeful grouping, however, ensures that individual learning needs continue to be met. Assigning students to groupings that account for their specific learning strengths allows them to engage and teach one another, thus allowing you to work with small groups of those who need to be re-taught concepts. As a result, purposeful grouping helps resolve a tough classroom challenge at Tier II—ensuring that all students are engaged even as teachers work specifically with small groups struggling with skill deficits.

Tier II groupings bring together students who are failing to meet grade-level benchmarks. These students should be grouped homogeneously by skill deficit area (rather than general ability). Herein lies the difference between this form of organizing students and ability grouping—children are grouped based on specific skill deficits rather than high, average, or low general ability. It's important to remember that Tier II instruction should take place outside of Tier I instructional time. Groups at Tier II should be fluid and flexible with students moving in and out of the small groups within eight to twelve weeks (as determined by frequent progress monitoring).

One administrative suggestion for overseeing groups at Tier II is to group across grade level. Here Grade Level Teams divide instructional areas among staff, allowing teachers to provide expert instruction in one or two skill areas. In this scenario, all grade-level teachers provide Tier II instruction at the same time so that students can move to the staff member specializing in their skill deficit areas.

RTI in Action

Reading Groups at Tier II

Ms. Ciaccio's Tier II instruction begins shortly after a language arts block of 120 minutes. She starts by explaining to the class that they will be working in their 3:00 groups to complete an assignment. While students work on group assignments, Ms. Ciaccio teaches a small homogeneous group in areas of phonemic awareness and letter recognition. The small group is made up of students from her classroom and the classrooms within her grade level. The grade-level expert in this area, Ms. Ciaccio works with this group of students three times a week for 40 minutes. As the other expert instructors do, she monitors student progress every two weeks. Students frequently move in and out of her group, as they do in the groups of her colleagues. The Grade Level Team meets weekly to discuss student progress.

RTI in Action

Science Groups at Tier II

Mr. Campbell realizes that some students in his third hour science class are really struggling to understand key vocabulary related to the unit on plant life. He decides to implement a targeted intervention aimed at teaching students these vocabulary words and the concepts behind the terms. He elicits help from his colleague's teaching aide, Miss Payton, who is working on a teaching degree and majoring in biology at the local university. She volunteers in the school two days a week. Miss Payton will teach a series of lessons every Monday and Wednesday for the next three weeks in Mr. Campbell's class while Mr. Campbell uses Vocabulary Picture Cards (page 193) with the students who are struggling with the vocabulary terms. He will monitor their progress once a week.

Tier III

Students receiving instruction in Tier III typically demonstrate inadequate progress after Tier II interventions have been implemented. These students are in need of more intense instruction within a structured, research-based program. Tier III instruction will most often take place outside of the classroom, though in close collaboration with the classroom teacher.

Tier III is similar to Tier II where students needing more intense instruction work with one "expert" in a given area at a particular time. Tier III instruction can also be offered at the same time as Tier II instruction. As students move to the appropriate classroom for Tier II instruction, Tier III students can go to the specialist trained to provide more intensive instruction in their deficit areas.

 RTI in Action

Reading Groups at Tier III

Ms. Ciaccio's struggling students receive Tier III instruction at the same time she teaches Tier II groups. Two of her students spend 30 minutes with the reading specialist. Later in the afternoon, these Tier III students return to the reading specialist for an additional 30 minutes of intense instruction. As a result of the afternoon instruction, the Tier III students miss 30 minutes of classroom instruction (but not in the areas of reading or writing). Both Tier II and Tier III groups change often throughout the school year so there is constant movement in and out of the groups and tiers

 RTI in Action

Science Groups at Tier III

A student in Mr. Campbell's sixth hour science class has fallen behind despite his efforts to intervene at a Tier II level and his routine differentiation. He is working with the school's interventionist, Mr. Garrett, to get the student up to speed. Mr. Campbell, Mr. Garrett, and the Evaluation Team have reviewed the student's work samples and have identified lack of content area reading comprehension as one of the primary reasons the student is falling behind. She is also struggling in her English and social studies classes. Analysis of her results on the Gray Oral Reading Test confirms their initial evaluation. The team decides that Mr. Garrett will provide instruction on content area reading strategies, such as Reciprocal Teaching (see page 187), for the student during her science class. Mr. Garrett will use material from the science curriculum in his instruction so the student doesn't continue to fall further behind.

Resources for Grouping and Differentiating Instruction

Differentiating Instruction in the Regular Classroom: How to Reach and Teach All Learners (Grades 3–12) by Diane Heacox (Minneapolis: Free Spirit Publishing, 2002). Differentiating instruction is all about changing the pace, level, or type of instruction to meet diverse needs in the classroom. This book provides general education teachers with a full menu of instruction and grouping strategies to deliver appropriate instruction and manage the classroom.

Differentiation: From Planning to Practice (Grades 6–12) by Rick Wormeli (Portland, ME: Stenhouse Publishers, 2007). This resource provides step-by-step instructions for differentiating instruction for middle and high school classrooms. Discover how to craft lesson plans that foster academic achievement in all types of learners, including students who are gifted, struggling, or learning English.

Fair Isn't Always Equal: Assessing and Grading in the Differentiated Classroom by Rick Wormeli (Portland, ME: Stenhouse Publishers, 2006). Differentiating instruction is increasingly common in classrooms, but one aspect of differentiation continues to give many teachers trouble: grading. This resource offers guidelines for making difficult grading decisions in middle and high school classrooms.

How to Differentiate Instruction in Mixed-Ability Classrooms by Carol Ann Tomlinson (Alexandria, VA: Association for Supervision and Curriculum Development, 2004). This title on differentiating instruction provides guiding principles and hands-on strategies for designing lesson plans for diverse classrooms. From curriculum planning to tips for overseeing learning groups, this book offers a comprehensive look at differentiated instruction.

Integrating Differentiated Instruction and Understanding by Design: Connecting Content and Kids by Carol Ann Tomlinson and Jay McTighe (Alexandria, VA: Association for Supervision and Curriculum Development, 2006). In an era of education emphasizing standards, many educators are looking for ways to ensure students fully understand concepts from the curriculum and can apply them in meaningful ways. This book helps teachers foster this kind of learning while maintaining standards and targeting students' specific areas of academic strength and weakness.

Making Differentiation a Habit: How to Ensure Success in Academically Diverse Classrooms by Diane Heacox (Minneapolis: Free Spirit Publishing, 2009). This resource provides easy-to-use tools, checklists, and surveys to incorporate differentiation principles into the everyday curriculum. Find specific strategies for assessment, tiering assignments, grading, and differentiating for gifted learners. The book also offers research connecting differentiation and RTI.

Class Profile

Student Name	Relative Academic Strengths	Relative Academic Needs	Accommodations and Modifications	Multiple Intelligence Preferences	Learning and Thinking Styles	Documented Disabilities	Special Interests

Research-Based Teaching

*I*t's important that research-based teaching methods and curriculum resources be used throughout the tiers of RTI—from universal level classroom instruction to the intense and strategic interventions addressing severe academic difficulties at Tier III. This provision for use of proven instructional strategies and education programs is intended to eliminate poor instruction or weak curricula as potential sources of a student's academic difficulties.

This chapter features research-based instructional methods, strategies, and programs that support the RTI model across grade level and subject area. These are practices you can use in conjunction with assessment and instructional decision-making tools detailed throughout this book. The "What to Try When" charts help you identify strategies that address specific learning deficits in students while also accounting for their respective areas of strength.

Research-Based Instructional Methods

Before addressing teaching strategies designed for meeting specific learning difficulties within particular subject areas, let us first look at some productive instructional methods that can be used across the curricula at all grade levels. Some of these practices form the basis of specific strategies appearing later in the section. (For example, Story Face on page 188 incorporates visual representations.)

Set Learning Goals

We all have learning goals for our students. We want to help them succeed—and demonstrate their achievement—in myriad ways over the course of the school year. In fact, the process of setting goals is vital toward establishing a direction for learning.*

Purposefully working with students to set goals at school can help them focus their academic efforts. When expectations are clear to students, they are more likely to meet them. These learning goals should be specific enough to direct learning, while also being flexible if changes need to be made. Allowing student interests to influence goals is also a good idea. You might establish learning objectives in broad terms and encourage students to personalize them based on individual preferences.

Letting students influence goal setting can be a powerful motivating factor. For example, a seventh-grade language arts teacher may set a common goal that students exhibit personal style and voice in their writing to enhance an expository piece of writing. A student might take that common goal and adapt it to something like, "I want to know more about how to use humor and my strong opinions to make my papers more interesting."

Spotlight

Selection of Research-Based Instructional Methods

These instructional methods have been carefully selected based on the findings of multiple researchers, including the Mid-Continent Research for Education and Learning and Harold Pashler and his colleagues' work for the U.S. Department of Education's Institute of Education Sciences. The strategies have been chosen for this book because they have demonstrated effectiveness in multiple content areas with students of diverse backgrounds (including varying ages, ability levels, and cultural backgrounds). For more information on the instructional methods listed here, see *Classroom Instruction that Works* by Robert Marzano, Debra Pickering, and Jane Pollock and *Organizing Instruction and Study to Improve Student Learning* (available at http://ies.ed.gov). The "References and Resources" section (pages 225–238) has more information on these sources.

---

*Marzano, Pickering, and Pollock (2001).

Once learning goals are set, it's important to provide students with timely feedback on how they are doing. Feedback should be corrective, meaning that you fully explain what the student is doing correctly and incorrectly. Another note on providing feedback: It's important we address how students are progressing toward goals, rather than how their performance compares to that of other students.*

Activate Prior Knowledge

Asking students to "show what they know" through classroom activities and discussion is an important technique most of us use on a regular basis. When we request information of students, we provide valuable opportunities for them to recall and reflect on what they already know about a topic. Additionally, when we bring up new topics within the context of previously known information, we help them make connections with other topics of study. Following are a few effective ways to activate student knowledge:

- **Cueing.** Cues provide students with hints or clues about what they are about to learn or experience. You can provide these in an introduction that precedes more complete discussion of new material. Cues can alert students to what they might already know about the topic and prepare them to process more developed information about it. In a sense, it sets the stage for learning to happen.

- **Questioning.** Similar to cueing, questions can help students form context around what they are learning (or about to learn). Questioning learners about a particular topic activates prior knowledge while still framing discussion around a topic.

- **Advance organizers.** Advance organizers offer students a preview of information in the form of an outline. You can share organizers with students before lessons to prepare them to learn about a particular topic. Advance organizer methods include notes, graphic representations, and scanning (looking at headings, subheadings, and bold text within a passage before reading).

Cues, questions, and advance organizers should focus on what is most important in overall understanding of the topic (rather than obscure facts and details). The goal with these teaching methods is to help students realize and analyze what they already know. Pre-tests can also be used to identify important material and determine knowledge of a subject that has yet to be taught.** Activating prior knowledge through questions, cues, and advance organizers can be especially beneficial for global thinkers; these learners like to understand context (the big picture) before taking in new information.

---

*Marzano, Pickering, and Pollock (2001).
**Pashler, et al. (2007).

Use Visual Representations

Visual representation is a powerful way to communicate new material to students—particularly learners who process information best when they are able to see it. Allowing these students to demonstrate their knowledge through visual means is also a good idea. In fact, research shows that use of visual representations helps students extend their knowledge and elaborate on thinking in ways they might not otherwise be able to show.[*] Among these important tools are:

- pictures
- charts
- video clips
- graphic organizers (for example, story maps)
- mental images
- physical models
- Web sites
- kinesthetic activities (for example, acting out a scene from a book)

> **Visual representations can be useful in helping students understand concepts from all subject areas.**

It's important that visual representations be accompanied by verbal descriptions, thus combining two learning modalities (auditory and visual).[**]

Assign Practice Opportunities

As educators, we all understand the importance of student practice toward mastery of academic skills. It is not surprising, then, that research bears out the effectiveness of multiple exposures to material over an extended period of time. Studies show that exposing students to key concepts, then re-exposing them to the same content weeks or months later, promotes learning.[†] Charting accuracy and speed with curriculum-based measurements (see page 102) is one effective way to infuse student practice into instruction and assessment. Another common and effective method, of course, is quizzing students on what has been taught. Quizzes have also been shown to be a strong motivator of student study.

While questions around the effectiveness of homework are periodically raised, studies show that it is effective toward reinforcing learning, particularly in secondary settings.[††] It's important that homework be thoughtfully assigned. Homework, for example, should cover information taught in class. Students should be able to complete it relatively independently (with

---

[*]Anderson (1990) as cited in Marzano, Pickering, and Pollock (2001).
[**]Pashler et al. (2007).
[†]Pashler et al. (2007).
[††]Marzano, Pickering, and Pollock (2001).

Tech Tools

Classroom response systems (commonly known as clicker systems) can be useful tools in helping students practice material. In classrooms with these systems, students input answers on handheld devices within group settings. They might provide answers to teacher-created multiple-choice questions, for example, or mathematical solutions, depending upon the subject being studied. These handheld devices communicate responses to a teacher's computer where software records, analyzes, graphs, and displays results. These systems allow teachers to check for understanding and provide students with immediate feedback. They can be a powerful motivating factor in subject review. See the "References and Resources" section for where you can find classroom response systems.

minimal parent support at most). Students should also be made aware of why they must complete assignments. Of perhaps greatest importance is the need for teachers to provide specific and timely feedback on student work. In all contexts, activities assigned for student practice should help them adapt, adjust, change, and extend their knowledge base. This often requires that you issue various forms of practice (rather than a single method).

Promote Higher-Level Thinking

While repeated practice can help students remember key information, we know simple recall of facts does not demonstrate true understanding. Rather, students benefit from being challenged by questions and activities that promote higher-level thinking. When we encourage students to examine subjects within the curriculum from different perspectives, we help them to think critically. After students have acquired basic knowledge about a certain concept, it's important to engage them in problem solving and analysis about it. Some methods for stimulating higher-level thinking include:

- Asking students to generate and test hypotheses on a subject

- Encouraging learners to connect abstract and concrete concepts (including real-life situations)

- Asking students to identify similarities and differences between two concepts, ideas, or artifacts

- Discussing solutions to problems and brainstorming other potential ways they might be solved

Provide Strategy Instruction

Without guidance, most students cannot accurately determine how well they have mastered new material; in fact, they often over-estimate what they know and the depth of their knowledge.* This is especially true for students with learning disabilities.** Strategy instruction supplies these students with the tools and techniques that efficient learners use. With the method, you will instruct learners on strategies that improve metacognition (the ability to judge how well we have learned new concepts and ideas) until their use becomes automatic. A plethora of approaches to teach students to use strategies are available, but one comprehensive approach that has a particularly strong research base is the Self-Regulated Strategy Development Model. This model is designed to ensure that all crucial aspects of strategy instruction are addressed. It involves the following stages:

1. Activate background knowledge.

2. Lead the class in another discussion of the strategy including the purpose of the strategy, who it is designed for, and the expected benefits.

3. Model the strategy.

4. Memorize the strategy.

5. Work together with another student to practice the strategy until learner is able to independently perform it. Provide multiple opportunities for practice and gradually release responsibility to the student.

6. Direct students to use the strategy on their own.

Examples of strategies that can be taught using this model include Directed Reading–Thinking (page 184) and the RIDD Strategy (page 220). When students can self-regulate learning (set learning goals, self-instruct, self-monitor, and provide themselves with positive reinforcement), they are able to make greater academic gains.[†] It's important to monitor students' use of a strategy throughout the stages so that they do not skip steps or otherwise distort the strategy.

Use the Gradual Release of Responsibility Framework

The Gradual Release of Responsibility Framework[††] shifts from a teacher-led instructional model to cooperative learning and, ultimately, individual student application of the material. These shifts in instructional focus must occur purposefully and carefully to ensure student understanding. The four main components of this method are:

- Focus Lessons (I do it). Administer focus lessons to establish a purpose for learning the new material, model the thinking process (through think alouds), and explain new concepts.

*Pashler, et al. (2007).
**Swanson (2001).
†Graham and Harris (2005).
††Based on the work of Pearson and Gallagher (1983).

- Guided Instruction (We do it). During the guided instruction phase you meet with small groups, providing practice and feedback based on learner needs. Encourage students to ask questions and share their thoughts about the material.

- Collaborative Learning (You do it together). In this phase, students interact with peers to consolidate their thinking and learning.

- Independent Learning Tasks (You do it alone). Build in opportunities for students to work with the material on their own. This helps them become more self-directed. Students need this individual practice time to gain confidence in completing tasks on their own.

Use Direct Instruction

Direct instruction, developed by Siegfried Engleman and Wesley Becker, is a teacher-centered instructional model. It emphasizes carefully developed and thoroughly planned lessons that break down learning into steps. Each step must be mastered before students are allowed to move on. Direct instruction demands that you deliver information with continuous modeling. The initial lesson involves fast-paced instruction and is followed by guided practice, and, reduced support until a student demonstrates mastery of the material. Direct instruction is most effective for developing isolated skills in students* and is ideally suited for those who need teacher support in grasping new material.** Generally, the sequence of a direct instruction lesson involves following these steps:

1. State the objectives of the lesson and explain why these objectives are important.
2. Review skills or knowledge necessary to learn the new information.
3. Present the new information in an organized manner.
4. Question students or infuse activities that check for understanding.
5. Provide guided practice.
6. Provide independent practice.
7. Assess.
8. Provide more opportunities for practice in the form of homework.

Direct instruction is a traditional model of teaching that should be used on a limited basis. Other forms of instruction (such as through grouping or interactive classroom activities) can often better meet the unique needs of diverse learners.

---

*Kroesbergen and VanLuit (2003).
**Sousa (2004).

Integrate Problem-Based Learning

Problem-based learning is a student-centered instructional model in which learners work in collaborative groups to solve problems and reflect on their experiences. Your role here is to pose high-level, open-ended problems and provide support. In this method, you serve as a facilitator of learning (rather than a provider of knowledge). Problem-based learning entails the following steps:

1. Explain the problem or present a realistic scenario with the problem embedded.

2. Set up students in heterogeneous collaborative groups (3–4 students per group).

3. Instruct students to discuss what they know about the topic, set learning goals, explore the problem, generate and test possible hypotheses, and arrive at a solution.

> **Problem-based learning represents an excellent opportunity to incorporate students' interests into instruction.**

4. Intersperse worked-out examples of the problems as models and challenge students' thinking.

5. Help students reflect on the problem-solving process and discuss the solutions different groups worked out.

During problem-based learning, you should fade support as students successfully generate and test hypotheses. You can achieve this by beginning with worked out examples and then introducing students to less complex problems. As the process evolves, you can alter problems by adding components that make them more realistic.* This progression and fading of support encourages self-directed learning and application of new knowledge to novel situations.**

Research-Based Programs and Strategies

Just like the preceding methods for delivering instruction, it's important that education programs and intervention strategies in place at your school also be grounded in research. In this section you will find information on ready-to-use, proven teaching strategies and research-based programs that address reading decoding and word recognition, reading fluency, reading comprehension, written expression, math computation, and math reasoning.

---

*Merrill (2007).
**Hemlo-Silver (2004).

You'll notice that the programs and strategies included in this chapter incorporate the instructional methods previously listed that are grounded in research. For example, the The Story Face strategy uses visual representations. The SQ3R strategy involves setting learning goals, advance organizers, collaborative grouping, and higher-level thinking. These instructional methods are the main ingredients needed to create a proven program or strategy. While not exhaustive in listing every program and strategy, there are dozens of intervention sources that can be used for instruction across RTI's tiers.

The "What to Try When" charts can assist you in selecting appropriate interventions. These charts list common academic problems and provide suggestions for which programs or strategies may most effectively address different learning challenges. During RTI meetings, pick several potential strategies from each academic area before determining which might work best based on students' academic deficit areas, interests, and learning strengths. Familiarize yourself and students with selected interventions until they begin to generalize them into other subject areas and content lessons. The "What to Try When" charts are broken down by skill area:

- Reading Decoding and Word Recognition (pages 159–161)

- Reading Fluency (pages 168–169)

- Reading Comprehension (pages 176–179)

- Written Expression (pages 194–195)

- Math Computation (pages 206–207)

- Math Reasoning (pages 213–215)

Remember, no instructional strategy or program will be 100 percent effective in promoting student success. Rather, student needs will vary; interventions may not always lead to the hoped-for result. Despite decades of educational research on pedagogical best practices, teaching remains more of an art than a science. Truly masterful teaching uses proven practices, but it is still flexible. No matter how well you know students and how thoroughly versed in research-based teaching, you still may not reach all of the students all of the time. Yet every small success moves students forward. These strategies and programs can help.

Reading Decoding and Word Recognition

What to try when a student has difficulty hearing and/or manipulating sounds in words:

Strategy	Multiple Intelligences Preferences and Key Learning Styles	Page Number
Letterboxes	Visual/Spatial Auditory	162
Four Square	Visual/Spatial Auditory	165
Reading Recovery	Verbal/Linguistic Auditory	165
Kaplan SpellRead	Verbal/Linguistic Auditory	162

What to try when a student cannot rhyme:

Strategy	Multiple Intelligences Preferences and Key Learning Styles	Page Number
Word Families	Verbal/Linguistic Auditory	163
Pattern Sorts	Bodily/Kinesthetic Visual/Spatial	167
Kaplan SpellRead	Verbal/Linguistic Auditory	162

What to try when a student has difficulty with letter-sound correspondence:

Strategy	Multiple Intelligences Preferences and Key Learning Styles	Page Number
Letterboxes	Visual/Spatial Auditory	162
Four Square	Visual/Spatial Auditory	165
Word Families	Verbal/Linguistic Auditory	163
Reading Recovery	Verbal/Linguistic Auditory	165
Kaplan SpellRead	Verbal/Linguistic Auditory	162

What to try when a student tries to sound out words letter by letter:

Strategy	Multiple Intelligences Preferences and Key Learning Styles	Page Number
DISSECT	Logical/Mathematical Visual/Spatial	164
Word Families	Verbal/Linguistic Auditory	163
Reading Recovery	Verbal/Linguistic Auditory	165
Strategy Access Rods	Intrapersonal Tactile	166

What to try when a student cannot generalize words he or she knows to read new words:

Strategy	Multiple Intelligences Preferences and Key Learning Styles	Page Number
Word Families	Verbal/Linguistic Auditory	163
Pattern Sorts	Bodily/Kinesthetic Visual/Spatial	167
Four Square	Visual/Spatial Auditory	165

What to try when a student guesses at unknown words, using no visual cues:

Strategy	Multiple Intelligences Preferences and Key Learning Styles	Page Number
Pattern Sorts	Bodily/Kinesthetic Visual/Spatial	167
Letterboxes	Visual/Spatial Auditory	162
Word Families	Verbal/Linguistic Auditory	163
DISSECT	Logical/Mathematical Visual/Spatial	164
Strategy Access Rods	Intrapersonal Tactile	166
Four Square	Visual/Spatial Auditory	165

What to try when a student over relies on phonics to read words:

Strategy	Multiple Intelligences Preferences and Key Learning Styles	Page Number
Pattern Sorts	Bodily/Kinesthetic Visual/Spatial	167
DISSECT	Logical/Mathematical Visual/Spatial	164
Strategy Access Rods	Intrapersonal Tactile	166

What to try when a student guesses at words using only the first letter:

Strategy	Multiple Intelligences Preferences and Key Learning Styles	Page Number
Strategy Access Rods	Intrapersonal Tactile	166
Letterboxes	Visual/Spatial Auditory	162
Word Families	Verbal/Linguistic Auditory	163
DISSECT	Logical/Mathematical Visual/Spatial	164

Kaplan SpellRead

Area Addressed: Reading Decoding and Word Recognition

Appropriate Grade Level: 2–12

Strategy Summary:

Kaplan SpellRead is a phonological auditory training program for struggling readers in grades 2 and above. It is designed as a remedial program for students who are at least two years below grade level in reading. The program combines sound-level work with language-based reading and writing by first working with the sounds that are the easiest to hear and manipulate and then progressing to more difficult sound combinations. The program focuses on phonological processing. The teacher discusses the underlying meaning of a word problem and has students role-play the problem.

Teacher Notes:

- The program has been tested and proven to be effective with English language learners and students with reading disabilities.

- The length of the training will vary depending on the student's initial assessment but typically takes about 100 hours to complete. Younger students will likely be able to progress more quickly.

- Kaplan SpellRead builds phonological awareness and spelling skills.

What Works Clearinghouse (2007). Document available at www.whatworks.ed.gov. Kaplan SpellRead is a commercially produced program. For more information visit spellread.com.

Letterboxes

Area Addressed: Reading Decoding and Word Recognition

Appropriate Grade Level: K–2

Strategy Summary:

Letterbox lessons help students isolate phonemes and learn the alphabetic code by placing letters in boxes that show the number of phonemes and graphemes in words. It is based on D.B. Elkonin's sound boxes.

1. Give each student his or her own empty letterbox worksheet that corresponds with the words the teacher is about to present. These worksheets can be created by hand or with a word processor.

2. Give each student his or her own set of letters to manipulate or a pencil to write the letters in the boxes.

3. Call out the words. Say them slowly and put emphasis on the phonemes. The emphasis of this lesson is on hearing the sounds.

4. Have students place or write the letters in the boxes as they hear the sounds in the word.

5. Check to make sure students have the correct letters in the boxes. *Note:* two or more letters can be in one box if those letters are needed to make the one phoneme.

6. Instruct the students to read the word.

L	O	CK

Teacher Notes:

- This is a hands-on activity that gives students a chance not only to make words but also break them into individual phonemes.

- Select words that have 2–6 phonemes.

- Tie the Letterbox strategy into spelling instruction.

- If the student is not ready to use letters (lacks letter recognition), have students move tokens (pennies, cardboard squares) into the boxes instead of letters. Instruct the student to say the sounds while pushing the tokens into the boxes one sound at a time.

Murray, B.A., and T. Lesniak. "The Letterbox Lesson: A Hands-On Approach for Teaching Decoding." *The Reading Teacher,* 52(6), 644–650 (1999). Adapted with permission.

Word Families

Area Addressed: Reading Decoding and Word Recognition

Appropriate Grade Level: K–2

Strategy Summary:

This strategy is designed to have engaging, meaningful, and enjoyable activities that help children actively attend to the phonological structure of oral language.

1. Introduce rhyming words as two words that share the rime of a word after the first letter sound, as in *at* in *cat, hat, sat, pat, bat,* and *splat.*

2. Read a book that uses rhyming words (for example, *The Cat in the Hat* by Dr. Seuss).

3. Discuss rhyming words.

4. Have students list rhyming words on 3" x 5" index card.

5. Punch cards and put on a ring.

6. Practice daily and add to the cards.

7. Point out to students that if they can read a word like cat, they can also read words like fat and sat because they contain the same rime.

Teacher Notes:

- Create bulletin board of rhyming words.

- Make a book of rhyming words and have students illustrate their books.

- Have students work in pairs and write sentences using their rhyming words.

- Discuss how words can rhyme, but have different rimes (for example, light and kite).

Pullen, P.C., and L.M. Justice. "Enhancing Phonological Awareness, Print Awareness, and Oral Language Skills in Preschool Children." *Intervention in School and Clinic,* 39, 87–98 (2003).

DISSECT

Area Addressed: Reading Decoding and Word Recognition

Appropriate Grade Level: 6–12

Strategy Summary:

The Strategic Instruction Model (SIM) by Deshler and Schumaker is an instructional system designed to provide learning strategies related to six areas (reading, remembering information, expression, demonstration, social interaction, and math). The DISSECT method, created by Lenz and Hughes, is within the reading portion of SIM. It is used to assist struggling readers with decoding unfamiliar words by using a combination of context clues and word analysis strategies. The mnemonic DISSECT stands for the following:

Discover the context. This step requires the student to skip over any unknown words and read to the end of the sentence. The student uses the context of the sentence to guess the unknown word. If the guess does not match, the student moves on to the next step.

Isolate the prefix. The student looks at the first few letters of the word to see if there is a common prefix that he or she is able to pronounce. If a prefix is identified, the student draws a box around it.

Separate the suffix. After the student has isolated the prefix, the next step is to separate the suffix in the same way.

Say the stem. The student attempts to read the stem of the word (the part that is left from steps 2 and 3). If the stem is recognized, the student says the prefix, stem, and suffix together. If the stem cannot be named, the student moves on to the next step.

Examine the stem. The student divides the letters and applies phonics rules, including:

- Rule 1: If the stem or part of the stem begins with a vowel, separate the first two letters and pronounce. If it begins with a consonant, separate the first three letters and pronounce. Continue to apply rule until the end of the stem is reached.

- Rule 2: If the stem is still not identifiable after using Rule 1, take off the first letter of the stem and use Rule 1 for the remainder of the stem.

- Rule 3: When two vowels are together, use what you know about pronunciation and try the different possibilities.

Check with someone. The student checks with a teacher, parent, or classmate.

Try the dictionary. The student looks up the word so he or she can use pronunciation information or is able to figure out the word by reading the definition.

Teacher Notes:

- Create a poster which reminds student of the DISSECT steps.

Lenz, B.K., C.A. Hughes. "A Word Identification Strategy for Adolescents with Learning Disabilities." *Journal of Learning Disabilities,* 23(3), 149–158, 163 (1990). Adapted with permission.

Reading Recovery

Area Addressed: Reading Decoding and Word Recognition

Appropriate Grade Level: 1

Strategy Summary:

Reading Recovery, developed by Marie Clay, is a short-term intervention of one-on-one tutoring for low-achieving beginning readers. Individual students receive a half-hour lesson every day for 12 to 20 weeks with a specially trained Reading Recovery teacher. As soon as students can meet grade-level expectations and demonstrate that they can continue to work independently in the classroom, their lessons are discontinued, and new students begin individual instruction. Each lesson consists of:

- reading familiar books

- reading yesterday's new book and taking a running record

- learning letter/sound relationships by working with letters and/or words using magnetic letters

- writing a story

- assembling a cut-up story

- reading a new book

The teacher creates opportunities for the student to apply problem-solving skills and provides just enough support to help the student develop strategic behaviors to use on texts in both reading and writing.

Teacher Notes:

- The intervention is most effective when it is available to all students who need it and is used as a supplement to good classroom teaching.

Clay, M. *Reading Recovery: A Guidebook for Teachers in Training*. Portsmouth, NH: Heinemann, 1993; Schwartz, R.M., B.J. Askew, and F.X. Gómez-Bellengé. *What Works? Reading Recovery: An Analysis of the What Works Clearinghouse Intervention Report*. Worthington, OH: Reading Recovery Council of North America, 2007. Reading Recovery is a commercially produced program. More information on Reading Recovery can be found at www.readingrecovery.org.

Four Square

Area Addressed: Reading Decoding and Word Recognition

Appropriate Grade Level: 1–5

Strategy Summary:

This teaching strategy considers how the use of graphic organizers helps students understand difficult concepts about literacy. The four-square strategy integrates specific aspects of phonics instruction, penmanship, spelling, and vocabulary building. The following example shows how to use the four-square strategy to teach phonetic concepts.

1. Target a phonetic element to use as a basis for a lesson (example "th"). It may be best to use an element that is associated with other readings.

2. Have students separate notebook paper into four sections.

3. Each section will have a different theme that students are to use with the phonetic element. *Example:* Develop a sentence that uses words that begin or end with "th," write a sentence that uses words that end with "th," or draw a picture of a word that begins with "th."

The visual organization of new information helps students remember, recall, and apply new knowledge to new situations.

Teacher Notes:

• Allow students to work in collaborative groups to generate their sentences or come up with lists of words that correspond with the phonetic element of focus.

• The four-square strategy can be used in multiple contexts.

Brunn, M. "The Four-Square Strategy." *The Reading Teacher,* 55(6) 522–525 (2002). Adapted with permission.

Strategy Access Rods (SARs)

Area Addressed: Reading Decoding and Word Recognition

Appropriate Grade Level: 3–5

Strategy Summary:

This strategy guides students to find their own answers so they will not rely on external support. It promotes independence and the opportunity for good choice-making. When the student comes to a word he or she does not know, the teacher prompts the student with "What strategies could you use to figure out that word?" The first step is to review the strategies the student knows and write them down in first person. There are seven strategies:

• I can sound it out

• I can look at the pictures

• I can read on and go back to the words I don't know

• I can find a little word in a big word

• I can say the parts of a word I know

• I can put in a word I know that makes sense

• I can ask for help

Next, the seven strategies are written out on rectangular wooden rods (popsicle sticks may also be used). Daily reading instruction begins with a quick review of the word recognition strategies. During the review, the children identify and hold up the correct strategy on their own set of strategy access rods. The students learn to try each of the seven strategies.

Teacher Notes:

• Help each student create their own set of SARs and keep them in a carrying case to take home.

• Encourage parents to take part in the use of the SARs and to practice them during reading at home.

Worthing, B., and B. Laster. "Strategy Access Rods: A Hands-On Approach." *The Reading Teacher,* 56(2), 122–124 (2002). Adapted with permission.

Pattern Sorts

Area Addressed: Reading Decoding and Word Recognition

Appropriate Grade Level: 1–8

Strategy Summary:

This teaching strategy helps students recognize common patterns in words.

1. List a variety of words that share common patterns (vowel digraphs, beginning blends, consonant digraphs, etc.).

2. Ask the students what these words have in common. Emphasize that you are looking for common letter combinations, not the meanings of the words.

3. Have the students do an open sort (sort the words without providing them specific categories) or a closed sort (place the words in predetermined categories).

4. Once the words have been sorted, discuss the common features.

Teacher Notes:

• This activity can be done to review previous patterns that have been introduced in combination with a newly introduced pattern.

• Students can complete the pattern sort in pairs, small groups, or as a class.

• Pocket charts can be useful if the pattern sort is done classwide.

Gillet, J., and M.J. Kita. "Words, Kids, and Categories." *The Reading Teacher,* 32, 538–546 (1979).

Reading Fluency

What to try when a student reads quickly, but inaccurately:

Strategy	Multiple Intelligences Preferences and Key Learning Styles	Page Number
Audio-Assisted Reading	Auditory Tactile	170
Readers Theatre	Verbal/Linguistic Bodily/Kinesthetic	170
Read Naturally	Visual/Spatial Auditory	171
PALS + Fluency	Verbal/Linguistic Interpersonal	172

What to try when a student reads quickly and accurately, but with little prosody (for example, struggles with expression and proper phrasing):

Strategy	Multiple Intelligences Preferences and Key Learning Styles	Page Number
Audiobooks	Auditory Tactile	175
Read Aloud	Verbal/Linguistic Auditory	173
Audio-Assisted Reading	Auditory Tactile	170
Readers Theatre	Verbal/Linguistic Bodily/Kinesthetic	170
Read Naturally	Visual/Spatial Auditory	171
Closed-Caption TV	Visual/Spatial Verbal/Linguistic	174

What to try when a student reads with such limited fluency that comprehension is lost:

Strategy	Multiple Intelligences Preferences and Key Learning Styles	Page Number
Audio-Assisted Reading	Auditory Tactile	170
Repeated Reading	Visual/Spatial	174
Read Naturally	Visual/Spatial Auditory	171

What to try when a student stops at every unfamiliar word:

Strategy	Multiple Intelligences Preferences and Key Learning Styles	Page Number
Readers Theatre	Verbal/Linguistic Bodily/Kinesthetic	170
Read Naturally	Visual/Spatial Auditory	171
Closed-Caption TV	Visual/Spatial Verbal/Linguistic	174

What to try when a student lacks confidence when reading aloud:

Strategy	Multiple Intelligences Preferences and Key Learning Styles	Page Number
Read Aloud	Verbal/Linguistic Auditory	173
Audio-Assisted Reading	Auditory Tactile	170
Readers Theatre	Verbal/Linguistic Bodily/Kinesthetic	170
Audiobooks	Auditory Tactile	175
Read Naturally	Visual/Spatial Auditory	171
PALS + Fluency	Verbal/Linguistic Interpersonal	172

Audio-Assisted Reading

Area Addressed: Reading Fluency

Appropriate Grade Level: 4–12

Strategy Summary:

This strategy allows students to listen to a selection of text that has been recorded by a fluent reader.

1. Students will use their own copy of the passage to follow along with the audio recording, pointing to each word the reader says.

2. When the entire passage has been read, students will choose a particular section to practice.

3. Cue the recording to that particular section.

4. Students will practice reading the section along with the recording. They will continue this step until they achieve fluency and can read the section independently.

5. The student will read the section to the teacher.

Teachers should monitor students while listening to the recording to ensure they are not off-task. The recorded reading should be at the instructional level of the student and should be read at a pace all students will be able to follow. Finally the recording should have clear sound and be at a suitable volume.

Teacher Notes:

*   This strategy can be used for one-on-one support or in a small group setting.

*   In a group setting, separate students who may distract each other.

*   Ensure each step is followed, so students begin to make connections with the reading and the audio selection.

*   You might allow use of MP3 players during silent sustained reading to practice fluency skills.

*   Research supports the use of this strategy with English language learners.

Eldredge, J.L. "Increasing the Performance of Poor Readers in the Third Grade with a Group-Assisted Strategy." *Journal of Educational Research,* 84(2), 68–76 (1990).

Readers Theatre

Addressed Area: Reading Fluency

Appropriate Grade Level: 1–12

Strategy Summary:

Readers Theatre incorporates repeated exposure to text while giving students an authentic means for practicing reading with expression, appropriate pace and volume, and in meaningful phrases. It involves the following components:

1. The teacher picks a book that can easily be adapted to a script format.

2. The teacher assigns character roles to as many students as possible to involve all students in some way.

3. Students rehearse their part while infusing appropriate tone, pace, and volume.

4. The teacher explains that each student must assume his or her character by trying to speak like the character. The students can decide how a character will talk according to the assigned character's role within the book.

5. The teacher controls the content and difficulty of the text selected and which roles are assigned to each student. Students with difficulties can easily be integrated into this strategy by assigning them less demanding roles if necessary.

6. Students should be given plenty of time to practice.

7. Students who do not end up with reading roles can be assigned noises or animal characters. The students can facilitate the car door slamming or the barking of the dog. Adding in a dog who talks, or a cat who gets into mischief can add excitement for elementary-age students.

8. Assessment can be measured by students' active engagement.

Teacher Notes:

• Both fiction and nonfiction can be adapted to Readers Theatre scripts.

• This strategy promotes reading fluency, comprehension, and motivation.

Martinez, M., N. Roser, and S. Strecker. "I Never Thought I Could Be a Star: A Readers Theatre Ticket to Fluency." *The Reading Teacher*, 52, 326–333 (1999). Adapted with permission.

Read Naturally

Area Addressed: Reading Fluency

Appropriate Grade Level: K–8

Strategy Summary:

1. Each student sets a reasonable, achievable fluency goal.

2. Start with an unpracticed "cold reading" of a student-selected passage from their targeted level. Students set a timer for 1 minute to assess themselves on the passage. As they read, they keep track of the words they don't know or stumble over (by putting up a finger or making a light pencil mark underneath the problem word). At the end of 1 minute, students note how many words they read and subtract all the marked words or "errors," leaving the total wcpm (words correct per minute). They then graph this first, unpracticed wcpm score on a bar graph using a blue colored pencil.

3. Students practice reading the same passage 3–4 times along with a fluent model. This model can come from an audio recording or a trained reader.

4. Students read the text independently again. A timer is set for 1 minute and students read the text several times until they reach their predetermined goal level.

5. The student reads the passage for 1 minute and this time the teacher keeps track of the errors. At the end of 1 minute, the total number of errors is subtracted from the total number of words read. The student "passes" if three criteria are met: (a) the wcpm score meets or exceeds the predetermined goal, (b) three or fewer errors were made, and (c) the student read the passage with correct phrasing with attention to punctuation. When students "pass" a story, they move on to another passage at the same level; if the goal was not met, they continue practicing this same story. After passing, the students graph this new score onto their graph, on the same bar with their original, unpracticed score, using a red colored pencil.

6. Students continue reading passages of equivalent difficulty for approximately 10–12 stories. At that point the teacher examines the data on the student's graph to decide what step to take next. The student may move up or down a level.

Teacher Notes:

- It can be helpful to encourage students to use a tracking stick to point to the text being read and follow along.

- Add comprehension activities to this process such as having students write a sentence or two before reading a story to indicate their prior knowledge of the topic and answering 4–5 questions about the content of the story after reading it.

Hasbrouck, J., C. Ihnot, and G. Rogers. "Read Naturally: A Strategy to Increase Oral Reading Fluency." *Reading Research and Instruction*, 39, 27-37 (1999). Read Naturally is a commercially produced program. More information regarding Read Naturally can be found at www.readnaturally.com.

PALS + Fluency

Area Addressed: Reading Fluency

Appropriate Grade Level: 1–2

Strategy Summary:

PALS + Fluency is part of the Peer Assisted Learning program. It involves the following steps:

1. Use Rapid Letter Naming from DIBELS to project the more fluent and less fluent readers.

2. Pair a fluent reader (or a "coach") with a reader who is struggling with reading fluency.

3. Teacher instructs for the first 3 minutes each time PALS is implemented.

4. Four peer mediated activities are utilized:

- letter-sound correspondence: coach points to letter, reader says the sound

- blending or decoding: coach points to words, reader decodes and blends it

- sight words: coach prompts and times reader

- passages of old and new words: coach prompts reader to read and times him or her for 1 minute

5. The coach will correct the reader if he or she makes a mistake.

6. The reader has three tries to complete the activity.

7. After third attempt, the coach marks five points and a smiley face when all items are correct; if incorrect, the coach marks a stopping point.

8. Roles switch and the activity is repeated.

Model PALS + Fluency to entire class, then provide the pairs with guided practice. When the student chart shows the reader has mastered the skill, the student can go on to a more difficult activity.

Teacher Notes:

• Monitoring charts could be used to chart student progress.

• PALS + Fluency is timed.

• Change pairs after 4 weeks for effectiveness.

• Teacher should monitor constantly.

Fuchs, D., et al. "Developing First-Grade Reading Fluency Through Peer Mediation." *Teaching Exceptional Children,* 34(2), 90–3 (2001). PALS is a commercially produced program. More information regarding PALS can be found at http://kc.vanderbilt.edu/pals.

Read Aloud

Area Addressed: Reading Fluency

Appropriate Grade Level: K–8

Strategy Summary:

A read aloud or shared reading is a general practice aimed at improving students' language and literacy skills. It is one of the best ways for students to hear fluent reading and gain an appreciation for books. It involves an adult reading a book to students without extensive interactions with them. Recommendations for use of read aloud are found below:

1. Teachers (or guest readers) should read to their students in class every day.

2. Reading should not come from the text book, it should be done for one of the following reasons:

   • Building students' background knowledge

   • Providing them with interesting vocabulary words

   • Assuring that they hear fluent reading

3. During a Read Aloud students should be doing one of the following:

   • Listening to the teacher read

   • Following along with a duplicate text as the teacher reads

4. Examples of a Read Aloud:

   • Read a picture book

   • Read a newspaper article and discuss

Teacher Notes:

• *The Read Aloud Handbook* by Jim Trelease is a wonderful resource that provides research behind reading aloud to children and gives practical tips for teachers and parents using read aloud strategies in the classroom and home environment.

Lonigan, C.J., et al. "Effects of Two Shared-Reading Interventions on Emergent Literacy Skills of At-Risk Preschoolers." *Journal of Early Intervention,* 22(4), 306–322 (1999).

Closed-Caption TV

Area Addressed: Reading Fluency

Appropriate Grade Level: 2–12

Strategy Summary:

This strategy is a simple but effective way to build literacy skills. It involves the following steps:

1. Enable the closed-caption option on the television in the classroom.

2. Instruct students to read along silently with the text as it scrolls the bottom of the screen.

3. Ask students how following along with the closed-captioning will help them with their reading. Discuss how it can help both their reading rate and reading prosody.

Teacher Notes:

- Inform parents of this tip so students can practice reading at home during their favorite television shows.

- This strategy should be explained and modeled in the classroom before it is presented as an at-home fluency strategy.

- Research supports use of this strategy with English language learners.

Koskinen, P.S., R.M. Wilson, and C.A. Jensema. "Closed-Captioned Television: A New Tool for Reading Instruction." *Reading World,* 24(4), 1–7 (1985).

Repeated Reading

Area Addressed: Reading Fluency

Appropriate Grade Level: 2–12

Strategy Summary:

This strategy builds fluency by repeatedly exposing students to words until the words become part of the students' sight word vocabularies.

1. The student chooses a short selection (50–200 words) from a text written at their instructional level.

2. The student reads the passage several times either silently or orally.

3. The student reads the passage aloud to a peer or a teacher.

4. The peer or teacher monitors the student while he or she reads.

Repeated reading builds confidence with reading because the more the students read the passage, the smoother their reading becomes, and the more comfortable they become with reading. However, care should be taken not to overuse repeated reading. Students should not lose sight of the overall goals of reading: to learn new information and for enjoyment.

Teacher Notes:

- This strategy can be used in combination with Readers Theatre or Audio-Assisted Reading.

- Students can select a poem to practice using the repeated reading method and then read the poem for an audience.

Samuels, S.J. "The Method of Repeated Readings." *The Reading Teacher,* 32, 403–408 (1972).

Audiobooks

Area Addressed: Reading Fluency

Appropriate Grade Level: 2–12

Strategy Summary:

Audiobooks can be used to promote an interest in reading and to model reading prosody. Commercially produced audiobooks are often read by trained orators and professional actors. They are both engaging to listen to and offer a unique opportunity to improve sight word vocabulary; and therefore, increase reading fluency. Try integrating audiobooks in the follow ways:

1. **Classroom listening centers:** allow students to listen to audiobooks during sustained silent reading time or free time.

2. **Book clubs:** allow students who might not be reading at grade level to listen to a book on CD or MP3 player so they can participate in book club discussions with their peers.

3. **Teasers:** introduce students to new books by playing the first chapter aloud for the whole class. Listening to the introduction might encourage the students to pick up the book on their own and read it independently.

4. **Take-home packs:** let students bring home audiobooks for at-home reading and listening.

Teacher Notes:

- Encourage students to read along while tracking the text with a tracking tool or their finger.

- Audiobooks can be found at most public libraries, downloaded from Web sites like audible.com and recordedbooks.com, or purchased at bookstores for use at home with parents.

- Parents can sign off on reading time spent at home for incentives given at school.

- Research supports use of this strategy with English language learners.

Esteves, K.J. "Audio-Assisted Reading with Digital Audiobooks for Upper Elementary Students with Reading Disabilities." Ed.D. dissertation, Western Michigan University (Publication No. AAT 3293166) (2007).

Reading Comprehension

What to try when a student's attention wanders during reading:

Strategy	Multiple Intelligences Preferences and Key Learning Styles	Page Number
Jigsaw	Interpersonal Verbal/Linguistic	185
Peer-Tutoring	Interpersonal Verbal/Linguistic	186
Directed Reading–Thinking Activity	Analytic	184
Reciprocal Teaching	Interpersonal Verbal/Linguistic	187
SQ3R	Verbal/Linguistic	190
Literature Circles	Interpersonal Verbal/Linguistic	181

What to try when a student struggles to remember what was read:

Strategy	Multiple Intelligences Preferences and Key Learning Styles	Page Number
Book in a Box	Visual/Spatial Bodily/Kinesthetic	181
Jigsaw	Interpersonal Verbal/Linguistic	185
Subtext Strategy	Bodily/Kinesthetic Interpersonal	188
THIEVES	Intrapersonal Visual/Spatial	190
Directed Reading–Thinking Activity	Analytic	184
SQ3R	Verbal/Linguistic	190
Literature Circles	Interpersonal Verbal/Linguistic	181

What to try when a student cannot make inferences:

Strategy	Multiple Intelligences Preferences and Key Learning Styles	Page Number
How Do You Know?	Verbal/Linguistic Analytic	184
Picture Walks	Visual/Spatial Verbal/Linguistic	187
Linking Literacy and Technology	Intrapersonal Verbal/Linguistic	186
Peer-Tutoring	Intrapersonal Verbal/Linguistic	186
THIEVES	Intrapersonal Visual/Spatial	190
Directed Reading-Thinking Activity	Analytic	184
Subtext Strategy	Bodily/Kinesthetic Interpersonal	188
Multicultural Reading and Thinking	Interpersonal Intrapersonal	180
Question-Answer Relationships	Verbal/Linguistic Analytic	191

What to try when a student cannot summarize or retell:

Strategy	Multiple Intelligences Preferences and Key Learning Styles	Page Number
Reciprocal Teaching	Interpersonal Verbal/Linguistic	187
Jigsaw	Interpersonal Verbal/Linguistic	185
Peer-Tutoring	Interpersonal Verbal/Linguistic	186
Subtext Strategy	Bodily/Kinesthetic Interpersonal	188
THIEVES	Intrapersonal Visual/Spatial	190
Summarizing by Drawing	Visual/Spatial	189
Literature Circles	Interpersonal Verbal/Linguistic	181

What to try when a student does not understand the key elements of a story (setting, characters, problem, solution, theme) or story structure:

Strategy	Multiple Intelligences Preferences and Key Learning Styles	Page Number
Book in a Box	Visual/Spatial Bodily/Kinesthetic	181
Story Face	Visual/Spatial	188
Picture Walks	Visual/Spatial Verbal/Linguistic	187

What to try when a student cannot draw conclusions after reading an informational piece:

Strategy	Multiple Intelligences Preferences and Key Learning Styles	Page Number
Jigsaw	Interpersonal Verbal/Linguistic	185
Linking Literacy and Technology	Intrapersonal Verbal/Linguistic	186
Peer-Tutoring	Interpersonal Verbal/Linguistic	186
Directed Reading–Thinking Activity	Analytic	184
THIEVES	Intrapersonal Visual/Spatial	190
Multicultural Reading and Thinking	Interpersonal Intrapersonal	180

What to try when a student cannot determine what is important in informational text:

Strategy	Multiple Intelligences Preferences and Key Learning Styles	Page Number
Linking Literacy and Technology	Intrapersonal Verbal/Linguistic	186
THIEVES	Intrapersonal Visual/Spatial	190
SQ3R	Verbal/Linguistic	190
Reciprocal Teaching	Interpersonal Verbal/Linguistic	187
Multicultural Reading and Thinking	Interpersonal Intrapersonal	180
Question-Answer Relationships	Verbal/Linguistic Analytic	191

What to try when a student has limited vocabulary:

Strategy	Multiple Intelligences Preferences and Key Learning Styles	Page Number
Vocabulary Picture Cards	Verbal/Linguistic Visual/Spatial	193
Read Aloud	Verbal/Linguistic Auditory	173
Text Talk	Verbal/Linguistic Auditory	180
Vocabulary Problem-Solving	Verbal/Linguistic	182
Word Sorts	Bodily/Kinesthetic Visual/Spatial	183
Reciprocal Teaching	Interpersonal Verbal/Linguistic	187

What to try when a student has difficulty choosing appropriate books for his or her reading level:

Strategy	Multiple Intelligences Preferences and Key Learning Styles	Page Number
Selecting an Appropriate Book	Verbal/Linguistic	192
The Five Finger Test	Verbal/Linguistic Bodily/Kinesthetic	192

Text Talk

Area Addressed: Reading Comprehension

Appropriate Grade Levels: K–3

Program Summary:

Text Talk uses carefully selected words from read alouds to build and expand students' oral language and listening comprehension. It involves the following steps:

1. Select a story to read aloud.

2. Choose three words that are unfamiliar to the majority of students but are not words related to a specific subject area.

3. Read the story.

4. Go back and reread the sentence which contains the first new word in order to provide a context of the story. Have the students repeat the word aloud.

5. Explain the meaning of the word in student-friendly terms.

6. Extend the meaning by using the word in a sentence that would be meaningful to the class. This helps the students make a new connection between the new word and their background knowledge.

7. Have the students provide sentences and a personal context for the word.

8. Tell the students to say the word again.

Repeat the process to teach the other two words. Bring the activity to a close by reminding the students of the three words and asking questions about the words.

Teacher Notes:

• Keep a vocabulary word wall of words introduced through the Text Talk lessons.

Beck, I.L., and M.G. McKeown. "Text Talk: Capturing the Benefits of Read Aloud Experiences for Young Children." *The Reading Teacher,* 55, 10–20 (2001). Text Talk is a commercially produced program. For more information on Text Talk go to www.teacher.scholastic.com/products/texttalk.

Multicultural Reading and Thinking (McRAT)

Area Addressed: Reading Comprehension

Appropriate Grade Levels: 3–8

Program Summary:

McRAT focuses on four kinds of reasoning (analysis, comparison, inference/interpretation, and evaluation). These reasoning skills are used across the curriculum and also transfer into everyday life. The program involves teaching at least one lesson per week pertaining to a multicultural concept, such as cultural assimilation. The lessons are designed around the direct instruction framework and include explanations of the thinking strategies, teacher modeling, guidance, and feedback. The lessons can be incorporated into thematic units involving parents and the community. Progress is measured through students' writing.

Teacher Notes:

• Teachers can use visual mapping, cooperative learning, and story retelling in conjunction with the McRAT lessons.

Quellmalz, E.S., and J. Hoskyn. "Making a Difference in Arkansas: The Multicultural Reading and Thinking Project." *Educational Leadership,* 45(7), 52 (1988). Copyright by ASCD; www.ascd.org. McRAT requires 9 days of training. For more information on McRAT, contact the Reading Program at the Arkansas Department of Education, 501-682-4232. Adapted with permission.

Book in a Box

Area Addressed: Reading Comprehension

Appropriate Grade Levels: K–5

Strategy Summary:

This strategy involves a creative response to literature which incorporates visual representations of key elements of a story or information on a specific author.

1. Each student will need to get a box or make one from an empty shoe or cereal box.

2. This box will focus on a specific book or author.

3. The box should illustrate major points of the book such as characters, setting, conflicts, or focus on an author. It could also provide detailed information about the book and/or author including fun activities.

For example, for *Charlotte's Web,* the student might have a spider on one side, and the following sides could spell out *pig, terrific,* or *humble.* Another side may be a maze that leads Templeton to the fair. The remaining sides might display a significant quote from the book and information about the author.

Teacher Notes:

- The students can present the boxes in class and place them on display for classmates to see.

- Students can place items related to the book on the inside of the box.

- Various assignments related to the book may be placed in the box.

Kovarik, M. "Meaningful Responses to Literature." *Kappa Delta Pi Record,* 42(4), 178-182 (2006).

Literature Circles

Area Addressed: Reading Comprehension

Appropriate Grade Level: 2–12

Strategy Summary:

Literature circles are a guided approach to student-led discussions on both fiction and informational literature. The strategy involves three to five readers who gather to discuss what they have read. Students use "job sheets" to guide their discussion and practice the application of key reading comprehension strategies.

1. Select four to five different books and present them to the class.

2. Let students submit a 1, 2, and 3 choice. Place students in groups of three to five, depending on class size, based on interest in the books presented.

3. Students divide the book into five equal parts (usually by chapter).

4. Schedule one day for reading and completing the job sheets and one day for discussion. Continue this rotation until all five parts have been read and discussed.

5. The following jobs are assigned to members of the group on each reading day. Jobs rotate so each student has an opportunity to do each job. Teachers can create their own jobs based on comprehension strategies they are teaching. Sample jobs include:

- *Discussion Director:* responsible for developing questions regarding the text
- *Vocabulary Master:* responsible for defining new or interesting words
- *Literary Luminary:* responsible for highlighting and explaining key events or important information
- *Connector:* responsible for making connections between what was read and other text, current events, and/or their prior experiences
- *Illustrator/Mapper:* responsible for creating a visual representation of a key event in the story or drawing a picture of information presented

6. On reading days, the students are to read and prepare for the discussion based on their individual job. On discussion days, students are to take turns, focusing on their specific job, to carry out a discussion on the reading.

Teacher Notes:

- Students can also be placed in groups according to reading level.
- A leader may have to be appointed if the group is not discussing the text appropriately.
- Follow-up or extension activities can be developed after the entire book has been read.
- Teacher should monitor constantly and provide feedback on the discussions.
- The effectiveness of Literature Circles hinges on its replication of authentic book clubs (involve choice of books, personal response through discussion, responsibility to contribute to the discussion).

Daniels, H. "What's the Next Big Thing with Literature Circles?" *Voices from the Middle,* 13(4), 10–15 (2006). Research on Literature Circles and similar strategies has been widely conducted (e.g., Dupuy, 1997; Klinger, Vaughn, and Schumm, 1998; Pardo, 1992). The strategy as described here builds on the work of Harvey Daniels. To read more about implementing Literature Circles, see *Literature Circles: Voice and Choice in Book Clubs and Reading Groups* (Stenhouse Publishers, 2002).

Vocabulary Problem-Solving

Area Addressed: Reading Comprehension

Appropriate Grade Level: 1–8

Strategy Summary:

This strategy helps students independently learn new words.

1. Beep it: When students are reading out loud or silently and they come across a word that they do not know, they would say BEEP in place of the word.

2. Frame it: When students try to figure out the word they did not understand they isolate the word from the rest of the sentence by placing their fingers around the word.

3. Begin it: Students look at the beginning of the word.

4. Split it: Next they divide the word into syllables and pronounce each syllable in the word.

5. Find it: If students are unable to figure out the pronunciation of the word they would look it up in the dictionary.

Teacher Notes:

- This activity would be good to complete in a small group setting. The students would need a highlighter or some sort of way to keep track of the word(s).

Smith, C. "Successful Techniques of Vocabulary." *Eric Clearinghouse on Reading, English and Communication,* TBC30013, 1–6 (2003).

Word Sorts

Area Addressed: Reading Comprehension

Appropriate Grade Level: K–12

Strategy Summary:

This strategy helps students understand the relationships between words by having learners sort words by common features.

1. Choose ten to twenty content area words or words for a selected text. Have students write the words on index cards.

2. Arrange students in groups to identify and discuss similarities and differences between the words.

3. Have students conduct a closed sort or an open sort.

Closed Sorts

Students sort the terms according to given categories that have been pre-determined by the teacher. Examples include: same parts of speech; multiple meaning words; number of syllables; contains prefixes or suffixes.

Open Sorts

Provide students with the words to be sorted and have them create as many categories for these words as possible. For example, if the terms were "bees, wasps, hornets, yellow jackets, fire ants" the students could come up with the following categories: "Insects," "Things that buzz," "Things that sting."

Teacher Notes:

- Students can perform word sorts individually or in pairs.

- Word Sorts is a nonthreatening activity that can be adapted to almost any grade level and subject matter.

- For an added challenge during closed sorts, teachers can introduce new words related to the categories, or even include words that have no relation to any of the given categories.

Greenwood, S. "Content Matters: Building Vocabulary and Conceptual Understanding in the Subject Areas." *Middle School Journal,* 35(3), 27–34 (2004).

Directed Reading–Thinking Activity

Area Addressed: Reading Comprehension

Appropriate Grade Level: 1–6

Strategy Summary:

The Directed Reading-Thinking Activity (DR-TA) helps students make predictions while reading.

1. Select a story or passage for students to read. Ask students "What do you think this story will be about?" Write down students' comments on chart paper or a white board.

2. Instruct students to read a portion of the passage. Give them a clear stopping point. Tell students to read until they reach that stopping point.

3. Ask students these three questions:

   • What has happened so far in the story?

   • What do you think will happen next?

   • Why do you think that will happen?

4. Have students share their predictions/justifications in small groups. Encourage discussion of the text.

5. Repeat the DR-TA process one or two more times throughout the story.

With DR-TA, students learn how to form, state, support, discuss, and adjust personal predictions and opinions.

Teacher Notes:

• DR-TA can be used with fiction or nonfiction.

• Carefully choose stopping points so students have read enough of the story to make solid predictions.

• Remind students that making predictions aids in active reading, regardless if predictions are accurate.

• Encourage students to use the DR-TA strategy while they are reading independently.

Stauffer, R.G. *The Language Experience Approach to the Teaching of Reading.* New York: Harper and Row, 1980.

How Do You Know?

Area Addressed: Reading Comprehension

Appropriate Grade Level: 1–6

Strategy Summary:

This strategy involves explicit instruction of inferring, combining prior knowledge with the text clues to draw conclusions.

1. Tell the students they are going to learn a new way to understand stories by making inferences.

2. Model the strategy by reading aloud a picture book and stopping at a place in the story where an inference can and should be made.

3. Ask a question that prompts students to infer important information.

4. When students respond, confirm their answer and ask, "Does the author say that?"

5. When students reply, ask them, "How do you know?"

6. When students are familiar with the strategy, ask them, "Are there any inferences you can make in this paragraph? Explain how you figured out the connections."

Teacher Notes:

- Before introducing this questioning strategy, teachers should choose quality children's literature to identify types of inferential connections that could be made.

- Student discussions about their inferences provide opportunities for English language learners to hear peers' language and consider peers' different views and thinking.

- This strategy can also benefit older struggling readers with content material by stopping throughout the text and asking comprehension questions.

Richards, J.C., and N.A. Anderson. "How Do You Know? A Strategy to Help Emergent Readers Make Inferences." *The Reading Teacher,* 57, 3, 290 (2003).

Jigsaw

Area Addressed: Reading Comprehension

Appropriate Grade Level: 4–12

Strategy Summary:

Jigsaw, originally developed by Elliot Aronson (1978), incorporates cooperative grouping and a shared responsibility for reading. The teacher assigns students different selections of text. Students read their selection and share what they have read with a small group.

1. Organize all of the students in the class into cooperative groups.

2. Each group member is responsible for reading one selection.

3. After reading the selections, all students who read the same selection should gather to discuss the information. They are the experts on this selection.

4. Next, the students should go back to their original groups and share the information they have read and discussed in their expert groups.

Teacher Notes:

- The advantage to this strategy is that students gain exposure to different material in less time than independently reading each selection.

- Different points of view or different formats of text can be used.

- Students can become experts in their assigned selection by listening and sharing information within their expert group.

Poindexter, C.C. "Classroom Strategies That Convinced Content Area Teachers They Could Teach Reading, Too." *Journal of Reading,* 38(2), 134 (1994). Adapted with permission.

Linking Literacy and Technology

Area Addressed: Reading Comprehension

Appropriate Grade Level: 3–12

Strategy Summary:

The strategies for reading text on the Internet are very similar to those for traditional text, only with some modifications. It helps to become familiar with navigating the Internet before trying to use it as a research tool.

1. Activate prior knowledge: recall experiences and information relating to topic.

2. Monitor comprehension: skim and scan larger volume texts.

3. Determine important ideas: analyze which parts are important for understanding text.

4. Synthesize: sift out unimportant ideas to determine main idea of text.

5. Draw inferences: read between the lines, using text and background information to fill in gaps.

6. Ask questions: keep questions relating to purpose of text in forefront of mind to avoid being distracted.

7. Navigate: reader figures out features of Internet in order to search for information.

Teacher Notes:

- Students should be taught how to use keys to skim material.

- Students should be taught how to use tools for the thesaurus and language features.

Schmar-Dobler, E. "Reading on the Internet: The Link Between Literacy and Technology." *Journal of Adolescent and Adult Literacy*, 47, 80–85 (2003).

Peer-Tutoring

Area Addressed: Reading Comprehension

Appropriate Grade Level: 4–12

Strategy Summary:

There are different ways to use peers within a class to enhance the comprehension of reading text. For each option, the teacher pairs two students, one student with strong comprehension skills and one student who struggles with reading comprehension.

1. **Partner Reading:** Students take turns reading paragraphs of assigned text. They help each other out if one becomes stuck on a word or has a question about what they are reading.

2. **Paragraph Shrinking:** Students ask each other (a) who or what is the paragraph about, and (b) the most important thing about the "who or what" at the end of each paragraph.

3. **Prediction Relay:** One person makes a prediction about what will happen or be learned on the next page. The other person reads the next page and either confirms or disconfirms the prediction.

Teacher Notes:

- These steps can be used in small teacher-led groups as well as in pairs.

- Features of this strategy include direct instruction using guided and independent practice.

- Strategy should be implemented consistently to build partnering skills.

Mastropieri, M.A., T.E. Scruggs, and J.E. Graetz. "Reading Comprehension Instruction for Secondary Students: Challenges for Struggling Students and Teachers." *Learning Disability Quarterly*, 26(2), 103–116 (2003).

Picture Walks

Area Addressed: Reading Comprehension

Appropriate Grade Level: K–3

Strategy Summary:

This strategy helps students activate their prior knowledge and make predictions about what they will be reading.

1. When introducing any new picture book to the class (basal, read aloud, any text), turn through all of the pages before beginning to read.

2. Talk about pictures and what may be happening in the pictures.

3. Ask questions to the students like, "What do you think this is about?" and "What is happening in this picture?"

4. Ask students to make predictions about what they are going to be reading about.

Teacher Idea:

*   This can be used as an anticipatory set.

Ogle, D. "Reading and Learning About Our Wonderful World: Informational Rich Resources and Strategies to Engage Readers." *The New England Reading Association Journal*, 39(2), 7–10 (2003).

Reciprocal Teaching

Area Addressed: Reading Comprehension

Appropriate Grade Level: 4–12

Strategy Summary:

Reciprocal Teaching is a strategic approach built upon student interaction with text. There are four stages to this strategy: questioning, summarization, clarification, and prediction. Before students proceed through the steps, the teacher should divide the text into several short passages (one to two paragraphs for younger students, one to two pages for older students). The students read a passage from their text and then proceed through the four stages within a group or in pairs.

1. **Questioning.** Students learn to create why and how questions in order to understand a specific passage. The questions will lead to further questions and a discussion among the group.

2. **Summarizing.** Student finds the main idea of the text or passage, but does not include details or unimportant information.

3. **Clarifying.** Student recognizes and questions any words or phrases that are unclear, unfamiliar, or misinterpreted.

4. **Predicting.** Students are often encouraged to make a guess about what might occur next in the text. Predications are usually made using prior knowledge learned during previous steps. This allows the text to be easily remembered.

Teacher Notes:

*   Teacher should teach students the stages/strategies and lead the group at the beginning.

*   Once students have a better understanding they can be responsible for leading the group.

Palincsar, A.S., and A.L. Brown. "The Reciprocal Teaching of Comprehension-Fostering and Comprehension-Monitoring Activities." *Cognition and Instruction*, 1, 117–175 (1984). There are many variations of Reciprocal Teaching, but the original research on the strategy is credited to Annemarie Palincsar and Ann Brown.

Story Face

Area Addressed: Reading Comprehension

Appropriate Grade Level: K–12

Strategy Summary:

Story Face is a strategy in which students read a story and generate a map of its events, ideas, and key elements. The teacher models how to fill in the map, or create an original map, then provides the opportunity for guided practice. There are many ways to map a story. An example is provided below.

Example

The Story Face strategy is an adaptation of story mapping, which also uses a visual framework for understanding, identifying, and remembering elements in narrative text.

The Story Face is constructed by:

1. **Making the eyes:** two circles representing the setting and main characters

2. **Eyelashes:** specific descriptors and secondary characters

3. **Nose:** problem

4. **Mouth:** comprises a series of circles representing the main events that lead to the solution

The teacher will fill out the story map as a visual for the students as both teacher and students read and reread the text to identify important information for the Story Face.

Teacher Notes:

- Story mapping helps prepare students for retelling key elements of a story.

- Variations of story maps can be learned through discovery. It also is flexible in how it accommodates resolutions, events, construction, and varies with student ages and abilities.

- It is an easy-to-use model for narrative writing composition.

Staal, L.A. "The Story Face: An Adaptation of Story Mapping That Incorporates Visualization and Discovery Learning to Enhance Reading and Writing." *The Reading Teacher,* 54(1), 26–31 (2000). Adapted with permission.

Subtext Strategy

Area Addressed: Reading Comprehension

Appropriate Grade Level: K–12

Strategy Summary:

This strategy is for students to go beyond the literal text and to make stories personal by actually putting themselves in the story.

1. Start by picking a story. The teacher takes the students through the story by doing a "picture walk." The teacher uses the illustrations to make predictions about the story before reading it aloud to the students.

2. The teacher tells the students that they are going to act out the story, but not the way you would normally do it. This time they will add what the characters are thinking and feeling.

3. As the story is read the teacher will pause and give each character a chance to tell the class what they are thinking and feeling.

4. After the students understand what to do they are divided up into groups, each group gets a stack of sticky notes. They write down what they were thinking or feeling and put the sticky notes in appropriate spots in the book.

5. Next the students perform in front of the class offering their subtext (thinking and feelings) to other students.

Teacher Notes:

• Students are able to make connections to characters beyond the usual read.

• Students will reach a deeper understanding or empathy for characters.

Clyde, J. "Stepping Inside the Story World: The Subtext Strategy: A Tool for Connecting and Comprehending." *The Reading Teacher,* 57(2), 150–160 (2003). Adapted with permission.

Summarizing by Drawing

Area Addressed: Reading Comprehension

Appropriate Grade Level: K–12

Strategy Summary:

This strategy involves creating visual representations to summarize text.

1. Give students informational reading passages at their reading level (this could be a section from the science or social studies text book, or an article from another source).

2. Have students read the passage silently, in groups, or read the passage together as a class.

3. Give students paper and have them draw pictures that depict the main points of the reading passage. The picture should either be an overall scenario of what the article was teaching or a sequence of events.

4. Have students answer comprehension questions about the passage using only their pictures as a guide.

Teacher Notes:

• The pictures can become a study guide and linking the picture to the information works as a mnemonic device that students have created on their own.

• This strategy works well with science and social studies texts where a lot of information is given that students need to remember.

Elliot, J. "Summarizing with Drawing a Reading-Comprehension Strategy." *Science Scope,* 30, 23–27 (2007).

THIEVES

Area Addressed: Reading Comprehension

Appropriate Grade Level: 3–12

Strategy Summary:

This strategy activates prior knowledge and the steps serve as an advance organizer for the text.

1. **T**itle is the first look into a chapter. What do I think I will be reading about? What do I already know about this topic? How does it relate to preceding chapters?

2. **H**eadings are the gateway to general subject areas within the chapter. Does this heading tell me anything? Does it give me a clue to what I am going to be reading? Can I turn this heading into a question that is likely to be answered in the actual content?

3. **I**ntroduction provides the framework for the chapter. Does the first paragraph introduce what I will be reading? Do I have any prior knowledge on this subject?

4. **E**very first sentence in a paragraph. Preview by reading the first sentence of each paragraph. This may result in eliminating some portions of the text that do not seem to merit further examination.

5. **V**isuals and vocabulary. Perusing photographs, charts, graphs, maps, or tables provides an insight into reading. Is there narrative in the text to further explain the visuals? How do the captions help me better understand the meaning of the visual? Is there a list of key vocabulary terms and definitions? Are important words in bold type and defined? Do I know what these key words mean?

6. **E**nd-of-the-chapter questions. Important points and concepts in the reading can be alerted from questions. What information do I learn from the questions? Where are potential answers to the questions located within the text?

7. **S**ummary. Give attention to the conclusion of the chapter.

Teacher Notes:

- This strategy can be an individualized learning tool.

- It is readily applicable to a wide range of content material.

Manz, S.L. "A Strategy for Previewing Textbooks: Teaching Readers to Become THIEVES." *The Reading Teacher,* 55(5), 434–435 (2002). Adapted with permission.

SQ3R

Area Addressed: Reading Comprehension

Appropriate Grade Level: 3–12

Strategy Summary:

SQ3R stands for Survey, Question, Read, Recite, Review. It incorporates preview, predicting, and establishing a purpose for reading.

1. **Survey.** Tell students to survey the text by looking at key features such as: title, headings, subheadings, pictures, bold print, and key words.

2. **Question.** Ask students to think about what they now know about the text based on the survey. Given what they now know, have students write questions they have that might be answered by reading the entire passage.

3. **Read.** Have the students read the passage.

4. **Recite.** Ask students to recite or write the answers to the questions they wrote in step 2.

5. **Review.** Have students review what they learned by reading and apply it to another context. This review could involve creation of a poster that visually represents the information, participating in a group discussion about the topic, or summarizing the information in a written report.

Teacher Notes:

- Use SQ3R repeatedly until the process becomes internalized by the student.

Martin, M.A. "Student's Application of Self-Questioning Study Techniques: An Investigation of Their Efficiency." *Reading Psychology,* 6, 68–83 (1985).

Question-Answer Relationships

Area Addressed: Reading Comprehension

Appropriate Grade Level: 3–12

Strategy Summary:

This strategy helps students understand various questioning techniques and how to comprehend at various levels.

1. The teacher should begin by introducing the four question types:

   - *Right There.* These are questions with answers that can be found "right there" in the text.

   - *Think and Search.* These questions require the reader to derive the answer from more than one sentence, paragraph, or page.

   - *Author and You.* These questions require the reader to connect his or her prior knowledge with the text to come up with the answer. These questions are more inferential in nature.

   - *On Your Own.* These questions require the reader to apply background knowledge and may not even require reading the actual text in order to answer the question correctly.

2. Ask students to answer different types of questions after reading a passage. Have students identify the types of questions and discuss the different strategies they may use to answer the question.

3. Have students write their own questions relating to the passage. Make sure students use all of the question types.

Teacher Notes:

- Partners or teams can write questions for each other to answer.

- Students could be asked to highlight or underline where they found Right There and Think and Search answers.

Raphael, T.V. "Teaching Question-Answer Relationships, Revisited." *The Reading Teacher,* 39(6), 516–522 (1986). Adapted with permission.

Selecting an Appropriate Book

Area Addressed: Reading Comprehension

Appropriate Grade Level: K–4

Strategy Summary:

In order to select a book that is appropriate to the ages and ability/achievement levels of the students, the teacher can use the following six questions:

- Is the book relevant to the child?

- Is the story predictable?

- Is the language level appropriate?

- Are the illustrations attractive and supportive of the text (i.e., can the student use picture cues to help read the words)?

- Is the book an appropriate length for repeated reading?

- Is the amount of text on a page and the font size appropriate for the child?

Teacher Notes:

- Encourage the student to read the book repeatedly. This deepens comprehension and helps build fluency.

- Use the "Goldilocks" rule to explain to students the importance of finding a book that is appropriate for them. Tell them you are looking for a book that is not TOO HARD or TOO EASY. They need a book that is JUST RIGHT.

Bellon, M.L., and B.T. Ogletree. "Repeated Storybook Reading as an Instructional Method." *Intervention in School and Clinic*, 36, 75–81 (2000).

The Five Finger Test

Area Addressed: Reading Comprehension

Appropriate Grade Level: K–5

Strategy Summary:

Teach students this easy strategy for determining if a book is at a reading level appropriate for them.

- Choose a book you are interested in based on the title and cover.

- Find a page of text somewhere in the middle of the book. The page should have a lot of words and few or no pictures.

- Read the page aloud or in a whisper.

- Every time you come to a word you don't know, hold up one finger.

- If you have all fingers up before you get to the end of the page, the book is too hard. Try it again later in the year.

- If you have no fingers up, ask yourself if the book is too easy. It is okay to pick books that are easy, but it is better to challenge yourself a little.

- If you have two, three, or four fingers up, chances are the book is just right for you.

Teacher Notes:

- Encourage students to use this strategy when picking out books from the school or classroom library.

- Teach parents the five finger test so they can reinforce the importance of selecting appropriate books at home.

Wutz, J.A., and L. Wedwick. "Bookmatch: Scaffolding Book Selection for Independent Reading." *The Reading Teacher,* 59, 16–32 (2005).

Vocabulary Picture Cards

Area Addressed: Reading Comprehension

Appropriate Grade Level: K–8

Strategy Summary:

Vocabulary Picture Cards incorporate visual representations of words and multiple exposures to the words.

1. Present a new vocabulary word.

2. Work together to find an understandable definition (dictionary, Internet, etc.).

3. Provide examples of how the word is used.

4. Elicit student-generated responses in which the words are used in context.

5. Direct the students to write the vocabulary word and its definition on one side of the card. On the other side of the card, write a sentence using the word in context and draw a picture illustrating the sentence.

6. Students can pair up with other students to quiz each other.

Accomplish
To achieve
To gain with effort

She accomplished her goal despite many setbacks.

Teacher Notes:

- Once students have acquired new vocabulary words, teachers should promote automaticity of word recognition and definition retrieval.

- Vocabulary Picture Cards can be used in combination with Word Sorts.

Alber, S.R., and C.R Foil. "Fun and Effective Ways to Build Your Students' Vocabulary." *Intervention in School and Clinic,* 37(3), 131–39 (2002).

Written Expression

What to try when a student has difficulty coming up with topics on which to write:

Strategy	Multiple Intelligences Preferences and Key Learning Styles	Page Number
Thinking and Self-Questioning	Analytic	202
Brainstorm to Break the Idea Logjam	Verbal/Linguistic	199
Drama and Writing	Interpersonal Visual/Spatial	203
Classroom Publishing House	Interpersonal Visual/Spatial	198
Collins Writing Program	Verbal/Linguistic Analytic	196

What to try when a student has difficulty writing stories:

Strategy	Multiple Intelligences Preferences and Key Learning Styles	Page Number
TAG (Writer's Workshop)	Verbal/Linguistic	200
Thinking and Self-Questioning	Analytic	202
Thinking Maps	Visual/Spatial Logical/Mathematical	198
6 + 1 Trait Writing	Visual/Spatial Analytic	196

What to try when a student has difficulty writing an informational piece:

Strategy	Multiple Intelligences Preferences and Key Learning Styles	Page Number
FIST	Visual/Spatial Bodily/Kinesthetic	201
STOP and DARE	Verbal/Linguistic	200
Thinking and Self-Questioning	Analytic	202
The Process Approach	Verbal/Linguistic Analytic	204
WRITE UP	Analytic	202
Thinking Maps	Visual/Spatial Logical/Mathematical	198

Collins Writing Program	Verbal/Linguistic Analytic	196
6 + 1 Trait Writing	Visual/Spatial Analytic	196

What to try when a student cannot or does not edit papers:

Strategy	Multiple Intelligences Preferences and Key Learning Styles	Page Number
TAG (Writer's Workshop)	Verbal/Linguistic	200
Peer Editing	Interpersonal	205
Classroom Publishing House	Interpersonal Visual/Spatial	198
Collins Writing Program	Verbal/Linguistic Analytic	196
6 + 1 Trait Writing	Visual/Spatial Analytic	196

What to try when a student's writing is dull or dry:

Strategy	Multiple Intelligences Preferences and Key Learning Styles	Page Number
Brainstorm to Break the Idea Logjam	Verbal/Linguistic	199
TAG (Writer's Workshop)	Verbal/Linguistic	200
Peer Editing	Interpersonal	205
6 + 1 Trait Writing	Visual/Spatial Analytic	196

What to try when a student's writing lacks structure:

Strategy	Multiple Intelligences Preferences and Key Learning Styles	Page Number
Thinking and Self-Questioning	Analytic	202
WRITE UP	Analytic	202
Thinking Maps	Visual/Spatial Logical/Mathematical	198
Collins Writing Program	Verbal/Linguistic Analytic	196
6 + 1 Trait Writing	Visual/Spatial Analytic	196

Collins Writing Program

Area Addressed: Written Expression

Appropriate Grade Level: K–12

Strategy Summary:

The Collins Writing Program presents a model for writing across the curriculum and writing to learn. Key aspects of the program are frequent informal writing about thoughts and observations, writing across the curriculum regularly, planning and organizing ideas before writing, and keeping compositions in a cumulative writing folder. The Collins Writing Program uses five types of writing assignments, each of which are based on clear expectations and outcomes. The cumulative writing folder is used to keep track of the skills each student demonstrates for each type of writing. The five types of writing are:

Type One: Capture Ideas

Type one writing is designed to brainstorm and get ideas on paper. It is timed and requires a minimum number of items or lines to be generated.

Type Two: Respond Correctly

Type two writing demonstrates that the writer knows something about a topic. It is a correct answer to a specific question.

Type Three: Edit for Focus Correction Areas

Type three writing is substantive content that meets specific standards called Focus Correction Areas (FCA). Examples of FCAs include: use a clear topic sentence and a strong conclusion; vary sentence beginnings and lengths; and use end marks and commas correctly.

Type Four: Peer Edit

Type four writing is a type three paper that has been critiqued by a peer and revisited by the author.

Type Five: Publish

Type five writing is of publishable quality. It usually takes many drafts to get to this type of writing.

Teacher Notes:

- The Collins Writing Program has been used effectively with students who receive special education, gifted and talented students, and English language learners.

Collins, J.J. "Developing Writing and Thinking Skills Across the Curriculum." *Collins Education Associates* (1992); Hillocks, G. "Synthesis of Research on Teaching Writing" *Educational Leadership*, (1987). The Collins Writing Program is a commercially produced research-based program. For more information on the Collins Writing Program go to www.collinseducationassociates.com.

6 + 1 Trait Writing

Area Addressed: Written Expression

Appropriate Grade Level: K–12

Strategy Summary:

The 6 + 1 Trait Writing model uses a common language to refer to characteristics of writing and creates a common vision of what quality writing looks and sounds like. It is both an assessment method and a teaching strategy. The 6 + 1 Trait Writing definitions listed as follows are adapted from the Northwest Regional Educational Laboratory Web site (www.nwrel.org).

Ideas

The ideas are the heart of the message, the content of the piece, the main theme with all the details that enrich and develop that theme. The ideas are strong when the message is clear, not garbled. The writer chooses details that are interesting, important, and informative—often the kinds of details the reader would not normally anticipate or predict.

Organization

Organization is the internal structure of a piece of writing, the thread of central meaning, the pattern, so long as it fits the central idea. When the organization is strong, the piece begins meaningfully and creates in the reader a sense of anticipation that is, ultimately, systematically fulfilled. Events proceed logically; information is given to the reader in the right doses at the right times so that the reader never loses interest. Connections are strong, which is another way of saying that bridges from one idea to the next hold up. The piece closes with a sense of resolution, tying up loose ends, bringing things to closure, answering important questions while still leaving the reader something to think about.

Voice

The voice is the writer coming through the words, the sense that a real person is speaking to us and cares about the message. It is the heart and soul of the writing, the magic, the wit, the feeling, the life and breath. When the writer is engaged personally with the topic, he or she imparts a personal tone and flavor to the piece that is unmistakably his or hers alone.

Word Choice

Word choice is the use of rich, colorful, precise language that communicates not just in a functional way, but in a way that moves and enlightens the reader. In good descriptive writing, strong word choice clarifies and expands ideas. In persuasive writing, careful word choice moves the reader to a new vision of things. Strong word choice is characterized not so much by an exceptional vocabulary that impresses the reader, but more by the skill to use everyday words well.

Sentence Fluency

Sentence fluency is the rhythm and flow of the language, the sound of word patterns, the way in which the writing plays to the ear, not just to the eye. How does it sound when read aloud? Fluent writing has cadence, power, rhythm, and movement. It is free of awkward word patterns that slow the reader's progress. Sentences vary in length and style, and are so well crafted that the reader moves through the piece with ease.

Conventions

Conventions are the mechanical correctness of the piece—spelling, grammar and usage, paragraphing (indenting at the appropriate spots), use of capitals, and punctuation. Writing that is strong in conventions has been proofread and edited with care. Handwriting and neatness are not part of this trait.

Presentation

Presentation combines both visual and verbal elements. It is the way we "exhibit" our message on paper. All great writers are aware of the necessity of presentation, particularly technical writers who must include graphs, maps, and visual instructions along with their text.

Teacher Notes:

- Each trait can be linked to the steps in the writing process (prewriting, drafting, revising, editing, and publishing).

Culham, R. "6 + 1 Trait Writing." *Northwest Regional Educational Laboratory* (2005); Jarmer, D., et al. "Six-Trait Writing Model Improves Scores at Jennie Wilson Elementary." *Journal of School Improvement* (2000). 6 + 1 Traits is a research-based program produced by the Northwest Regional Educational Laboratory. For more information on 6 + 1 Traits go to www.nwrel.org. Adapted with permission.

Thinking Maps

Area Addressed: Written Expression

Appropriate Grade Level: 2–12

Strategy Summary:

David Hyerle identified eight different patterns of language used by teachers and students. He developed graphic organizers that visually represent these eight thinking processes. They are:

- Circle Map—used for defining in context

- Bubble Map—used for describing with adjectives

- Double Bubble Map—used for comparing and contrasting

- Flow Map—used for sequencing and ordering

- Multiflow Map—used for analyzing cause and effect

- Brace Map—used for identifying part-whole relationships

- Tree Map—used for classifying and grouping

- Bridge Map—used for seeing analogies

These visual tools can aid written expression, reading comprehension, and mathematical thinking skills by helping students organize their ideas on paper or on a computer.

Teacher Notes:

- Thinking Maps can be used in multiple content areas and grade levels. School-wide use can provide a consistent tool that helps students organize their thought processes and see relationships between otherwise abstract concepts.

Hyerle, D. "Thinking Maps: Seeing Is Understanding." *Educational Leadership*, 53(4), 85–89 (1996). Copyright by ASCD; www.ascd.org. Adapted with permission.

Classroom Publishing House

Area Addressed: Written Expression

Appropriate Grade Level: 1–12

Strategy Summary:

This writing strategy motivates students to learn to write and do their best work. They are able to get money for their published pieces and use multiple resources to create the product.

1. Students create writing pieces with their own ideas.

2. They turn the writing pieces into books, games, charts, and/or audio tapes.

3. These published pieces are sold at school assemblies and workshops.

Teacher Notes:

• Have multiple supplies for creating a published piece.

• Have a book sale scheduled far in advance and help students reach their goals prior to the event.

• If real money is not available, create classroom money that students can earn with their writing to cash in for privileges or classroom incentives.

Hoover, M.R., and E.M. Fabian. "Problem-Solving—Struggling Readers." *Reading Teacher,* 53, 474–476 (2000).

Brainstorm to Break the Idea Logjam

Area Addressed: Written Expression

Appropriate Grade Level: 3–12

Strategy Summary:

Brainstorming can be done as a collaborative process or individually. Four ideas are provided below to help break the idea logjam.

1. **Freewriting.** The student sets a time limit or length limit and spontaneously writes until the limit is reached. The writer does not judge the writing but simply writes as rapidly as possible, capturing any thoughts that come to mind on the topic. Later, the student reviews the freewriting to pick out any ideas, terms, or phrasing that might be incorporated into the writing assignment.

2. **Listing.** The student selects a topic based on an idea or key term related to the writing assignment. The writer then rapidly brainstorms a list of any items that might possibly relate to the topic. Finally, the writer reviews the list to select items that might be useful in the assigned composition or trigger additional writing ideas.

3. **Similes.** The student selects a series of key terms or concepts linked to the writing assignment. The student brainstorms, using the framework of a simile: "___ is like ___." The student plugs a key term into the first blank and then generates as many similes as possible.

4. **References.** The student jots down key ideas or terms from the writing assignment. He or she then browses through various reference works (dictionaries, encyclopedias, specialized reference works on specific subjects) looking randomly for entries that trigger useful ideas. (Writers might try a variation of this strategy by typing assignment-related search terms into an online search engine.)

Teacher Notes:

• This can help students generate motivating topics for writing assignments and uncover new ideas.

The Writing Center, University of North Carolina at Chapel Hill. "Brainstorming." Retrieved April 15, 2009, from www.unc.edu/depts/wcweb/handouts/brainstorming.html.

TAG (Writer's Workshop)

Area Addressed: Written Expression

Appropriate Grade Level: 3–5

Strategy Summary:

This strategy helps students learn how to give constructive feedback after listening to a classmate's story. The most effective way to implement would be in a writer's workshop format. This strategy assists the writer by giving suggestions on how and where to add more details to strengthen the story. The acronym reminds the listener/reader to:

1. **T**ell what he or she liked.

2. **A**sk questions.

3. **G**ive ideas (offer suggestions to improve the piece).

Examples of questions students can ask each other during a writer's workshop conference:

1. Where did you get that idea? Is your story fiction or nonfiction?

2. What is the main idea?

3. What was the problem? How was it solved?

4. Who is your favorite character(s)? Can you tell me more about your character(s)?

5. What is your setting?

6. What part do you think needs more work?

Teacher Notes:

• Feedback should be provided in the order of the letters in TAG.

• Teachers play an important role in modeling the procedure for students by telling what they liked, asking relevant questions, and giving ideas that might help students expand or clarify their writing.

• After the peer reader has asked the writer the TAG questions, he or she can also consider these three questions for additional feedback:

  1. Is there anything that is hard to understand?

  2. Where could more information be added?

  3. Tell what you liked best about the story.

Marchisan, M.L., and S.R. Alber. "The Write Way: Tips for Teaching the Writing Process to Resistant Writers." *Intervention in School and Clinic,* 36(3), 154–162 (2001).

STOP and DARE

Area Addressed: Written Expression

Appropriate Grade Level: 6–12

Strategy Summary:

This strategy helps students create a process for writing an opinion about a given idea or passage just read in class.

- **S**uspend judgment: Write down bits of information about a given idea. However, keep an open mind.

- **T**ake a side: Decide which side of the topic to be on.

- **O**rganize ideas: Select a number of ideas to support your view and at least one that does not support your view.

- **P**lan more as you write: Remember to make additions and changes as you write.

- **D**evelop your topic sentence.

- **A**dd supporting details.

- **R**eject arguments.

- **E**nd with a conclusion.

Teacher Notes:

- Help students learn the strategy's mnemonics STOP and DARE.

- Feedback should be provided in the order of the letters STOP and DARE.

De La Paz, S. "STOP and DARE: A Persuasive Writing Strategy." *Intervention in School and Clinic,* 36(4), 234–243 (2001). Adapted with permission.

FIST

Area Addressed: Written Expression

Appropriate Grade Level: 3–8

Strategy Summary:

FIST is a visual and kinesthetic tool that helps students remember the parts to a five-sentence paragraph using their fist.

1. Begin with an open hand, first fold down your little finger.
   Little finger. The topic sentence is short and to the point. It leads to other things in the paragraph.

2. Next fold down three middle fingers.
   Middle fingers. The middle three sentences are each different and stand alone. They are longer than the first with details and facts that expand the topic sentence. They fill in the middle.

3. Finally fold down your thumb, you should now have a fist.
   Thumb. It does not work like the other fingers, so use different words.
   This is the conclusion, so fold up everything and cover the three fingers and the sentences.

Teacher Notes:

- When you have completed you should have a fist and a piece of writing that packs a punch!

- This strategy gives students a way to organize their thoughts.

Arthur, B., and N. Zell. "WRITE UP: A Strategy for Teaching Creative Writing Skills to Emotionally Disturbed Students." *Preventing School Failure,* 134(4), 26–31 (1990).

Thinking and Self-Questioning

Area Addressed: Written Expression

Appropriate Grade Level: 3–12

Strategy Summary:

This strategy is designed for individual use while writing. Before students start to write have them ask themselves these questions.

1. Who am I writing for? This will help them determine their purpose.

2. Why am I writing this? This will help them activate background knowledge.

3. What do I know about my topic? This will help generate ideas.

4. How can I group my ideas? This will help with organization.

During drafting, writers take ideas gathered in planning and translate those ideas to conform to their audience and purpose. After the first draft is complete, the writer should ask themselves a couple more questions.

1. Does everything make sense?

2. Did I accomplish my plan?

When these questions have been answered, students can implement their editing plans to add, delete, substitute, and modify their ideas.

Teacher Notes:

- It may take some time and extended practice for students to internalize this strategy.

Englert, et al. "Making Strategies and Self-Talk Visible: Writing Instruction in Regular and Special Education Classrooms." *American Educational Research Journal,* 28(2), 337–372 (1991).

WRITE UP

Area Addressed: Written Expression

Appropriate Grade Level: 4–12

Strategy Summary:

This strategy helps students overcome traditional difficulties with creative writing by helping them organize their thoughts.

- **W**hat is the topic of your paper?

- **R**ead and record notes from literature and reference books pertaining to the subject of your paper.

- **I**s it interesting? Are there adjectives and other describing words? Do sentences vary in structure and length?

- **T**hesis statement and opening paragraph: Does the opening paragraph describe what you will be discussing in your paper?

- **E**xpand the middle three paragraphs, with one paragraph for each topic.

- **U**niversal Statement, Ending Paragraph, Original Title: This should include a summary of the proof in one or two sentences and a universal statement. The universal statement is a summary sentence that is applied to the theme and generally is true in other life situations, for instance, "People that are wise get along with everyone." The title should be formulated after the theme has been written to highlight the main idea of the theme.

- **P**roofread the rough draft and make adjustments/corrections, then rewrite and proofread again.

Teacher Notes:

- Create a poster that reminds students of the WRITE UP mnemonic.

Arthur, B., and N. Zell. "WRITE UP: A Strategy for Teaching Creative Writing Skills to Emotionally Disturbed Students." *Preventing School Failure*, 134(4), 26–31 (1990). Adapted with permission.

Drama and Writing

Area Addressed: Written Expression

Appropriate Grade Level: 1–3

Strategy Summary:

Students are given an experience with creative drama prior to writing. The students first do a warm-up activity and then are able to focus on individual ideas.

1. Warm up with a narrative pantomime (children pantomime the action of a character in a story). Paired improvisation, mime, sensory exploration, poetry dramatization, or creative movement could be used.

2. Individual ideas for stories take place through discussion, individual role play, or paired improvisations of main scenes.

3. Students are allowed up to 30 minutes to write the first draft of a narrative composition. Additional time for editing is provided.

Teacher Notes:

- This strategy may not be appropriate for all students, and should not be used exclusively as a tool for increasing writing fluency. No student should be forced to participate. This strategy is helpful in generating ideas. It allows kinesthetic learners and children with high energy levels to channel energy and organize creative ideas.

- Writing time should always directly follow the drama work since this stimulates the creativity of the children and brings out their ideas.

Moore, B.H., and H. Caldwell. "Drama and Drawing for Narrative Writing in Primary Grades." *Journal of Educational Research*, 87(2), 100–110 (1993).

The Process Approach

Area Addressed: Written Expression

Appropriate Grade Level: 4–12

Strategy Summary:

This procedure includes modeling three stages of writing compositions: 1) The planning stage, 2) the draft stage, and 3) the evaluation and revision stage. The procedure should be modeled often in groups before students practice independently.

1. **Selection.** Teacher introduces the planning stage by selecting the topic and type of composition the group will write, which might include: descriptive, compare/contrast, or opinion.

2. **Create a planning guide.** The teacher and students brainstorm ideas that should appear in the composition. Summarize these ideas and list them on the board or overhead projector. Model self-questions such as: "Can we think of an example of this? Does the reader need to know more? What order should I put these in?"

3. **Supporting information.** The teacher prompts the students for information that will support the ideas listed. The information will include facts, details, reasons, examples, instances. Highlight the main ideas that are formulated.

4. **The first pass.** Introduce the draft stage by emphasizing that this will be the "first pass" at developing students' ideas and perfection is not the main concern at this time.

5. **Prewriting plan.** Discuss items on the planning guide. Ask questions such as, "What are we going to say about this?" Write the comments from the class on the board. Remind students that all comments can be clarified or restated later.

6. **Teacher-directed group draft.** Using the prewriting plan already developed, students and the teacher write a draft composition on the board.

7. **Critical analysis.** Introduce the evaluation and revision stage. Have the students read the compositions as if for the first time.

8. **Editing.** Teacher models self-questioning that will help assess the final draft.

Teacher Notes:

- Modeling this strategy a number of times will help students begin to use this process on their own.

Vallecorsa, A.L., R. Rice Ledford, and G.G. Parnell. "Strategies for Teaching Composition Skills to Students with Learning Disabilities." *Teaching Exceptional Children,* 13, 52–55 (1991).

Peer Editing

Area Addressed: Written Expression

Appropriate Grade Level: 3–12

Strategy Summary:

This strategy involves use of partnering to revise and edit student writing.

1. Students compose a rough draft of their paper. An extra copy should be made.

2. The editor listens to the composer read the paper and follows along on another copy.

3. The editor tells the composer what the paper was about and points out areas that he or she likes best.

4. Students then switch roles and students follow steps two and three.

5. Students work independently, rereading each others' draft. They look for areas that are unclear to them.

6. Students then discuss with one another areas of concern. The author makes final decisions regarding changes.

7. Students work individually on their own papers making revisions, using a word processor if available.

Teacher Notes:

- The evaluation in step five should be one of clarification, not an evaluation of mechanical errors.

- Revisions should be made the same day as the conference, so it is fresh in students' minds.

MacArthur, C. "Peers + Word Processing + Strategies." *Teaching Exceptional Children*, 27, 24–28 (1994).

Math Computation

What to try when a student has trouble with basic math skills (counting, adding, subtracting, multiplying, and/or dividing):

Strategy	Multiple Intelligences Preferences and Key Learning Styles	Page Number
TouchMath	Bodily/Kinesthetic Visual/Spatial	208
Minimum Addend Strategy	Bodily/Kinesthetic Auditory	210

What to try when a student does not follow the math operations signs:

Strategy	Multiple Intelligences Preferences and Key Learning Styles	Page Number
Partner Transcription	Visual/Spatial Auditory	210
Fast Fluency with Scaffolding	Visual/Spatial Auditory	211

What to try when a student has difficulty memorizing math facts:

Strategy	Multiple Intelligences Preferences and Key Learning Styles	Page Number
TouchMath	Bodily/Kinesthetic Visual/Spatial	208
Fast Fluency with Scaffolding	Visual/Spatial Auditory	211
Minimum Addend Strategy	Bodily/Kinesthetic Auditory	210

What to try when a student does not know or follow the appropriate steps to complete a math problem:

Strategy	Multiple Intelligences Preferences and Key Learning Styles	Page Number
Long Division Face	Visual/Spatial Logical/Mathematical	208
LAP Fractions	Logical/Mathematical Analytic	209
Making Math Less Monotone	Musical/Rhythmical	211
Graphic Organizers	Visual/Spatial	212

What to try when a student has difficulty spatially organizing multi-digit math problems:

Strategy	Multiple Intelligences Preferences and Key Learning Styles	Page Number
Graphic Organizers	Visual/Spatial	212

TouchMath

Area Addressed: Math Computation

Appropriate Grade Level: K–12

Strategy Summary:

This strategy is especially helpful for tactile, kinesthetic, and visual learners. It helps students solve basic math facts.

1. Numbers are taught to students with dots representing their value. For example, five gets five dots on it. Numbers higher than five receive a circle around the dot indicating to count it twice.

2. Students touch the dots, either with a pencil or their finger, when they are adding, subtracting, multiplying, or dividing.

3. Students are taught to find the bigger number, start at that number, touch and count the dots on the other number to get their answer.

4. Once students have this skill down, if possible, begin to fade out the dots out to encourage mastery.

Use this only when it is appropriate. Students should not rely on this strategy for all of their mathematics.

Teacher Notes:

• TouchMath is most commonly used for adding and subtracting.

Duris, A. "Using TouchMath for Students with Physical Impairments to Teach and Enhance Beginning Math Skills." *Physical Disabilities and Related Services,* 21 (1–2), 17–21 (2002). TouchMath is a commercially produced program. More information on TouchMath can be found at www.touchmath.com.

Long Division Face

Subject Area: Math Computation

Appropriate Grade Level: 3–12

Strategy Summary:

This strategy helps students remember the steps necessary to complete a long division problem.

1. Draw visual cue (long division face with goatee) Two division signs for eyes, multiplication sign for nose, subtraction sign for mouth, arrow facing down for goatee

Divide

Multiply

Subtract

Bring Down

2. Follow features on the face (from top to bottom) to solve long division problems

$$7\overline{)364}$$ with 52 above, −35, 14, −14, 0

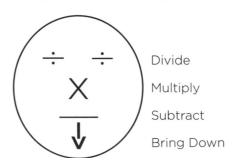

Divide: 7 goes into 36 5 times

Multiply: 5 x 7 to get 35

Subtract: 36 take away 35 to get 1

Bring Down: 4 to get 14

Repeat steps until there is nothing to bring down.

Teacher Notes:

• This strategy is especially helpful for visual learners.

• The idea of a "goatee" can help remind students to bring down numbers after subtracting.

Mercer, C.D., and A.R. Mercer. *Teaching Students with Learning Problems (Fifth Edition).* Upper Saddle River, NJ: Prentice-Hall, 1998.

LAP Fractions

Area Addressed: Math Computation (can also be found in Math Reasoning)

Appropriate Grade Level: 5–9

Strategy Summary:

Look at the sign and denominator

Make sure the sign is addition or subtraction. See if the denominators are the same or different. If they are the same, skip down to "Pick a fraction type," and pick Type 1. If they are different, go to the "Ask yourself the question" step.

Ask yourself the question

Will the smallest denominator divide into the largest denominator an even number of times? If your answer is yes, then go down to "Pick a fraction type" and pick Type 2. If your answer is no, then go to "Pick a fraction type" and pick Type 3.

Pick a fraction type

• Type 1: 1/4 + 3/4 Bottom numbers are the same. Its sign is addition or subtraction.

• Type 2: 1/8 + 1/2 Bottom numbers are different and the smallest bottom number will divide into the largest bottom number an even number of times. Its sign is addition or subtraction.

• Type 3: 2/3 + 3/4 Bottom numbers are different and the smallest number will not divide into the largest bottom number an even number. Its sign is addition or subtraction.

Identify denominator. Student points to denominator.

Divide denominator. Student is shown two denominators. Student divides the smallest denominator into the largest denominator.

Teacher Notes:

• Allow students to work in pairs for increased comprehension of LAP strategy.

• The LAP strategy shows that mnemonics can help a student remember the steps to solving a math problem.

• Students should find the LAP strategy easy to use and remember when solving addition and subtraction of fractions and be able to generalize to other subject areas using math computation skills.

Test, D.W., and M.F. Ellis. "The Effects of LAP Fractions on Addition and Subtraction of Fractions with Students with Mild Disabilities." *Education and Treatment of Children,* 28(1), 11–24 (2005). Adapted with permission.

Minimum Addend Strategy

Area Addressed: Math Computation

Appropriate Grade Level: K–2

Strategy Summary:

1. Student looks at a single digit addition problem such as 3 + 5.

2. Determine which number is larger (in this case it is 5).

3. Count on the number of units specified by smaller number (3).

4. Example: Start at 5 and count three more units 6 . . 7 . . 8 . . the answer is 8.

$$5 + \text{(image)} = 8$$

Teacher Notes:

- If a student comes up with an incorrect answer, review strategy with her or him again.

- This strategy may also be useful for students in higher grade levels who still struggle with simple addition.

Tournaki, N. "The Differential Effects of Teaching Addition Through Strategy Instruction Versus Drill and Practice to Students With and Without Learning Disabilities." *Journal of Learning Disabilities*, 36(5), 448–458 (2003).

Partner Transcription

Area Addressed: Math Computation

Appropriate Grade Level: 3–12

Summary:

1. One partner reads the symbolic expression or sentence from the textbook. See examples:

$2.3 \neq 2.7$

< 7

$\overline{)9+6}$

2. The other partner writes down the symbols that he or she hears.

3. Students compare the transcribed version to the oral version. Was the oral reading correct? Was the transcribed version correct?

4. Students then switch roles.

Teacher Notes:

- The teacher should model this strategy for the students so they do it correctly.

- Students need to be able to work collaboratively.

Rubenstein, R.N, and D.R. Thompson. "Learning Mathematical Symbolism: Challenges and Instructional Strategies." *Mathematics Teacher*, 94, 263–271 (2001).

Making Math Less Monotone

Area Addressed: Math Computation

Appropriate Grade Level: 3–12

Strategy Summary:

Songs in a math classroom can provide motivation and mnemonics along with enriching students' connections to mathematics.

1. Use Existing Popular Songs

    *   Take a song with some relation to mathematics and apply critical thinking skills to the mathematical concepts

    *   For example, to remember that one is the only natural number, neither prime nor composite, play Three Dog Night's, "One Is the Loneliest Number"

2. Use Raps

    *   Students make up their own raps or jingles to remember a mathematical concept

    *   Don't require rhythm or rhyme

    *   For example, "Dividin' fractions, easy as pie: flip the second and multiply!"

3. Use New Words with Old Tunes

    *   Replace original lyrics with mathematical lyrics

    *   For example, "We Will Rock You," changes to "We Will Graph You"

Teacher Notes:

*   Begin with having students write their own raps or jingles since they are typically easier.

*   Before students share their songs/raps, be sure that their information is factual.

*   This type of strategy facilitates self-expression, improves self-esteem, and develops linguistic skills.

Lesser, L.M. "Sum of Songs: Making Mathematics Less Monotone!" *Mathematics Teacher*, 93, 372–277 (2000). Adapted with permission.

Fact Fluency with Scaffolding

Area Addressed: Math Computation

Appropriate Grade Level: 3–12

Strategy Summary:

This strategy develops automaticity of math facts through practicing.

1. Create flash cards with basic math facts.

2. Present the student with one card at a time. The student must state the fact in 5 seconds or less. If the fact is stated correctly, the partner marks the back of the flashcard with a "+" sign. If the fact is missed or time runs out, the partner marks a "−" on the back. When a fact is missed, the correct answer should be stated by the partner and the student repeats it.

3. When a card accumulates 5 "+" marks, the fact is considered to be mastered and it may be set aside.

Teacher Notes:

- This activity is especially helpful for students who have attention issues.

- Looking at the facts, saying them aloud, and writing them down has shown increases in math fact fluency.

Fasko, S., and R. Leach. "A Math Fact Fluency Intervention with Scaffolding." Paper presented at the Annual Meeting of the Association for Behavior Analysis, Atlanta, GA (2006).

Graphic Organizers

Area Addressed: Math Computation

Appropriate Grade Level: 5–12

Strategy Summary:

Graphic organizers can be used to help students who have trouble organizing their work on multi-digit problems. Sometimes, something as simple as offering the student graph paper can help the student place numbers in the correct location. The example below is an advance organizer that would help a student solve a 3 digit by 1 digit division problem. Once the student has demonstrated the ability to solve the problem using the template, fade support by providing graph paper (be sure the boxes are large enough for the student to write the numbers).

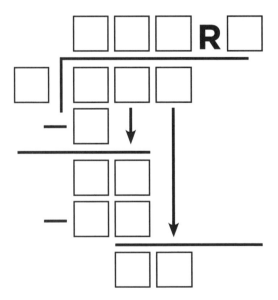

Teacher Notes:

- These templates can be created with the drawing tool on word processing software.

- Create a binder with templates for each type of problem the student may encounter in their current math unit. Place each template in a plastic page protector and have the student practice problems with a dry erase marker by writing right on the plastic page protector. After the teacher checks the student's work, the student can erase the page and try another problem.

Kooy, T. "The Effect of Graphic Advance Organizers on the Math and Science Comprehension with High School Special Education Students." B.C. Journal of Special Education, 16(2), 101–11 (1992).

Math Reasoning

What to try when a student has difficulty understanding the meaning of numbers (number sense):

Strategy	Multiple Intelligences Preferences and Key Learning Styles	Page Number
Snack Math	Interpersonal Tactile	219
Understanding Math Concepts	Logical/Mathematical	216

What to try when a student has trouble recognizing groups and patterns:

Strategy	Multiple Intelligences Preferences and Key Learning Styles	Page Number
Thinking Maps	Visual/Spatial Logical/Mathematical	198
Understanding Math Concepts	Logical/Mathematical	216

What to try when a student cannot identify critical information needed to solve equations and complex problems:

Strategy	Multiple Intelligences Preferences and Key Learning Styles	Page Number
Communication of Mathematical Thinking	Verbal/Linguistic Interpersonal	217
RIDGES	Visual/Spatial Logical/Mathematical	221
7 Steps to Solving Word Problems	Logical/Mathematical	222
Snack Math	Interpersonal Tactile	219
Understanding Math Concepts	Logical/Mathematical	216

What to try when a student has difficulty with mental math (i.e., solving math problems in his or her head):

Strategy	Multiple Intelligences Preferences and Key Learning Styles	Page Number
Thinking Maps	Visual/Spatial Logical/Mathematical	198
Snack Math	Interpersonal Tactile	219
RIDD Strategy	Visual/Spatial Logical/Mathematical	220

What to try when a student has difficulty comprehending story problems:

Strategy	Multiple Intelligences Preferences and Key Learning Styles	Page Number
7 Steps to Solving Word Problems	Logical/Mathematical	222
RIDGES	Visual/Spatial Logical/Mathematical	221
STAR Strategy	Visual/Spatial Logical/Mathematical	222
Mathematics Think-Aloud	Visual/Spatial Verbal/Linguistic	220
RIDD Strategy	Visual/Spatial Logical/Mathematical	220
The Math Poem	Verbal/Linguistic	218
Thinking Maps	Visual/Spatial Logical/Mathematical	198
Understanding Math Concepts	Logical/Mathematical	216

What to try when a student cannot decide on the mathematical operation for a story problem:

Strategy	Multiple Intelligences Preferences and Key Learning Styles	Page Number
Communication of Mathematical Thinking	Verbal/Linguistic Interpersonal	217
Making Math Less Monotone	Musical/Rhythmical	211
Understanding Math Concepts	Logical/Mathematical	216

What to try when a student has problems with fractions:

Strategy	Multiple Intelligences Preferences and Key Learning Styles	Page Number
Fraction Squares	Visual/Spatial Interpersonal	218
LAP Fractions	Logical/Mathematical Interpersonal	209

What to try when a student has trouble with estimation:

Strategy	Multiple Intelligences Preferences and Key Learning Styles	Page Number
Snack Math	Interpersonal Tactile	219
Communication of Mathematical Thinking	Verbal/Linguistic Interpersonal	217

What to try when a student doesn't understand the purpose of math outside of school:

Strategy	Multiple Intelligences Preferences and Key Learning Styles	Page Number
Basketball Math	Bodily/Kinesthetic Visual/Spatial	216
Snack Math	Interpersonal Tactile	219

Understanding Math Concepts

Area Addressed: Math Reasoning

Appropriate Grade Level: K–12

Strategy Summary:

This teaching strategy emphasizes understanding the concepts behind math facts (specifically, multiplication) versus memorizing the facts. In order for students to remember math facts, they need to understand the reasoning behind those facts. For example, students need to understand four interconnected concepts when multiplying. They are:

- Understanding quantity—students need to understand that numbers represent units which can be represented with objects or pictures

- Understanding multiplicative problem situation—students need to have experience figuring out the meaning of a word problem and see how various word problems are alike and different.

- Understanding equal groups—students need sufficient experience arranging objects into groups to understand the role of those groups in a multiplication problem.

- Understanding units relevant to multiplication—students need to have experience with counting and arranging objects into groups to understand the differences between the various units relevant to multiplication (for example, the number 30 is 3 sets of 10s).

Analyzing the concepts behind the math computation facts will help students remember math facts and understand the solutions, rather than just memorizing a series of numbers.

Teacher Notes:

- A valuable method for assessing students' conceptual understanding is to provide them with a math fact (for example, 9 – 7 =) and ask them to write a story problem and draw a picture that matches the fact.

Smith, S., and M. Smith. (2006). "Assessing Elementary Understanding of Multiplication Concepts." *School Science and Mathematics*, 106(3), 140–149.

Basketball Math

Area Addressed: Math Reasoning

Appropriate Grade Level: 5–12

Strategy Summary:

This is a math strategy designed to encourage students to think about connections between math, math words, and the relationship of math to the outside world.

1. Divide the class into groups of equal numbers of students. Go to the gym or outside. The teacher can also set up baskets in the classroom.

2. Each student takes ten of each shot: free throws, two pointers, three pointers.

3. Students track results on a student scoring chart, tracking shots made, shots missed, and percentage made of each shot.

4. Return to the classroom and compile total statistics by group.

5. Compare and analyze statistics individually and by group to determine which shot would be the best to take, and in what situation.

Teacher Notes:

- Before the activity, discuss historical or current basketball player statistics.

- Before the activity, go over how to figure percentages.

- Have charts ready, or make them up as a class beforehand. If this strategy has been introduced before, it could be completed in a station teaching format.

- This format of using real-life activities in math can be transferred to several other activities such as bowling, running scores, races, etc.

Watters, D.M. "Basketball Math." *Teaching Children Mathematics*, 6, 556–559 (2000). Adapted with permission.

Communication of Mathematical Thinking

Area Addressed: Math Reasoning

Appropriate Grade Level: 5–12

Strategy Summary:

This teaches students how to communicate mathematical reasoning by evaluating other student responses.

1. Present students with a mathematical word problem.

2. Give the students a set of responses to the problem.

3. Let the students act as evaluators of these responses. Have them write down whether they think the problem was answered correctly/completely and why.

4. If the response is incorrect, the students need to correct and revise it.

5. Discuss findings, and establish what determines useful mathematical reasoning and communication.

Teacher Notes:

- After the last step, write down what the class determines for quality math reasoning and communication and display in the classroom.

- This is an excellent way to model good and bad ways of problem solving and communication.

Cai, J., and P.A. Kenney. "Fostering Mathematical Thinking Through Multiple Solutions." *Mathematics Teaching in the Middle School*, 5(8), 534–539 (2000).

Fraction Squares

Area Addressed: Math Reasoning

Appropriate Grade Level: 4–12

Strategy Summary:

This is a game that can be used to help learners understand how to solve math problems incorporating fractions. Students use manipulatives (game tiles) to visualize and solve problems.

1	2	3	4
1	2	3	4
1	2	3	4
1	2	3	4
1	2	3	4
1	2	3	4
1	2	3	4
1	2	3	4
1	2	3	4
1	2	3	4

1. Create 40 game pieces. You may enlarge the box included here and cut out the numbers, or design game pieces of your own that incorporate the same number scheme (10 pieces with the numbers 1, 2, 3, and 4).

2. Students, in groups of 2–4, randomly pick 10 game pieces.

3. Each student should also be given a fraction kit containing:

    *   1 white tile that represents a whole

    *   multiple red tiles to represent halves

    *   multiple blue tiles to represent fourths

    *   multiple yellow tiles to represent eighths

4. Students use the game pieces they picked in step 2 to show different combinations of fractions that add up to one whole. These combinations of fractions are then represented using the pieces from the fraction kit. The white tile (representing one whole) is on the bottom, and students use the red, blue, and yellow tiles (depending on their choice of fractions) to create one whole on top.

In this example, students have added 1/2 and 1/2 to equal 1 whole.

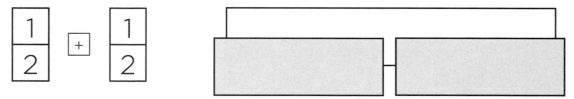

Teacher Notes:

*   Once students have mastered this game, try allowing students to trade pieces or using new game pieces such as 1, 3, 6, 12.

Ortiz, E. "A Game Involving Fraction Squares." *Teaching Children Mathematics*, 7(4), 218–222 (2000). Adapted with permission.

The Math Poem

Area Addressed: Math Reasoning

Appropriate Grade Level: 5–12

Strategy Summary:

By combining math terms and poetry writing, students can gain a new understanding and appreciation for both topics.

1. Provide a list of math terms from which students may select a minimum number for their individual poems.

2. Differentiate instruction by offering less advanced terms and poetry requirements to students at lower ability levels.

3. Students must write a poem about something other than math.

4. Give students several days to write a first draft.

5. Have students revise their poems, on later revisions allow students to be more flexible with the number and form of math terms used.

Teacher Notes:

- Give students the opportunity to help form the list of words to be used.

- If the project is successful, expand the project to allow students to use any word form of a particular math term.

Keller, R., and D. Davidson. "The Math Poem: Incorporating Mathematical Terms in Poetry." *Mathematics Teacher*, 94, 342–347 (2001). Adapted with permission.

Snack Math

Area Addressed: Math Reasoning

Appropriate Grade Level: K–2

Strategy Summary:

Combining snack time and mathematics time integrates the topics and maximizes the minutes in a busy day in a classroom.

1. Give a bag of snacks, such as animal crackers, to students in groups of 3 or 4. Each bag should contain enough crackers so that they cannot be distributed equally.

2. The teacher introduces the problem by asking "think about how many crackers might be in the bag," and guides students by asking how many crackers would need to be in the bag for everyone in a group to have two, three, four etc.

3. The point is not to model sharing strategies, but to see what the students come up with.

4. During the work time, the teacher meets with each group to discuss how they solved the snack problem.

Teacher Notes:

- Allow the students to discuss their solutions among their small groups, which demonstrates their ability to use the language of mathematics in meaningful ways.

- Everyday activities provide students with numerous opportunities to learn and practice math. The risk-free atmosphere during snack time offers an environment where children can become independent thinkers and discuss their ideas freely.

Roberts, S.K. "Snack Math: Young Children Explore Division." *Teaching Children Mathematics*, 9(5), 258–261 (2003).

RIDD Strategy

Area Addressed: Math Reasoning

Appropriate Grade Level: 6–12

Strategy Summary:

This strategy encourages students to make sure they read all parts of a word problem in math, but it can also extend to reading comprehension and other word problems presented cross-curriculum. The following steps make sure that all parts of the problem are addressed: the directions, the task, decision making, and actually performing the task being asked. The acronym device is great to help remind students the order of their work.

- **R**ead the passage from the first capital to the last end mark without stopping.

- **I**magine or make a mental picture of what you have read.

- **D**ecide what to do.

- **D**o the work.

Teacher Notes:

- Put the acronym at the front of the class to remind students on a continuous basis.

- If needed, put a checklist with RIDD at the top of the worksheet and have students check off each step as it is performed.

- This is a strategy that follows a sequential order and can train students to read carefully and plan ahead while they are doing their work.

Jackson, F.B. "Crossing Content: A Strategy for Students with Learning Disabilities." *Intervention in School and Clinic,* 37(5), 278–282 (2002). Adapted with permission.

Mathematics Think-Aloud

Area Addressed: Math Reasoning

Appropriate Grade Level: 4–8

Strategy Summary:

1. Student will read the problem aloud.

2. Student will circle the important words in the problem.

3. Student will draw a picture to explain what is happening in the problem.

4. Student will write out the mathematical problem.

5. Student will provide the answer.

Example: If Tom has two apples and Jerry has two apples, how many apples will they have if they add them together?

1. Student reads the problem aloud.

2. Student circles important words in the problem.

3. Student draws a picture to explain what is happening in the problem.

  +   =

4. Student will write out the mathematical problem.

2 + 2 =

5. Student will provide the answer.

2 + 2 = 4

Teacher Notes:

- Students eventually should be able to mentally go through this process in math and also be able to use this problem-solving technique in other subject areas.

- Teacher should go over what words to look for and circle while implementing this strategy.

Barrera, M., et al. "Math Strategy Instruction for Students with Disabilities Who Are Learning English." *ELLs with Disabilities Report,* 16, 2–5 (2006).

RIDGES

Area Addressed: Math Reasoning

Appropriate Grade Level: 3–12

Strategy Summary:

This strategy is a mnemonic device to help students solve math word problems step by step.

Read the problem for understanding

I know statement (list all the information given in the problem)

Draw a picture

Goal statement declared in writing beginning with, I want to know . . .

Equation development

Solve the equation

Example: Kaley and four of her friends were given a bag of candy. In the bag there were 15 pieces of candy. How many pieces of candy did Kaley and her four friends get when split equally?

R The problem asks how many pieces of candy can be split up

I I know that the candy has to be split among 5 people

D People = Candy =

G I want to know how many pieces of candy the 5 people will equally receive

E Equation: People = 5, Pieces of Candy = 15

S 15 divided by 5 equals 3 pieces of candy per person

Teacher Notes:

- This is a good strategy for visual learners to see what they are working with in math word problems.

- This strategy helps organizational skills and brings abstract concepts to life.

Snyder, K. "RIDGES: A Problem-Solving Math Strategy." *Academic Therapy,* 23(3), 261–263 (1988). Adapted with permission.

7 Steps to Solving Word Problems

Area Addressed: Math Reasoning

Appropriate Grade Level: 1–12

Strategy Summary:

This is a seven-step process that can be used when teaching students of different ages and abilities how to solve word problems. The seven steps are:

1. Go back to the word problem's question and ask yourself, "what is it asking for?"

2. Get rid of any extra data.

3. Look for and identify the key words.

4. Identify the essential numbers.

5. Think it through again; "what is it asking for?"

6. Solve the problem using paper and a pencil.

7. Always ask yourself: "Does my answer make sense?"

Teacher Notes:

- This strategy can be used in collaborative environments where flexible grouping and peer learning are being utilized.

- The technique is also well suited for use in multiage classrooms or situations where older students are tutoring younger students.

Hoffman, J. "Flexible Grouping Strategies in the Multiage Classroom." *Theory Into Practice,* 41(1), 47–52 (2002).

STAR Strategy (Search, Translate, Answer, Review)

Area Addressed: Math Reasoning

Appropriate Grade Level: 3–12

Strategy Summary:

1. **S**earch the word problem. Read the problem aloud carefully. Ask yourself the questions, "What do I know?" "What do I need to find?" Write down the facts.

2. **T**ranslate the word into an equation in picture form. Choose a variable. Check answer. Represent the problem with manipulatives (concrete application). Draw a picture of the representation (semi-concrete application). Write an algebraic equation.

3. **A**nswer the problem.

4. **R**eview the solution. Reread the problem. Ask the questions, "Does the answer make sense? Why?" Identify the operation(s).

Example: Jackie has 3 books on her desk. Her friend Joe gave her some more. She now has a total of 7 books on her desk. How many books did Joe give her?

3 + ? = 7

Teacher Notes:

• Many secondary school students with high-incidence disabilities are able to successfully progress to algebra and learn skills successfully through the STAR Strategy.

• Common to most interventions is the use of a mnemonic designed to help students recall steps or procedures.

• The STAR Strategy requires careful teaching and should be taught slowly, allowing students to grasp essential components.

Mancini, P., and K.L. Ruhl. "Effects of Graduated Instructional Sequence on the Algebraic Subtraction of Integers by Secondary Students with Learning Disabilities." *Education and Treatment of Children*, 23(4), 465–471 (2000). Adapted with permission.

A Final Word

We set out to write *RTI Success* as a way of sharing with teachers and administrators what we have learned about Response to Intervention in our work with schools. One thing we have realized in school efforts to make RTI work is that it can help to begin by imagining what the end result will be. Similar to putting a puzzle together, the process is much easier when you have the big picture in mind.

As you work to make RTI a reality at your school, imagine what success will look like: Administrators and teachers collaborate together and support one another to meet diverse student needs. A comprehensive assessment program and differentiation techniques ensure instruction is designed with students' learning strengths, skill deficits, and interest areas in mind. Research-based teaching and interventions limit the severity and duration of academic difficulties.

We hope that this book helps guide you toward your vision of RTI success. At times when the process might seem overwhelming, remember that every effort brings you one step closer to your goal. A thriving RTI initiative is one that is developed thoughtfully over time—it can come by adding one puzzle piece at a time. We have provided you with essential pieces to that puzzle. It's our hope that you will now take them and make them your own.

Elizabeth Whitten
Kelli J. Esteves
Alice Woodrow

References and Resources

Introduction

References

Batsche, G., et al. *Response to Intervention: Policy Considerations and Implementation.* Alexandria, VA: National Association of State Directors of Special Education, 2005.

Bender, W.N., and C. Shores. *Response to Intervention: A Practical Guide for Every Teacher.* Thousand Oaks, CA: Corwin Press, 2007.

Fuchs, D., and L.S. Fuchs. "Introduction to Response to Intervention: What, Why, and How Valid Is It?" *Reading Research Quarterly,* 41:1, 93–99 (2006).

Hughes, C., and D.D. Dexter "Response to Intervention: A Research Review." Retrieved April 15, 2009, from www.rtinetwork.org/Learn/Research/ar/ResearchReview.

Chapter 1

References

Batsche, G., et al. *Response to Intervention: Policy Considerations and Implementation.* Alexandria, VA: National Association of State Directors of Special Education, 2005.

Bender, W.N., and C. Shores. *Response to Intervention: A Practical Guide for Every Teacher.* Thousand Oaks, CA: Corwin Press, 2007.

Chapman, M.N. "Designing Literacy Learning Experiences in a Multiage Classroom." *Language Arts,* 72, 416–429 (1995).

Delquadri, J., et al. "Peer Assisted Learning Strategies." *Exceptional Children,* 52, 535–542 (1986).

Fuchs, D., and L.S. Fuchs. "Introduction to Response to Intervention: What, Why, and How Valid Is It?" *Reading Research Quarterly,* 41:1, 93–99 (2006).

Fuchs, D., et al. "Peer-Assisted Learning Strategies in Reading: Extensions for Kindergarten and First Grade and High School." *Remedial and Special Education,* 22, 15–21 (2001).

Fuchs, D., et al. "Responsiveness-to-Intervention: Definitions, Evidence, and Implications for the Learning Disabilities Construct." *Learning Disabilities: Research and Practice,* 18, 157–171 (2003).

Goodenow, C. "Classroom Belonging Among Early Adolescent Students: Relationships to Motivation and Achievement." *Journal of Early Adolescence,* 13, 21–43 (1993).

Greenwood, C.R., et al. "Class-Wide Peer Tutoring Learning Management System: Applications with Elementary Level English Language Learners." *Remedial and Special Education,* 22, 34–47 (2001).

Haager, D., J. Klinger, and S. Vaughn. *Evidence-Based Reading Practices for Response to Intervention.* Baltimore: Brookes Publishing Company, 2007.

Hall, S. *Implementing Response to Intervention: A Principal's Guide.* Thousand Oaks, CA: Corwin Press, 2007.

International Reading Association. "New Roles in Response to Intervention: Creating Success for Schools and Children." Retrieved September 20, 2007, from www.reading.org/downloads/resources/rti_role_definitions.pdf.

Kroeger, S.D., and B. Kouche. "Using Peer-Assisted Learning Strategies to Increase Response to Intervention in Inclusive Middle Math Settings." *Teaching Exceptional Children,* 38, 6–12 (2006).

Klern, A.M., and J.P. Connell. "Relationships Matter: Linking Teacher Support to Student Engagement and Achievement." *Journal of School Health,* 74, 262–273 (2004).

Ryan, A.M., and H. Patrick. "The Classroom Social Environment and Changes in Adolescents' Motivation and Engagement During Middle School." *American Educational Research Journal,* 38, 437–460 (2001).

Vaughn, S., and L.S. Fuchs. "Redefining Learning Disabilities as Inadequate Response to Instruction: The Promise and Potential Problems." *Learning Disabilities Research and Practice,* 18, 137–146 (2003).

Resources

Frequently Asked Questions About Response to Intervention: A Step-by-Step Guide for Educators by Roger Pierangelo and George A. Giuliani. Thousand Oaks, CA: Corwin Press, 2008. A valuable reference tool that answers some of the most common and basic questions educators have about RTI.

Response to Intervention: Principles and Strategies for Effective Practice by Rachel Brown-Chidsey and Mark W. Steege. New York: Guilford Press, 2005. A comprehensive guide that uses a 10-step model to implement RTI school-wide.

RTI Toolkit: A Practical Guide for Schools by Jim Wright. Port Chester, NY: National Professional Resources, 2007. An excellent resource for teachers and administrators, this book provides the framework to implement RTI.

Web Sites

Council for Exceptional Children's RTI Blog • cecblog.typepad.com/rti. This blog by the CEC features posts by leading experts in RTI. Anyone may comment on or ask questions regarding specific entries.

National Research Center on Learning Disabilities • www.nrcld.org. Go to the "SLD and RTI Tools" menu to gain access to more information and free downloads on how to implement RTI.

National Center on Response to Intervention • www.rti4success.org. This Web site provides extensive information on what RTI is, tools and interventions you can use (including a glossary of RTI terms), as well as discussion forums.

Regional Resource Center Program • www.rrfcnetwork.org. Access information about RTI under "Links Directory." Here you can find specific state activities and policies on education.

RTI Action Network • rtinetwork.org. Offering tips on how to get started, this site also details specific strategies for successful implementation of the RTI model. Go to "Professional Development" for Webinars, videos, and podcasts on RTI.

Teaching LD • www.teachingld.org. Part of the Council for Exceptional Children, this Web site is dedicated to helping educators who teach students with learning disabilities. Members of the CEC can gain access to information on RTI and how it specifically relates to those with LD.

U.S. Department of Education—IDEA • idea.ed.gov. Here you can find video clips and PowerPoint presentations about Early Intervening Services (EIS) and RTI.

Chapter 2

References

Bahr, M., E. Whitten, L. Dieker, C. Korcarek, and D. Manson. "A Comparison of School-Based Intervention Teams: Implications for Educational and Legal Reform." *Exceptional Children, 66,* 67–84 (1999).

Dettmer, P., L. Thurston, and N. Dyck. *Consultation, Collaboration and Teamwork for Students with Special Needs.* Boston, MA: Allyn & Bacon, 2005.

Dieker, L., and E. Whitten. "Intervention Assistance Teams: Tools for Success!" *Student Assistance Journal* (January–February, 1998).

Fullan, M. *The Six Secrets of Change.* San Francisco: Jossey-Bass, 2008.

Hart, L. "Mathematics and Science Teacher Education and School Reform: A Statewide Process in Georgia." *Action in Teacher Education, 19,* 16–27 (1997).

Individuals with Disabilities Education Improvement Act of 2004 (Public Law 108–446).

Knackendoffel, E.A. "Collaborative Teaming in the Secondary School." *Focus on Exceptional Children, 37*(5), 1–16 (2005).

Lyon, S., and G. Lyon. "Team Functioning and Staff Development: A Role Release Approach to Providing Integrated Educational Service for Severely Handicapped Students." *Journal of the Association for the Severely Handicapped 5,* 250–63 (1980).

McLaughlin, M.J. "Special Education Teacher Preparation: A Synthesis of Four Research Studies." *Exceptional Children, 55,* 215–21 (1988).

No Child Left Behind Act of 2001 (Public Law 107–110).

Siders, J.Z. "Training of Leadership Personnel in Early Intervention: A Transdisciplinary Approach." *Teacher Education and Special Education, 10*(4), 161–70 (1987).

Vonde, D.A.S., P. Maas, and T. McKay. "Teaming Up to Create Leaders." *Principal Leadership, 5*(8), 41–44 (2005).

Resources

Handbook of Response to Intervention: The Science and Practices of Assessment and Intervention edited by Shane R. Jimerson, Matthew K. Burns, and Amanda M. VanDerHeyden. New York: Springer, 2007. A compilation of research-based articles on many facets of RTI.

Implementing Response to Intervention: A Principal's Guide by Susan L. Hall. Thousand Oaks, CA: Corwin Press, 2007. This excellent resource highlights the specific role administrators play in ensuring academic success. The book largely focuses on improving all students' literacy skills.

Implementing Response-to-Intervention in Elementary and Secondary Schools: Procedures to Assure Scientific-Based Practices by Matthew K. Burns and Kimberly Gibbons. New York: Routledge, 2008. A wonderful how-to guide that's both practical and comprehensive. A companion CD-ROM includes examples of progress monitoring materials.

Response to Intervention: Enhancing the Learning of All Children edited by Sharon LaPointe and Diane Heinzelman. Petoskey, MI: Michigan Association of Administrators of Special Education, 2006. This guide can help administrators and teachers implement RTI at the district-wide level.

RTI: A Practitioner's Guide to Implementing Response to Intervention by Daryl F. Mellard and Evelyn Johnson. Thousand Oaks, CA: Corwin Press, 2007. A reference book for administrators, this book goes beyond the typical how-to guide and explores possible challenges when implementing RTI.

The RTI Guide: Developing and Implementing a Model in Your Schools by John E. McCook. Horsham, PA: LRP Publications, 2006. For administrators, this book features guidelines and hands-on tools for getting RTI up and running in schools.

Web Sites

See also Web Sites for Chapter 1.

Intervention Central • www.interventioncentral.org. This Web site offers many specific strategies for intervention that are arranged by subject.

National Center on Student Progress Monitoring • www.studentprogress.org. Progress monitoring can be implemented at any level and this site provides information for administrators, educators, and families on how to ensure success.

OSEP Technical Assistance Center on Positive Behavioral Interventions and Supports • www.pbis.org. Visit this comprehensive Web site for information on Positive Behavior Support (PBS), how its tiered structure correlates with RTI, and how the two can easily be implemented simultaneously.

Chapter 3

References

Heacox, D. *Differentiating Instruction in the Regular Classroom: How to Reach and Teach All Learners, Grades 3–12.* Minneapolis: Free Spirit Publishing, 2001.

Kolb, D.A. *LSI Learning Style Inventory.* Boston: McBer and Company, Training Resources Group, 1985.

Matte, N.L., and S.H. Green-Henderson. *Success, Your Style! Right- and Left-Brain Techniques for Learning.* Belmont, CA: Wadsworth Publishing Company, 1995.

O'Brien, L. *Learning Channel Preferences.* Rockville, MD: Specific Diagnostics, 1985.

Resources

Educating Everybody's Children: Diverse Teaching Strategies for Diverse Learners by Robert Cole. Alexandria, VA: Association for Supervision and Curriculum Development, 2008. This is a great hands-on resource for any educator, offering a wealth of strategies on how to differentiate instruction in reading, writing, mathematics, social studies, and science.

Frames of Mind: The Theory of Multiple Intelligences by Howard Gardner. New York: Basic Books, 1993. This groundbreaking, best-selling book details the theory of multiple intelligences as well as how to adapt education practices to different learning styles.

Multiple Intelligences Centers and Projects by Carolyn Chapman and Lynn Freeman. Thousand Oaks, CA: Corwin Press, 1996. This book is a great classroom resource, containing activities specifically tailored to each intelligence. Reproducibles are included.

Multiple Intelligences in the Classroom by Thomas Armstrong. Alexandria, VA: Association for Supervision and Curriculum Development, 2009. The updated edition of this classic resource features tips and strategies on how to apply the theory of multiple intelligences to the entire spectrum of education, from curriculum development to instruction and assessment.

Teaching and Learning Through Multiple Intelligences by Linda Campbell, Bruce Campbell, and Dee Dickinson. Boston: Allyn & Bacon, 2003. Expounding on the theory of multiple intelligences, this book offers ready-to-use strategies for educators on how to identify them in the classroom and modify their instruction.

Teaching Gifted Kids in the Regular Classroom: Strategies and Techniques Every Teacher Can Use to Meet the Academic Needs of the Gifted and Talented by Susan Winebrenner. Minneapolis: Free Spirit Publishing, 2001. A classic resource for teaching and meeting the needs of gifted children in mixed-ability classrooms. Includes a chapter on identifying gifted students as well as a chapter for parents.

Teaching Kids with Learning Difficulties in the Regular Classroom: Ways to Challenge and Motivate Struggling Students to Achieve Proficiency with Required Standards by Susan Winebrenner. Minneapolis: Free Spirit Publishing, 2005. Full of easy-to-use strategies, this book helps educators improve learning outcomes for all students—including those who struggle in the classroom. Reproducibles are included.

Web Sites

Abiator's Online Learning Styles Inventory • www.berghuis.co.nz/abiator/lsi/lsiframe.html. Visit this Web site for free tests on learning styles and multiple intelligences as well as suggested teaching strategies for each style.

LDPride.net • www.ldpride.net. This Web site provides information about learning styles and multiple intelligences. Features of the site include an interactive assessment and descriptions of learning styles and multiple intelligences.

Learning Styles Online • www.learning-styles-online.com. At this site, schools, colleges, and universities can administer a learning styles inventory to the entire classroom and chart the results.

Literacy Works • literacyworks.org/mi/home.html. The materials featured on this Web site include assessment tools for multiple intelligences as well as several links to online resources for more information.

Personal Thinking Styles • www.thelearningweb.net/personalthink.html. Visit this Web site for a different take on learning styles by assessing how students think versus how they learn.

Responsive Classroom • www.responsiveclassroom.org. This Web site by Northeast Foundation for Children highlights the important relationship between social-emotional learning and academic success. An array of professional development resources are available for a fee.

Chapter 4

References

Clay, M.M. *Running Records for Classroom Teachers*. Portsmouth, NH: Heinemann, 2000.

Ekwall, E., and J.L. Shanker. *Diagnosis and Remediation of the Disabled Reader*. Boston: Allyn & Bacon, 1988.

Fewster, S., and P.D. MacMillan. "School-Based Evidence for the Validity of Curriculum-Based Measurement of Reading and Writing." *Remedial and Special Education,* 23(3), 149–56, (2002).

Fountas, I.C., and G.S. Pinnell. *Leveled Books K–8: Matching Texts to Readers for Effective Teaching*. Portsmouth, NH: Heinemann, 2006.

Good, R., D.C. Simmons, and E.J. Kame'enui."The Importance and Decision-Making Utility of a Continuum of Fluency-Based Indicators of Foundational Reading Skills for Third-Grade High-Stakes Outcomes." *Scientific Studies of Reading,* 5(3), 257–288 (2001).

Gurganus, S.P. *Math Instruction for Students with Learning Problems*. Boston: Pearson, 2007.

Hosp, M.K., J.L. Hosp, and K.W. Howell. *The ABCs of CBM: A Practical Guide to Curriculum-Based Measurement*. New York: Guildford Press, 2007.

Jiban, C.L., and S.L. Deno. "Using Math and Reading Curriculum-Based Measurements to Predict State Mathematics Test Performance: Are Simple One-Minute Measures Technically Adequate?" *Assessment for Effective Intervention,* 32(2), 7889 (2007).

Johns, J. *Basic Reading Inventory*. Dubuque, IA: Kendall/Hunt Publishing Company, 2005.

Klauda, S.L., and J.T. Guthrie. "Relationships of Three Components of Reading Fluency to Reading Comprehension." *Journal of Educational Psychology,* 100(2), 310–321 (2008).

Scruggs, T.W., and M.A. Mastropieri. "On Babies and Bathwater: Addressing the Problems of Identification of Learning Disabilities." *Learning Disabilities Quarterly,* 25(2), 155–168 (2002).

Resources

Assessment as Learning: Using Classroom Assessment to Maximize Student Learning by Lorna Earl. Thousand Oaks, CA: Corwin Press, 2003. A timely resource that not only catalogs various assessment strategies but also provides real-life examples and case studies.

Checking for Understanding: Formative Assessment Techniques for Your Classroom by Douglas Fisher and Nancy Frey. Alexandria, VA: Association for Supervision and Curriculum Development, 2007. This is a great book for any educator and especially for those with students who are reluctant to speak up when they don't understand. Many different assessment techniques tailored to specific learning styles are explained.

Classroom Assessment and Grading That Work by Robert J. Marzano. Alexandria, VA: Association for Supervision and Curriculum Development, 2006. Based on extensive research, this book outlines an assessment program that will help students reach their learning goals and also details why traditional grading methods are often a poor reflection of student mastery.

Classroom Assessment for Student Learning: Doing It Right—Using It Well by Rick Stiggens, et al. Upper Saddle River, NJ: Prentice Hall, 2007. Individuals and learning teams alike can use this textbook. Activities and resources for implementing formative assessment are included on a CD-ROM and a DVD contains interactive training videos.

Fair Isn't Always Equal: Assessing and Grading in the Differentiated Classroom by Rick Wormeli. Portland, ME: Stenhouse Publishers, 2006. See the chapters on tiered assessments and grouping assignments. For middle and high school educators.

Handbook of Response to Intervention: The Science and Practice of Assessment and Intervention edited by Shane R. Jimerson, Matthew K. Burns, and Amanda VanDerHeyden. New York: Springer, 2007. A detailed and comprehensive volume of the RTI method. Includes chapters on psychometric measurement within RTI as well as transition planning.

How to Assess Authentic Learning by Kay Burke. Thousand Oaks, CA: Corwin Press, 2005. This book presents an array of assessment strategies that are an alternative to the traditional standardized test and are easy to implement.

Transformative Assessment by W. James Popham. Alexandria, VA: Association for Supervision and Curriculum Development, 2008. Step-by-step guidelines on how to integrate formative assessment show educators how to make instructional decisions that benefit individual learners.

Sources for Research Norms and Growth Rate Charts

AIMSWEB. Pearson Clinical Assessment Group (www.psychcorp.com/800-211-8378).

CBM Warehouse. Part of Intervention Central (www.interventioncentral.org), CBM Warehouse provides a number of teacher-created and commercially-produced CBMs across various subject areas. Multiple versions of K–12 CBMs in the areas of reading, writing, and math.

Deno, S.L., et al. "Using Curriculum-Based Measurement to Establish Growth Standards for Students with Learning Disabilities." *School Psychology Review, 30,* 507–527 (2001).

Fuchs, L.S., et al. "Formative Evaluation of Academic Progress: How Much Growth Can We Expect?" *School Psychology Review, 22,* 27–49 (1993).

Hasbrouck, J., and G.A. Tindal. "Oral Reading Fluency Norms: A Valuable Assessment Tool for Reading Teachers." *The Reading Teacher, 59,* 636–644 (2006).

Hosp, M.K., J.L. Hosp, and K.W. Howell. *The ABCs of CBM. A Practical Guide to Curriculum-Based Measurement.* New York: Guildford Press, 2007.

Academic Assessments

Accelerated Math. Grades 1–8. A software program that allows educators to create math assessments tailored to each student's current level of intervention. This system allows for individual progress monitoring. Administration time: varies depending on subject area. Renaissance Learning; www.renlearn.com; 800-338-4204.

Developmental Reading Assessment (Second Edition) (DRA-2). Grades K–8. A set of individually administered, criterion-referenced reading assessments modeled after an informal reading inventory. Administration time: 15–45 minutes. Pearson; www.pearsonassess.com; 800-211-8378.

Dynamic Indicators of Basic Early Literacy Skills (DIBELS). Grades PreK–3. A series of individually administered tests that are used to assess a student's fluency in five literary components: Phonological Awareness, Alphabetic Principle, Vocabulary, Comprehension, and Fluency with Connected Text. Since the tests are staggered, they effectively monitor students' progress and can be used to evaluate the need for intervention. Administration time: approximately 1–3 minutes per test. Dynamic Measurement Group; dibels.uoregon.edu/measures/index.php; 888-497-4290.

Edcheckup Progress Monitoring System. Grades K–8. A series of tests based on the CBM model that measure student growth in the basic skills of literacy and mathematics. This program features electronic scoring that allows instant access to progress reports. Administration time: varies depending on subject area. Edcheckup; www.edcheckup.com; 952-229-1440.

Gates-MacGinitie Reading Tests (GMRT). Ages 5–90+. A group administered survey designed to test students' achievement in reading. Can be used as a diagnostic or progress-monitoring tool and is developmentally appropriate for all learners. Administration time: 55–75 minutes. Riverside Publishing; www.riversidepublishing.com; 800-323-9540.

KeyMath-3: A Diagnostic Inventory of Essential Mathematics (KM-III). Grades K–12. An individually administered test designed to diagnose a student's level of math achievement. Administration time: 30–90 minutes. Pearson; www.pearsonassess.com; 800-211-8378.

Process Assessment of the Learner: Diagnostics for Math (PAL-II Math). Grades K–6. An individually administered test that measures the development of cognitive processes that are necessary for building math skills. Has applications at three tiers, ranging from prevention to diagnosis. Administration time: varies when assessed at Tier 1, Tier 2, or Tier 3. Pearson; www.pearsonassess.com; 800-211-8378.

Process Assessment of the Learner: Diagnostics for Reading and Writing (PAL-II Reading and Writing). Grades K–6. This individually administered assessment system can be used to diagnose dysgraphia, dyslexia, and oral and written language disability. Administration time: varies when used at Tier 1, Tier 2, or Tier 3. Pearson; www.pearsonassess.com; 800-211-8378.

Reading A–Z. Grades PreK–3. This Web site offers a series of individually administered assessment tools that can be used to evaluate student achievement and literacy skills. No special training is needed by the examiner and the tests may be accessed directly from the Web site. Administration time: varies depending on subject area. Reading A–Z; www.readinga-z.com; 866-889-3729.

Slosson-Diagnostic Math Screener (S-DMS). Grades 1–8. Individually administered test that assesses students' conceptual development, problem-solving, and computation skills in math. Available in five grade ranges. Administration time: approximately 45 minutes. Slosson Educational Publishers; www.slosson.com; 888-756-7766.

Star Math and Star Reading. Grades 1–12. A Web-based assessment that evaluates students' math and reading skills. Ideal for RTI screening and progress-monitoring tools are available. Administration time for each test: 15 minutes. Renaissance Learning; www.renlearn.com; 800-338-4204.

Wechsler Fundamentals: Academic Skills. Grades K–12. These individually administered tests assess reading abilities, spelling abilities, and math calculation skills. These tests can be useful in determining whether intervention is needed. Administration time: 45 minutes. Pearson; www.pearsonassess.com; 800-211-8378.

Woodcock-Johnson III NU Complete (WJ III NU). Ages 2–90+. The Cognitive Standard tests and Achievement Standard tests are individually administered and measure general intellectual abilities and cognitive functions. When used in conjunction, these tests can be used as a diagnostic means to identify specific skill strengths and deficiencies. Administration time: 60–120 minutes. Riverside Publishing; www.riversidepublishing.com; 800-323-9540.

Web Sites

See also Web Sites for Chapter 2.

Dibels Data System • dibels.uoregon.edu. Visit this Web site for free testing materials and scoring guides.

Fountas and Pinnell Leveled Books • www.fountasandpinnellleveledbooks.com. For a small fee, educators can access over 32,000 leveled books and guided reading instruction.

Reading A-Z • www.readinga-z.com. Visit this Web site for a variety of reading resources such as leveled books, reading assessments, and lesson plans.

Research Institute on Progress Monitoring • www.progressmonitoring.org. Funded by the Office of Special Education Programs, the Institute is currently researching the efficacy of individualized instruction. Go to "RIPM Products" for literature based on the most current findings.

Chapter 5

References

Block, M.E., B. Oberweiser, and M. Bain. "Using Classwide Peer Tutoring to Facilitate Inclusion of Students with Disabilities in Regular Physical Education." *Physical Educator,* 52, 47–56 (1995).

Fantuzzo, J.W., R.E. Riggio, S. Connelly, and L.A. Dimeff. "Effects of Reciprocal Peer Tutoring on Academic Achievement and Psychological Adjustment: A Component Analysis." *Journal of Educational Psychology,* 81, 173–177 (1989).

Fuchs, D., et al. "Peer-Assisted Learning Strategies in Reading." *Remedial and Special Education,* 22, 15–21 (2001).

Hansen, B. "Is the Bluebird Really a Phoenix?" *Reading Today,* 25(6), 19 (2008).

Johnson, D.W., and R.T. Johnson. *Learning Together and Alone. Cooperative, Competitive, and Individualist Learning.* Boston: Allyn & Bacon, 1999.

Johnson, D.W., and R.T. Johnson. "Mainstreaming and Cooperative Learning Strategies." *Exceptional Children,* 52, 552–61 (1986).

Kagan, S. *Cooperative Learning.* San Clemente, CA: Kagan Publishing, 1994.

Lou, Y., P.C. Abrami, J.C. Spence, C. Paulsen, B. Chambers, and S. d'Apollonio. "Within-Class Grouping: A Meta-Analysis." *Review of Educational Research,* 66, 423–458 (1996).

Palincsar, A.S., and A.L. Brown. "Reciprocal Teaching of Comprehension-Fostering and Comprehension-Monitoring Activities." *Cognition and Instruction,* 2, 117–175 (1984).

Resources

Designing Groupwork: Strategies for the Heterogeneous Classroom by Elizabeth Cohen. New York: Teachers College Press, 1994. For clear, easy-to-follow theory and examples of groupwork strategies in the classroom, you'll want to use this book.

Differentiation: From Planning to Practice (Grades 6–12) by Rick Wormeli. Portland, ME: Stenhouse Publishers, 2007. Written by a former classroom teacher, this book contains both the research and the examples to make differentiation doable. Includes over 24 strategies with special attention on how to help struggling learners.

Differentiating Instruction in the Regular Classroom: How to Reach and Teach All Learners, Grades 3–12 by Diane Heacox. Minneapolis: Free Spirit Publishing, 2001. Pick up this easy-to-use guide on differentiation for tiered assignments. The chapter on flexible group instruction is particularly helpful.

Differentiating Math Instruction: Strategies That Work for K–8 Classrooms by William Neil Bender. Thousand Oaks, CA: Corwin Press, 2009. Educators can use this resource to help their diverse classroom succeed in math.

Differentiating Textbooks: Strategies to Improve Student Comprehension and Motivation by Char Forsten, Jim Grant, and Betty Hollas. Peterborough, NH: Crystal Springs Books, 2003. This is a great resource for educators looking to differentiate instruction in content areas. Several classroom-ready grouping strategies are explained.

Flexible Grouping in Reading: Practical Ways to Help All Students Become Better Readers by Michael Opitz. New York: Scholastic, 1999. Includes many options for flexible grouping, such as arranging students by interest, random selection, and genre.

Great Grouping Strategies: Dozens of Ways to Flexibly Group Your Students for Maximum Learning Across the Curriculum by Ronit M. Wrubel. New York: Scholastic, 2002. This is a great resource for educators on how to plan and organize groups, and what to do when a particular grouping strategy isn't working.

How to Differentiate Instruction in Mixed-Ability Classrooms by Carol Ann Tomlinson. Alexandria, VA: Association for Supervision and Curriculum Development, 2004. The how-to chapters provide more information on grouping students according to levels of readiness, interest, and learning styles.

Integrating Differentiated Instruction and Understanding by Design: Connecting Content and Kids by Carol Ann Tomlinson and Jay McTighe. Alexandria, VA: Association for Supervision and Curriculum Development, 2006. Explains how to meet the varied learning needs of a diverse classroom by using preassessment techniques to group students.

Learning Together: A Manual for Multiage Grouping by Nancy Bacharach, Robin Christine Hasslen, and Jill Anderson. Thousand Oaks, CA: Corwin Press, 1995. This book presents the theory and strategies of a multiage classroom, with suggestions on curriculum and assessment.

Making Differentiation a Habit: How to Ensure Success in Academically Diverse Classrooms by Diane Heacox. Minneapolis: Free Spirit Publishing, 2009. Be sure to review the chapter on tiered assignments and flexible grouping for eight tips on how to group students effectively.

RTI: The Classroom Connection for Literacy by Karen A. Kemp and Mary Ann Eaton. Port Chester, NY: National Professional Resources, 2007. This book suggests ways to modify day-to-day instruction to include intervention and monitor student progress.

Strategies for Teaching Differently: On the Block or Not by Donna E. Walker. Thousand Oaks, CA: Corwin Press, 1998. This resource helps teachers leave lectures behind and connect with learners through active student engagement.

Chapter 6

References

Adams, G.L., and S. Engelmann. *Research on Direct Instruction: 25 Years Beyond DISTAR.* Seattle: Educational Achievement Systems, 1996.

Bereiter, C., and S. Engelmann. *Teaching Disadvantaged Children in the Preschool.* Upper Saddle River, NJ: Prentice Hall, 1966.

Carnine, D. "Effects of Two Teacher Presentation Rates on Off-Task Behavior, Answering Correctly, and Participation." *Journal of Applied Behavior Analysis,* 9, 198–206 (1976).

Cohen, P.A., J.A. Kulik, and C.C. Kulik. "Educational Outcomes of Tutoring: A Meta-Analysis of Findings." *American Educational Research Journal,* 19(2), 237–248 (1982).

Engelmann, S. "Student-Program Alignment and Teaching to Mastery." *Journal of Direct Instruction,* 7(1), 45–66 (2007).

Gersten, R., and T. Keating. "Long-Term Benefits from Direct Instruction." *Educational Leadership,* 44(6), 28–29 (1987).

Gersten, R., T. Keating, and W. Becker. "The Continued Impact of the Direct Instruction Model: Longitudinal Studies of Follow Through Students." *Education and Treatment of Children,* 11(4), 318–327 (1988).

Graham, S., and K.R. Harris. "Improving the Writing Performance of Young Struggling Writers: Theoretical and Programmatic Research from the Center on Accelerated Student Learning." *The Journal of Special Education,* 39, 18–33 (2005).

Heward, W.L. "Ten Faulty Notions About Teaching and Learning That Hinder the Effectiveness of Special Education." *Journal of Special Education,* 36(4), 186–205 (2003).

Hmelo-Silver, C.E. "Problem-Based Learning: What and How Do Students Learn?" *Educational Psychology Review,* 16, 235–266 (2004).

Kroesbergen, E.H., and J.E.H. Van Luit. "Mathematics Interventions for Children with Special Education Needs: A Metaanalysis." *Remedial and Special Education,* 24, 97–114 (2003).

Lienemann, T.O., and R. Reid. "Self-Regulated Strategy Development for Students with Learning Disabilities." *Teacher Education and Special Education,* 29, 3–11 (2006).

Marzano, R.J., D.J. Pickering, and J.E. Pollock. *Classroom Instruction That Works: Research-Based Strategies for Increasing Student Achievement.* Alexandria, VA: Association for Supervision and Curriculum Development, 2001.

Merrill, M.D. "A Task-Centered Instructional Strategy." *Journal of Research on Technology in Education,* 40(1), 33–50 (2007).

Pashler, H., et al. *Organizing Instruction and Study to Improve Student Learning* (NCER 2007–2004). Washington, DC: National Center for Education Research, Institute of Education Sciences, U.S. Department of Education, 2007. Retrieved from http://ncer.ed.gov.

Pearson, P.D., and M.C. Gallagher. "The Introduction of Reading Comprehension." *Contemporary Educational Psychology,* 8(3), 317–344 (1983).

Sousa, D.A. *How the Brain Learns to Read.* Thousand Oaks, CA: Corwin Press, 2005.

Swanson, H.L. "Searching for the Best Model for Instructing Students with Learning Disabilities." *Focus on Exceptional Children,* 34, 1–15 (2001).

Resources

The Art and Science of Teaching: A Comprehensive Framework for Effective Instruction by Robert J. Marzano. Alexandria, VA: Association for Supervision and Curriculum Development, 2007. This guide not only explains how to use certain teaching strategies but also when to use them. The included charts and rubrics are helpful.

Classroom Management for Elementary Teachers by Carolyn M. Evertson and Edmund T. Emmer. Boston: Allyn & Bacon, 2008. Based on over thirty years of research, this book of practical suggestions will be appreciated by any educator. Also includes a "Managing Special Groups" chapter with information on Autism Spectrum Disorders.

Classroom Management for Secondary Teachers by Edmund T. Emmer, Carolyn M. Evertson, and Murray E. Worsham. Boston: Allyn & Bacon, 2002. This book features examples, checklists, and activities for the educator teaching at the secondary level. This updated edition also encourages the use of technology to manage the classroom.

Creating Strategic Readers: Techniques for Developing Competency in Phonemic Awareness, Phonics, Fluency, Vocabulary, and Comprehension by Valerie Ellery. Newark, DE: International Reading Association, 2005. This comprehensive resource can be used to align reading instruction with current literacy education standards.

Improving Reading: Strategies and Resource by Jerry L. Johns and Susan Davis Lenski. Dubuque, IA: Kendall Hunt, 2005. This book and CD-ROM provide teachers with countless methods for helping students read better.

Looking in Classrooms by Thomas L. Good and Jere E. Brophy. Boston: Allyn & Bacon, 2007. A classic and comprehensive resource to be used by both educators and administrators alike. New chapters in this updated edition focus on ways to monitor student progress and active teaching.

Strategies That Work: Teaching Comprehension to Enhance Understanding by Stephanie Harvey and Anne Goudvis. Portland, ME: Stenhouse Publishers, 2000. This resource allows educators to teach thinking strategies that can help students thrive as independent readers.

Summarization in Any Subject: 50 Techniques to Improve Student Learning by Rick Wormeli. Alexandria, VA: Association for Supervision and Curriculum Development, 2004. A collection of summarization strategies that can be adapted for all learning styles and for individual or group instruction as well. Includes ready-to-use activity prompts.

Teaching What Matters Most: Standards and Strategies for Raising Student Achievement by Richard W. Strong, Harvey F. Silver, and Matthew J. Perini. Alexandria, VA: Association for Supervision and Curriculum Development, 2001. The authors of this text outline four standards: rigor, thought, diversity, and authenticity. Using practical, classroom-tested strategies, they show how most students can meet them.

Understanding by Design by Grant Wiggins and Jay McTighe. Alexandria, VA: Association for Supervision and Curriculum Development, 2005. This resource now includes a curriculum and assessment template for the Understanding by Design model.

Winning Strategies for Classroom Management by Carol Bradford Cummings. Alexandria, VA: Association for Supervision and Curriculum Development, 2000. Learn how to develop students' listening, cooperation, and self-management skills while maintaining achievement standards.

Web Sites

4Teachers • www.4teachers.org. The goal of 4Teachers is to help teachers bring technology into the classroom. The site offers online tools and resources such as rubrics, classroom calendars, and ready-to-use Web lessons. Also check out the "Classroom Architect," which enables teachers and students to design their own classroom.

AAA Math • www.aaamath.com. AAA Math offers basic K–8 math drills and practice, providing immediate feedback to student responses. Activities can be searched by grade level or skill area. A wide range of lessons ensures learners can find activities that match up with their abilities. The Web site is also available in Spanish.

ABC Teach • www.abcteach.com. This site contains thousands of free printable pages and worksheets, clip art, fonts, and teaching ideas for grades PreK–8. Educators can also create activities of their own, including word walls, word searches, word scrambles, crosswords, and sudoku puzzles (to help with math skills). Some downloads are available for free while others can only be accessed by paying members.

A Plus Math • www.aplusmath.com. This Web site is designed to help K–12 students improve their math skills. Among its features are games, flashcards, worksheets, and a homework helper where learners can check their answers.

BrainPOP • www.brainpop.com. This site provides curriculum-based content spanning seven main subjects: science, math, English, social studies, health, arts and music, and technology. For grades 3–12, the site also features hundreds of animated movies, which are supported by quizzes, comic strips, and other learning activities. BrainPOP Jr. is aimed at grades K–3. Activities at the site are available in Spanish. BrainPOP does require a subscription fee.

Center for Applied Special Technology (CAST) • www.cast.org. CAST has earned international recognition for its development of innovative, technology-based educational resources and strategies based on the principles of Universal Design for Learning (UDL). Online K–12 tools include the Lesson Builder, Strategy Tour, UDL curriculum self check, and a digital book library.

Dr. Jean—Songs and Activities for Young Children • www.drjean.org. Designed for teachers in early elementary classrooms, this site offers classroom ideas from educators and schools. Other features include an activity of the month, teaching ideas, downloadable books, science projects, phonics activities, games, craft ideas, and Web links.

EdHelper • www.edhelper.com. EdHelper provides lesson support to K–12 teachers in their planning. Information is organized by grade level and subject area. Among the offerings are specific units, test preparation, art activities, monthly themes, daily skills review, and art activities. Some of the resources are available for free while others require a fee.

Education World • www.educationworld.com. Education World is designed for preK–12 teachers and administrators. The site contains lesson plan ideas in all subjects, technology integration tips, professional development resources, Web site reviews, and ideas for increasing parent involvement. There are also virtual workshops, teacher tools and templates, education articles, and links to state and national education standards.

Enchanted Learning • www.enchantedlearning.com. Enchanted Learning provides lesson plans and theme ideas for all grade levels. Included at the site are printable books, coloring pages, songs, themes, worksheets, cooking activities, games, maps, dictionaries, and homework help. Some activities are free while others require paid membership.

Florida Center for Reading Research • www.fcrr.org. Teachers can find activities for teaching reading under the "Student Center Activities" section. Lesson plans with the corresponding reproducible forms are organized by primary area of reading instruction.

Funbrain • www.funbrain.com. This site features educational games designed to motivate student learning. Teachers using this tool with learners can select games based on subject area and grade level (K–8). There are also Web links to popular characters from comic books and children's literature.

GameGoo • www.earobics.com/gamegoo/gooey.html. GameGoo offers K–5 educational games that focus on early literacy and phonemic awareness. Key features include colorful graphics and the option to select games based on a player's skill level or area of need.

Hubbard's Cupboard • www.hubbardscupboard.org. Hubbard's Cupboard is devoted to beginning literacy. Visit the site for reading and writing lesson plans featuring photographs, supplies lists, room arrangements, and other pertinent information. There are also some math activities and ideas for connecting concepts across the curriculum.

The Iris Center • iris.peabody.vanderbilt.edu. This site provides high-quality resources on students with disabilities for college and university faculty and professional development providers. Key features include modules, case studies, and activities related to the education of students with disabilities.

Kaufman Children's Center • www.kidspeech.com. Search this site for information on young children struggling with listening and speaking skills. There is information on signs and symptoms, specialized treatment methods, language activities, and Web links.

Math Fact Cafe • www.mathfactcafe.com. Math Fact Cafe is a Web site designed for teachers, parents, and students (grades K–5) where visitors can create and complete various math drills and practice sheets. The site also contains games, online flashcards, and math trivia.

PBS Kids • pbskids.org. PBS Kids contains songs, games, coloring pages, and many more activities. The site offers resources for parents, teachers, and children in grades K–5. Many of the activities are associated with favorite characters from PBS shows.

PBS Teachers • www.pbs.org/teachers. PBS Teachers contains a wide variety of resources. Teachers can search for standards-based lesson plans and thematic units in all content areas and grade levels. Other features of the site include professional development trainings, PBS TV schedules, local resources, and blogs offering solutions to classroom challenges.

Promising Practices Network • www.promisingpractices.net. This site provides quality, evidence-based information about effective practices for improving the lives of children, youth, and families. Information on the site has been screened for scientific rigor, relevance, and clarity. Go to the "Programs that Work" link for research reviews of various programs used in schools.

read*write*think • www.readwritethink.org. This Web site, a joint venture between the International Reading Association (IRA) and the National Council of Teachers of English (NCTE), is dedicated to effective literacy instruction. The site features K–12 lesson plans, IRA/NCTE standards, Web resources, and online student materials.

Reading Rockets • www.readingrockets.org. Reading Rockets is a national program dedicated to researching how children learn to read and what can be done to help those who struggle. Go to the Web site for tips and techniques on how to teach reading.

Scholastic Teachers • www.teacher.scholastic.com. This Web site provides lesson plans, teaching strategies, and other resources. Teachers can search for thematic lessons and activities by grade level or subject. A blog features educators answering questions submitted by site visitors.

Starfall • www.starfall.com. Starfall is a research-based Web site that helps young children (grades K–2) learn to read. The Web site is an inexpensive resource for making the classroom more fun and inspiring students to read and write. Key features are the supports offered for literacy development using interactive books and letter/word recognition. Teachers also have the option to print out books, puzzles, activities, and reading awards.

TeacherVision • www.teachervision.fen.com. TeacherVision is a Web site that provides educators with thousands of printable lesson plans and classroom resources. Teachers can search for ideas and resources by grade, subject, and theme. There are also ideas for classroom management and professional development.

Teaching That Makes Sense • www.ttms.org. This Web site is a resource for teachers developing a content management system in literacy. Features include downloads, professional development workshops, and columns on issues in education.

Teachnology • www.teach-nology.com. Teachnology is a tool for K–12 teachers creating rubrics and lesson plans. The site includes teaching tips, craft ideas, and a program that generates worksheets and rubrics. There are also thousands of preformatted lesson plans, worksheets, and rubrics as well as games and Web site reviews.

What Works Clearinghouse • ies.ed.gov/ncee/wwc. The What Works Clearinghouse is a trusted source of scientific evidence on proven educational resources and techniques. Databases and user-friendly reports offer high-quality reviews of the effectiveness of educational interventions (programs, products, practices, and policies).

Index

Page numbers in **bold type** indicate reproducible forms; page numbers in *italics* indicate figures.

About the Authors

Elizabeth Whitten, Ph.D., is a professor in the Special Education and Literacy Studies Department at Western Michigan University in Kalamazoo, Michigan. Prior to her twenty years working in higher education, she served as a special and general education teacher and administrator. Elizabeth has consulted with school districts for the past fifteen years, providing training in areas of Response to Intervention, collaboration and teaming, co-teaching, curriculum-based assessment, differentiated instruction, and intervention strategies.

Kelli J. Esteves, Ed.D., is an assistant professor of education and is the director of the Learning Disabilities program at Aquinas College in Grand Rapids, Michigan. She specializes in literacy instruction and special education. Before joining the faculty at Aquinas, Kelli was a special education teacher and reading specialist in the Rockford Public Schools (Michigan), where she taught students at the elementary level. She is also a certified teacher consultant for the visually impaired and has worked with preschool through high school students and adults who are blind or have low vision.

Alice Woodrow, Ed.D., is the director of Special Education at the Allegan Area Educational Service Agency in Allegan, Michigan. She has a doctorate in special education with an emphasis on special education administration and quality programming for students with emotional impairments. She was formerly a middle school teacher and a supervisor of special education.

Kelli and Elizabeth offer on-site professional development on Response to Intervention and related topics in the form of one-day workshops, multiday institutes, and yearlong consultation services. To learn more, email speakers@freespirit.com.

More Great Books from Free Spirit

Differentiating Instruction in the Regular Classroom
How to Reach and Teach All Learners, Grades 3–12
by Diane Heacox, Ed.D.

This guide offers a menu of strategies, examples, templates, and tools teachers can use to differentiate instruction in any curriculum, even a standard or mandated curriculum. The included CD-ROM includes all of the forms from the book, plus additional materials.
176 pp.; softcover; 8½" x 11", grades 3–12

Teaching Gifted Kids in the Regular Classroom
Strategies and Techniques Every Teacher Can Use to Meet the Academic Needs of the Gifted and Talented
by Susan Winebrenner, foreword by Sylvia Rimm, Ph.D.

This is the definitive guide to meeting the learning needs of gifted students in the mixed-abilities classroom. It's full of proven, practical, classroom-tested strategies teachers love, plus many useful reproducibles. CD-ROM has forms from the book, plus extensions for several projects.
256 pp.; softcover; 8½" x 11", grades K–12

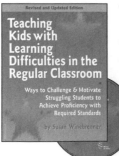

Teaching Kids with Learning Difficulties in the Regular Classroom
Ways to Challenge & Motivate Struggling Students to Achieve Proficiency with Required Standards
by Susan Winebrenner

A gold mine of practical, easy-to-use teaching methods to help teachers differentiate the curriculum in all subject areas to meet the needs of all learners, including those labeled "slow," "remedial," or "LD"; students of poverty; and English language learners. CD-ROM has forms from the book, plus additional content organization and vocabulary charts.
256 pp.; softcover; 8½" x 11", grades K–12

Making Differentiation a Habit
How to Ensure Success in Academically Diverse Classrooms
by Diane Heacox, Ed.D.

If you're a teacher with an academically diverse classroom (and what classrooms aren't today?), you need this resource. Framed around critical elements for success in academically diverse environments, this book gives educators specific, user-friendly tools to optimize teaching, learning, and assessment. This book offers new ideas, fresh perspectives, and research-based strategies designed to help teachers seamlessly integrate differentiation practices into their daily routines.
192 pp.; softcover; 8½" x 11", grades K–12

The Cluster Grouping Handbook: A Schoolwide Model
How to Challenge Gifted Students and Improve Achievement for All
by Susan Winebrenner, M.S., and Dina Brulles, Ph.D.

The authors explain how the Schoolwide Cluster Grouping Model (SCGM) differs from grouping practices of the past, and they present a wealth of teacher-tested classroom strategies along with detailed information on identifying students for clusters, gaining support from parents, and providing ongoing professional development. The CD-ROM features all of the forms from the book plus a PowerPoint presentation. An essential resource for administrators, gifted-education program directors, and classroom teachers.
224 pp.; softcover; 8½" x 11", grades K–8

Interested in purchasing multiple quantities?
Contact edsales@freespirit.com or call 1.800.735.7323 and ask for Education Sales.

Many Free Spirit authors are available for speaking engagements, workshops, and keynotes.
Contact speakers@freespirit.com or call 1.800.735.7323.

For pricing information, to place an order, or to request a free catalog, contact:

217 Fifth Avenue North • Suite 200 • Minneapolis, MN 55401-1299
toll-free 800.735.7323 • local 612.338.2068 • fax 612.337.5050
help4kids@freespirit.com • www.freespirit.com